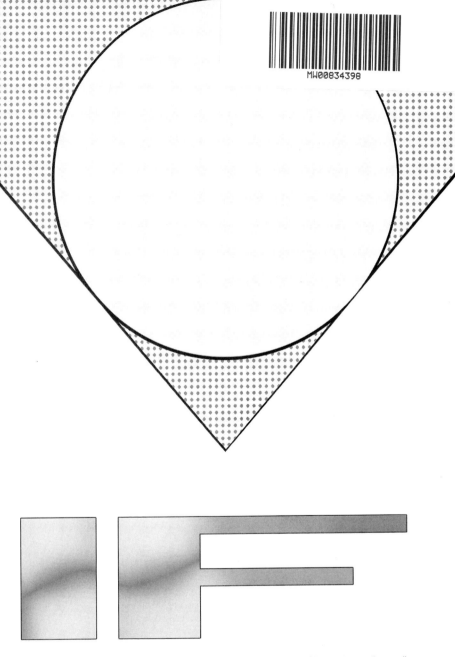

IF

*   *   *   A SCIENCE-FICTION ANTHOLOGY   *   *   *

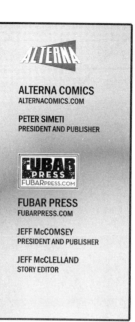

ALTERNA COMICS
ALTERNACOMICS.COM

PETER SIMETI
PRESIDENT AND PUBLISHER

FUBAR PRESS
FUBARPRESS.COM

FUBAR PRESS
FUBARPRESS.COM

JEFF McCOMSEY
PRESIDENT AND PUBLISHER

JEFF McCLELLAND
STORY EDITOR

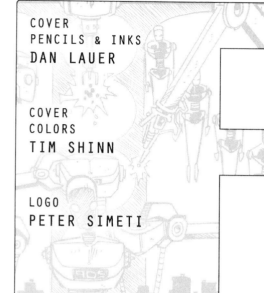

COVER
PENCILS & INKS
DAN LAUER

COVER
COLORS
TIM SHINN

LOGO
PETER SIMETI

A VERY SPECIAL THANKS TO THESE SUPPORTERS:

Anders M. Ytterdahl
Chris Bell
Ramel Rocket-Man Hill
Patrick Gerard
Robert "Sal" Mennella
William Robertson
Todd Good
Nicolas ANDRY
Vicky

41 Comics, Cards and Collectibles

IF
VOLUME 1
978-1-934985-46-5
2015 FIRST PRINTING
Published by Alterna Comics, Inc.

CREATORS

STORIES
ALEX ECKMAN-LAWN
BRANDON BARROWS
CASEY REECE
CHAS! PANGBURN
CHIP REECE
DINO CARUSO
GARRETT SNEEN
GLENN MATCHETT
JAMES E. ROCHE
JON CLARK
LOKI DeWITT
MICHAEL MALKIN
MIKE SALT
ROBERT MENEGUS
ZACH BASSETT

ART
ALEX ECKMAN-LAWN
DAN LAUER
DAVID BRAME
ERIC WEATHERS
FABIAN COBOS
GARRETT SNEEN
GEORGE ATHANASIOU
JON CLARK
MARIANO LACLAUSTRA
NOVO MALGAPO
PEEBO MONDIA
SALO FARIAS
SAM AGRO
UGUR SERTCELIK
TIM SHINN
ZACH BASSETT

EDITS
CANDICE WEATHERS
CLAIRE BENSON
PETER SIMETI

LETTERS
ADAM WOLLET
ALEX ECKMAN-LAWN
BRANT FOWLER
CHAS! PANGBURN
DEKARA
ERICA J. HEFLIN
GARRETT SNEEN
GEORGE ATHANASIOU
KENNY JEFFERY
NIC J. SHAW
UGUR SERTCELIK
ZACH BASSETT

\-

...in **IF** there are no questions...

only **answers**

\-

D IS FOR VICTORY

STORY
BRANDON BARROWS

ART
PEEBO MONDIA

LETTERS
NIC J. SHAW

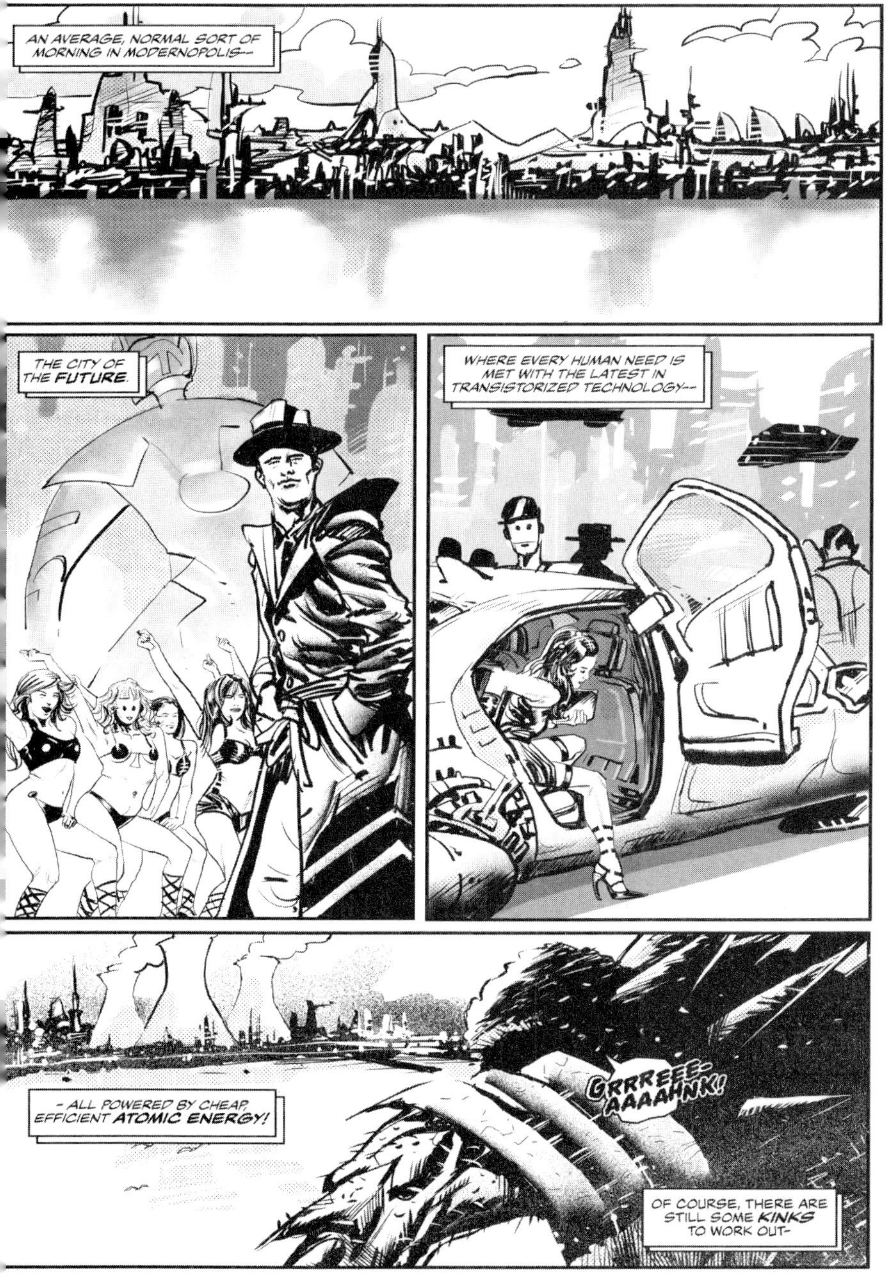
AN AVERAGE, NORMAL SORT OF MORNING IN MODERNOPOLIS--
THE CITY OF THE FUTURE.
WHERE EVERY HUMAN NEED IS MET WITH THE LATEST IN TRANSISTORIZED TECHNOLOGY--
- ALL POWERED BY CHEAP, EFFICIENT ATOMIC ENERGY!
GRRREEE-AAAAHNK!
OF COURSE, THERE ARE STILL SOME KINKS TO WORK OUT-

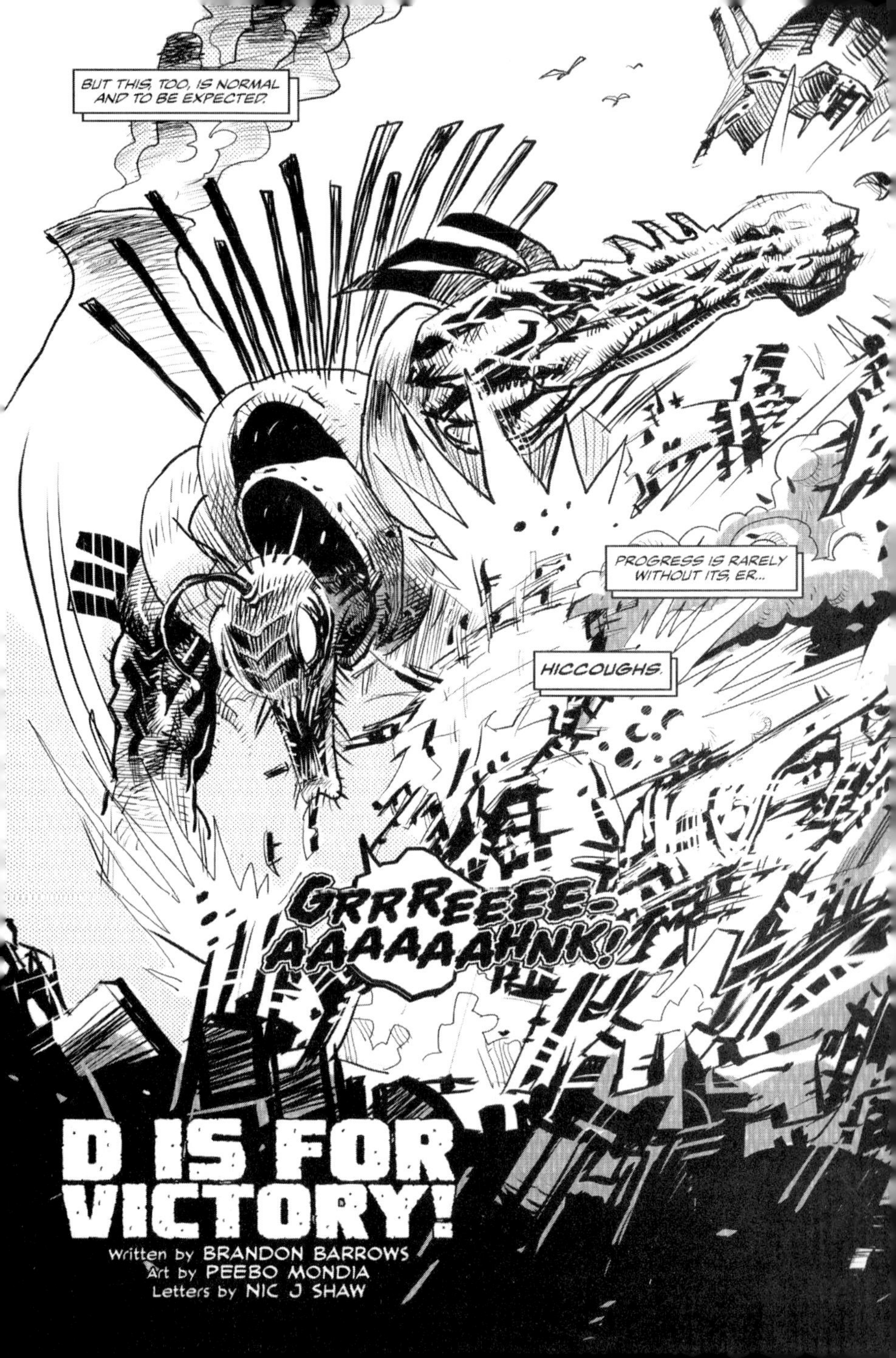
BUT THIS, TOO, IS NORMAL AND TO BE EXPECTED.
PROGRESS IS RARELY WITHOUT ITS, ER...
HICCOUGHS.
GRRREEEEE-AAAAAAHNK!
D IS FOR VICTORY!
Written by BRANDON BARROWS
Art by PEEBO MONDIA
Letters by NIC J SHAW

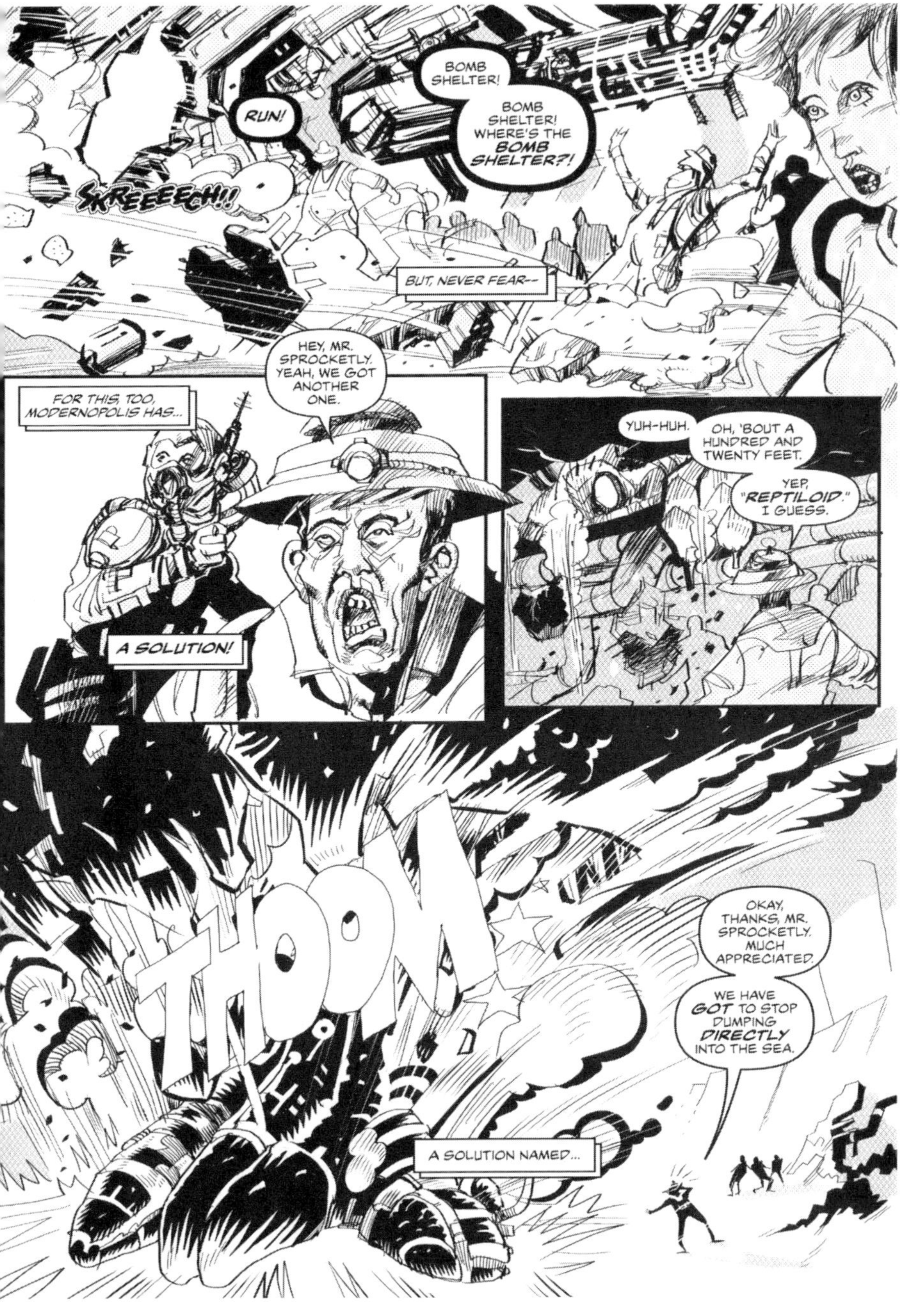
RUN!
BOMB SHELTER!
BOMB SHELTER! WHERE'S THE BOMB SHELTER?!
SKREEEECH!!
BUT, NEVER FEAR--
FOR THIS, TOO, MODERNOPOLIS HAS...
HEY, MR. SPROCKETLY. YEAH, WE GOT ANOTHER ONE.
A SOLUTION!
YUH-HUH.
OH, 'BOUT A HUNDRED AND TWENTY FEET.
YEP, "REPTILOID." I GUESS.
THOOM
OKAY, THANKS, MR. SPROCKETLY. MUCH APPRECIATED.
WE HAVE GOT TO STOP DUMPING DIRECTLY INTO THE SEA.
A SOLUTION NAMED...

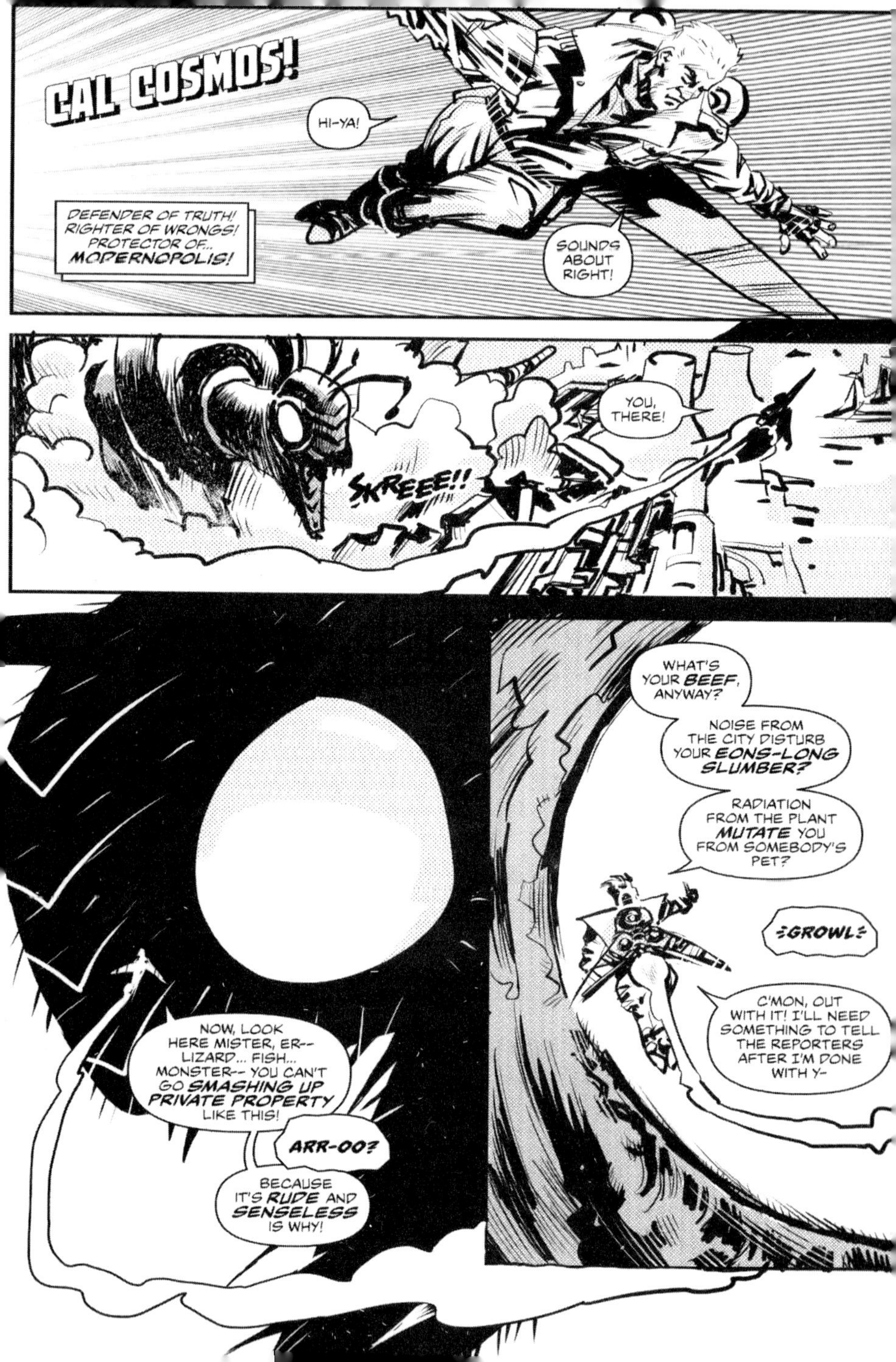
CAL COSMOS!
HI-YA!
DEFENDER OF TRUTH! RIGHTER OF WRONGS! PROTECTOR OF... MODERNOPOLIS!
SOUNDS ABOUT RIGHT!
YOU, THERE!
SKREEEE!!
WHAT'S YOUR BEEF, ANYWAY?
NOISE FROM THE CITY DISTURB YOUR EONS-LONG SLUMBER?
RADIATION FROM THE PLANT MUTATE YOU FROM SOMEBODY'S PET?
GROWL
C'MON, OUT WITH IT! I'LL NEED SOMETHING TO TELL THE REPORTERS AFTER I'M DONE WITH Y-
NOW, LOOK HERE MISTER, ER-- LIZARD... FISH... MONSTER-- YOU CAN'T GO SMASHING UP PRIVATE PROPERTY LIKE THIS!
ARR-OO?
BECAUSE IT'S RUDE AND SENSELESS IS WHY!

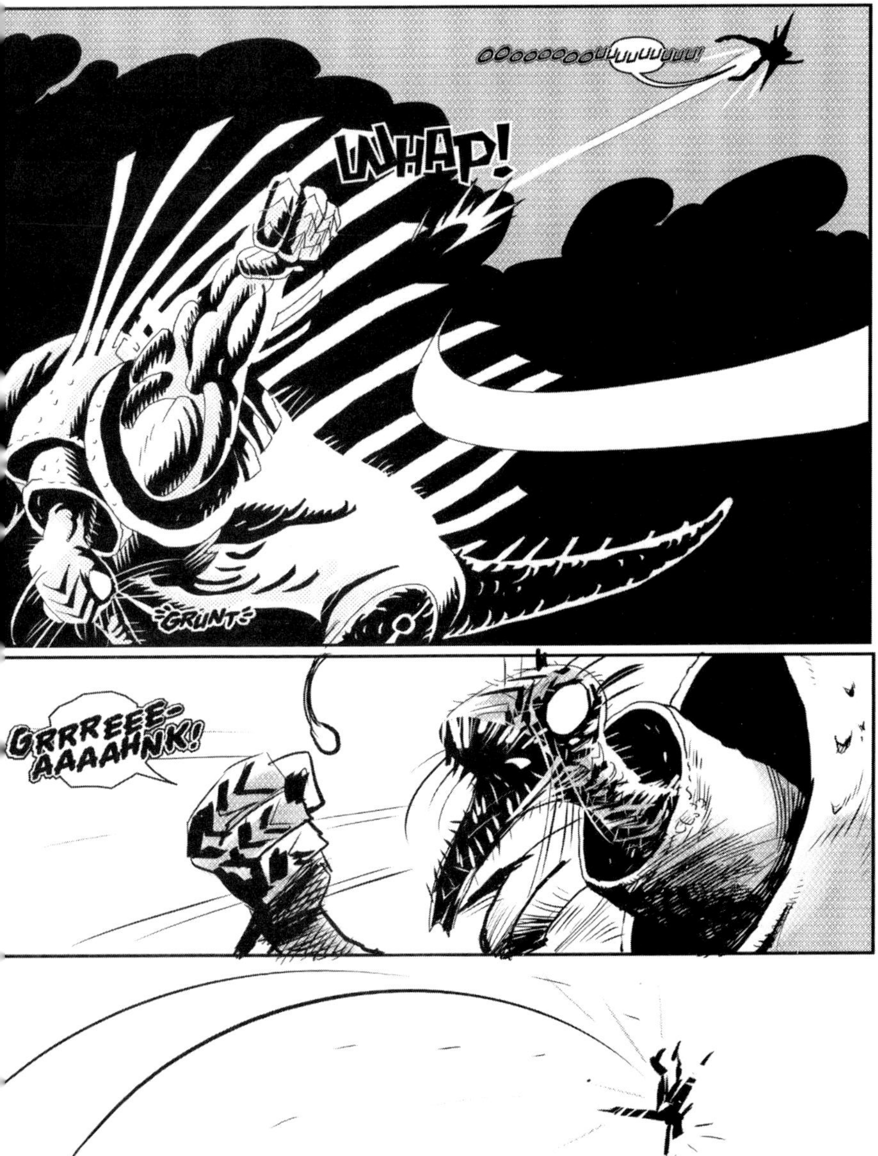

OOoooooouuuuuuuuuuu!
WHAP!
GRUNT
GRRREEE-AAAAAHNK!

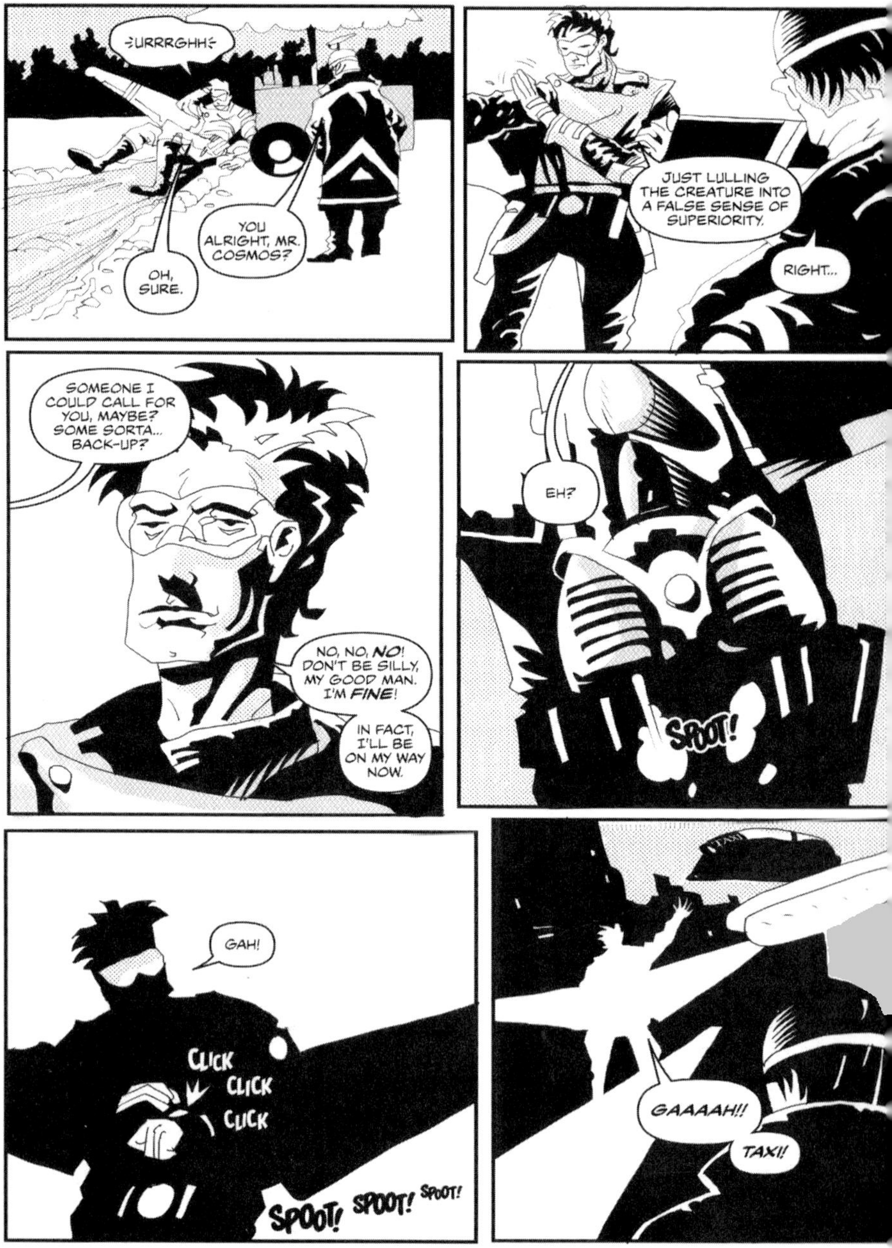
URRRGHH
YOU ALRIGHT, MR. COSMOS?
OH, SURE.
JUST LULLING THE CREATURE INTO A FALSE SENSE OF SUPERIORITY.
RIGHT...
SOMEONE I COULD CALL FOR YOU, MAYBE? SOME SORTA... BACK-UP?
NO, NO, NO! DON'T BE SILLY, MY GOOD MAN. I'M FINE!
IN FACT, I'LL BE ON MY WAY NOW.
EH?
SPOOT!
GAH!
CLICK
CLICK
CLICK
SPOOT! SPOOT! SPOOT!
TAXI
GAAAAH!!
TAXI!

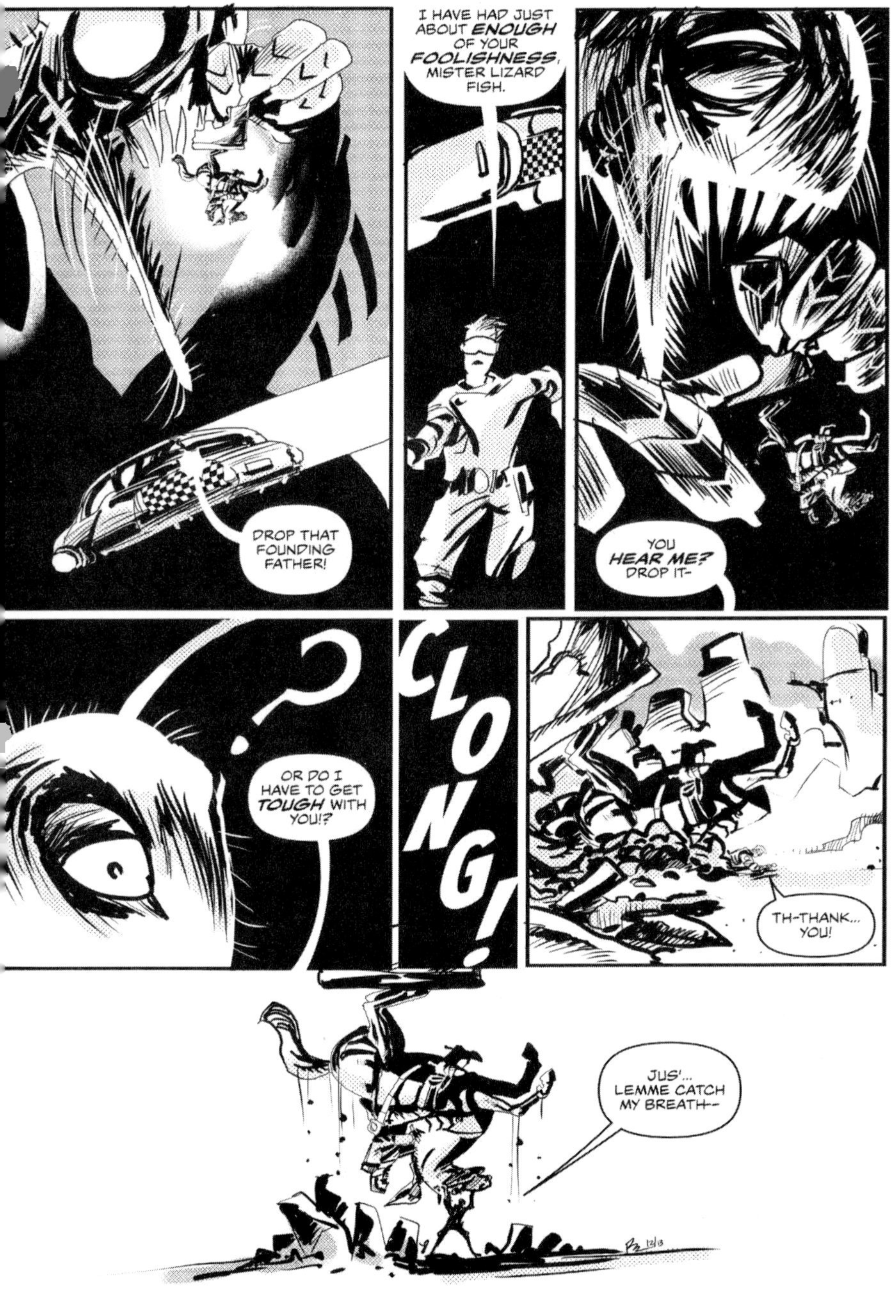
DROP THAT FOUNDING FATHER!
I HAVE HAD JUST ABOUT ENOUGH OF YOUR FOOLISHNESS, MISTER LIZARD FISH.
YOU HEAR ME? DROP IT-
OR DO I HAVE TO GET TOUGH WITH YOU!?
CLONG!
TH-THANK... YOU!
JUS'... LEMME CATCH MY BREATH--

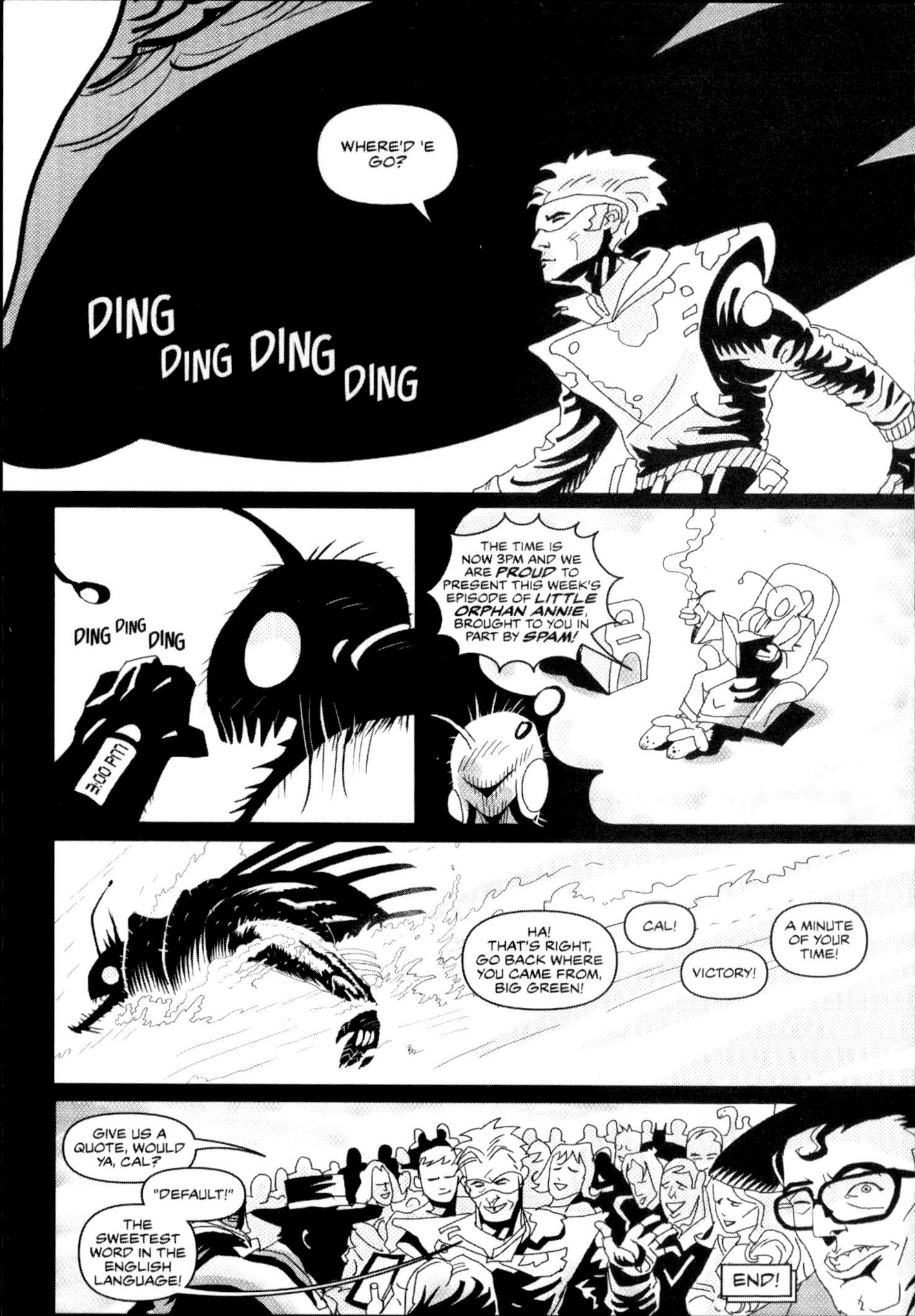
WHERE'D 'E GO?
DING DING DING DING
DING DING DING
3:00 PM
THE TIME IS NOW 3PM AND WE ARE PROUD TO PRESENT THIS WEEK'S EPISODE OF LITTLE ORPHAN ANNIE, BROUGHT TO YOU IN PART BY SPAM!
HA! THAT'S RIGHT, GO BACK WHERE YOU CAME FROM, BIG GREEN!
CAL!
VICTORY!
A MINUTE OF YOUR TIME!
GIVE US A QUOTE, WOULD YA, CAL?
"DEFAULT!"
THE SWEETEST WORD IN THE ENGLISH LANGUAGE!
END!

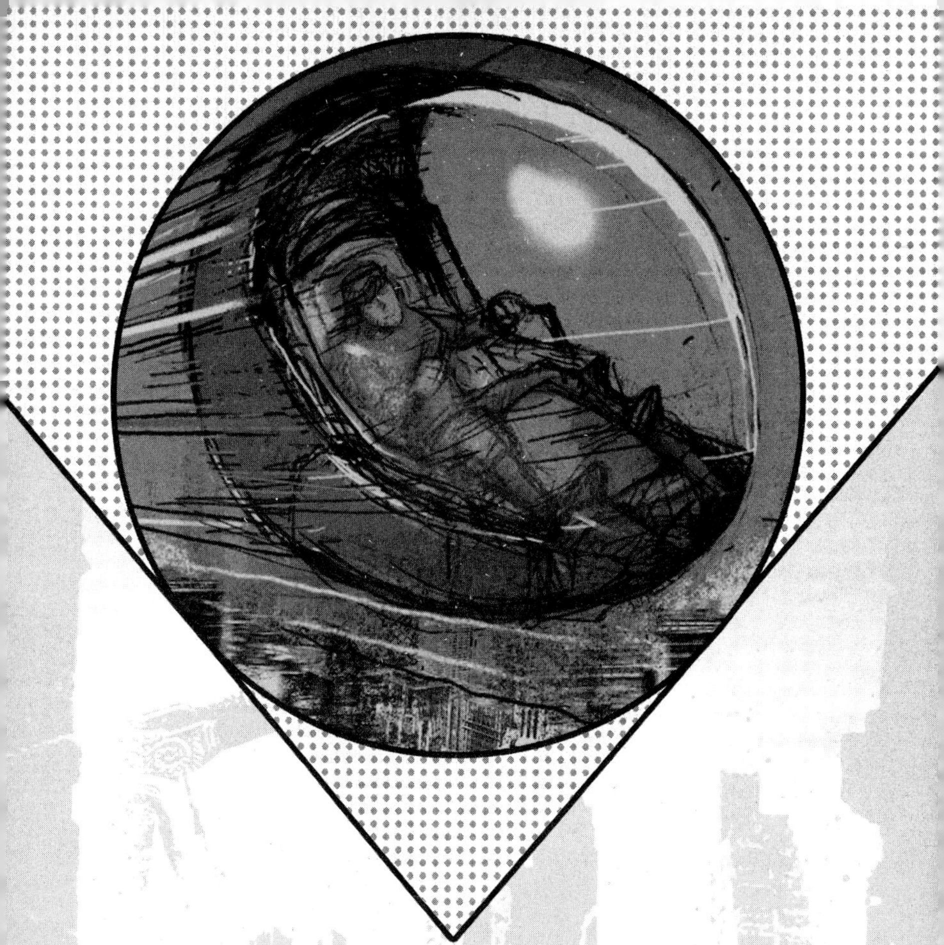

MOON

STORY - ART - LETTERS
ALEX ECKMAN-LAWN

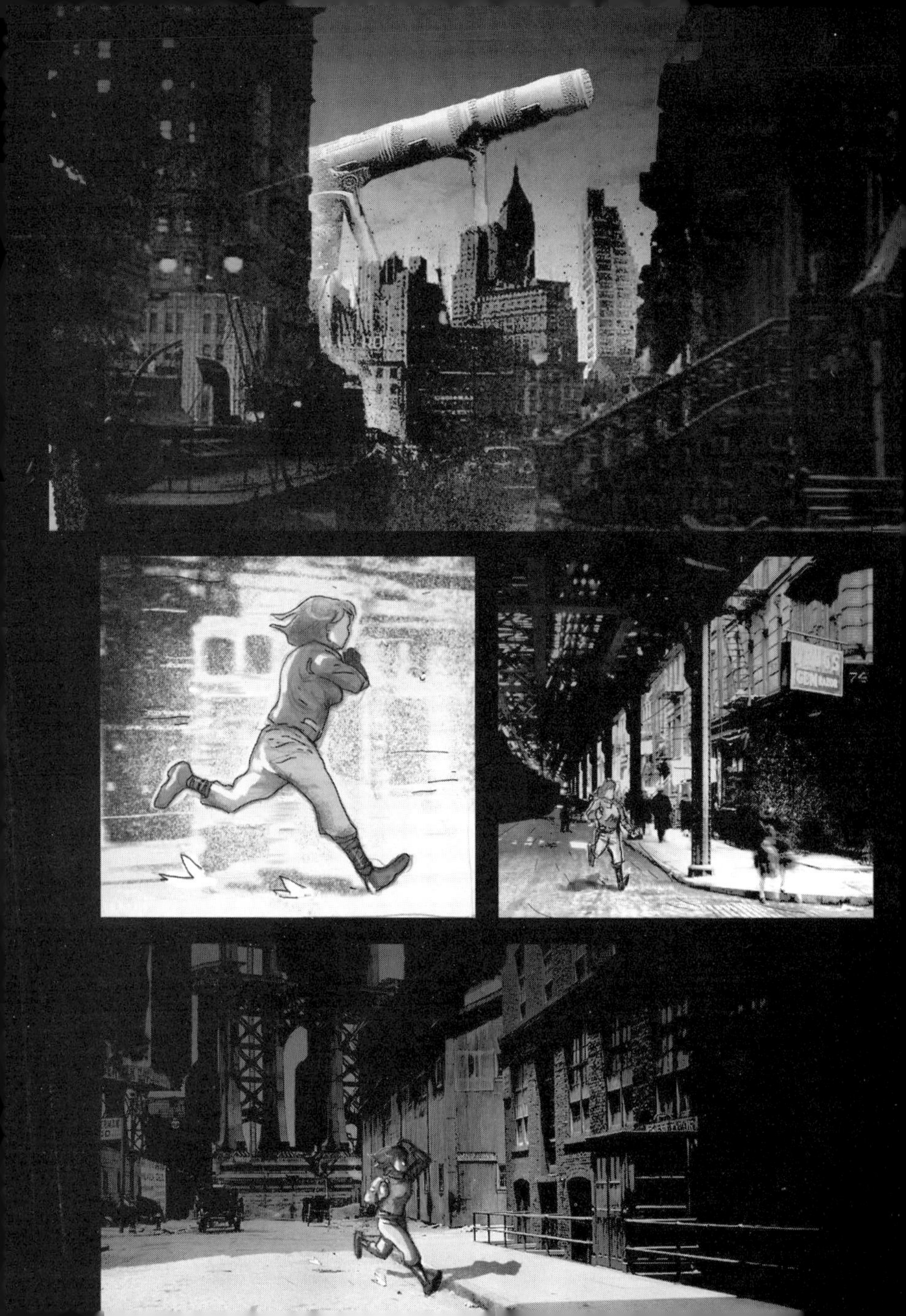

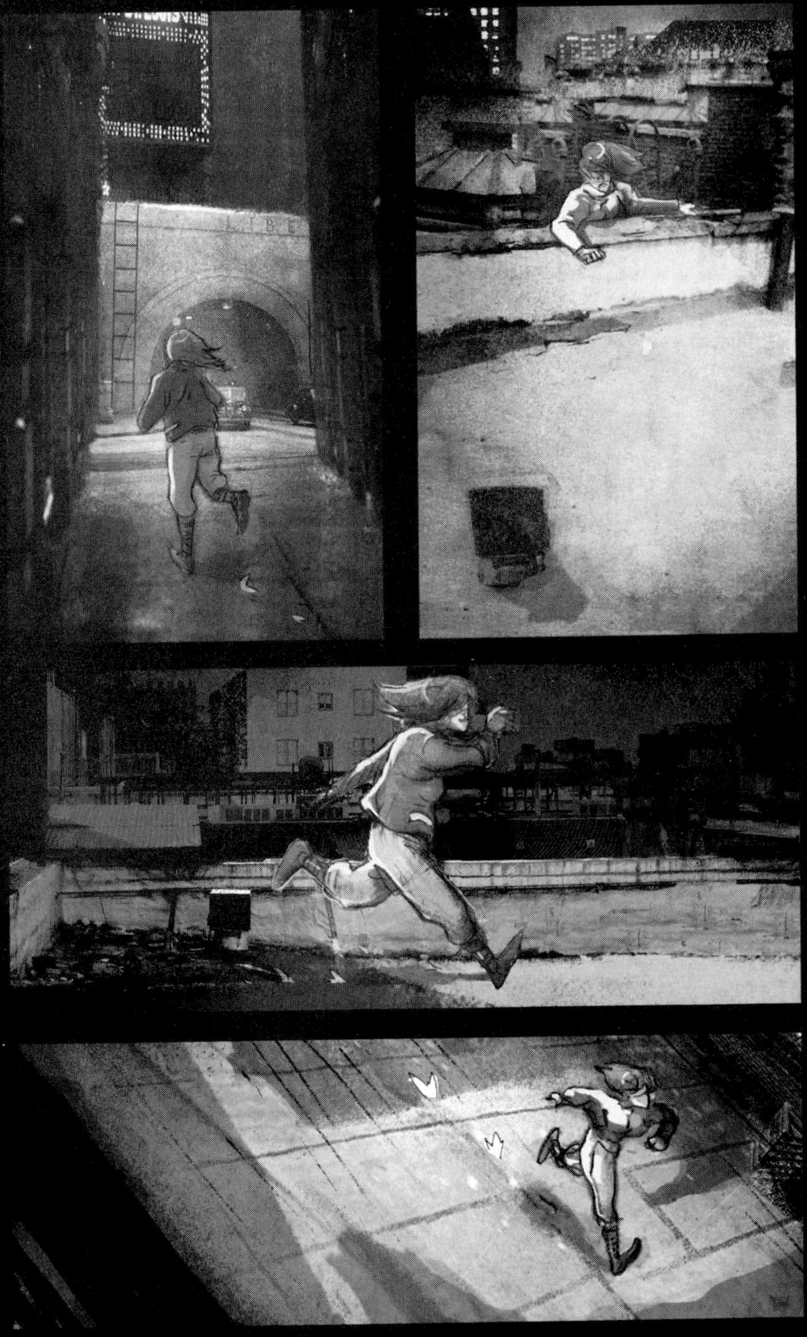

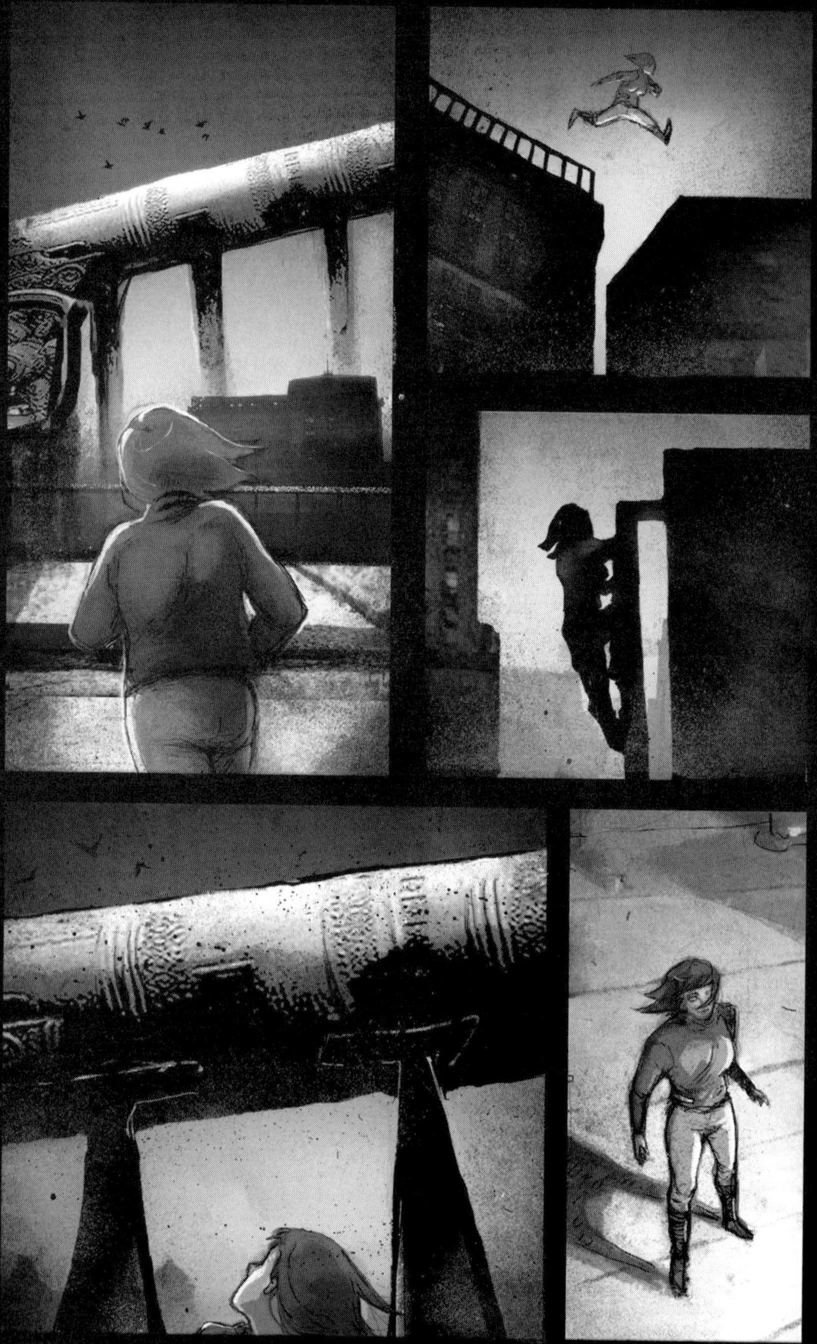

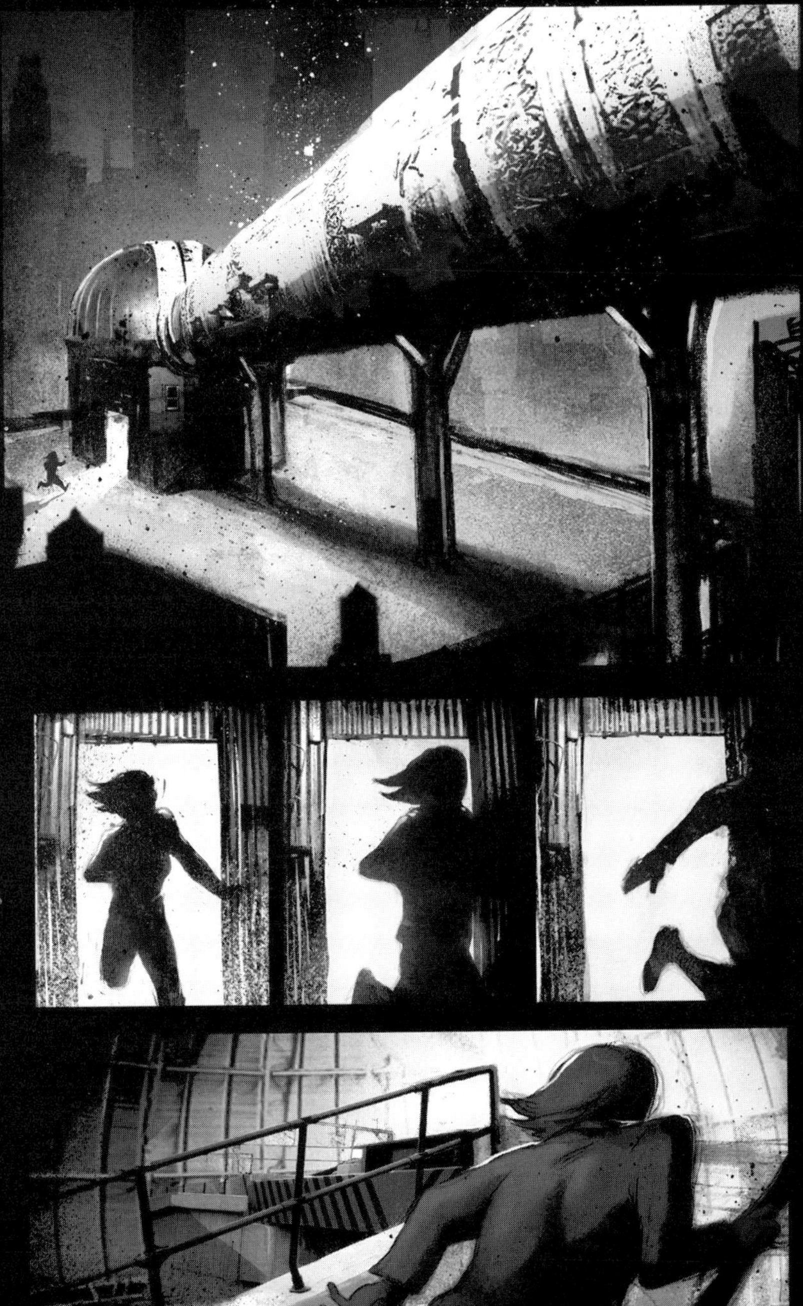

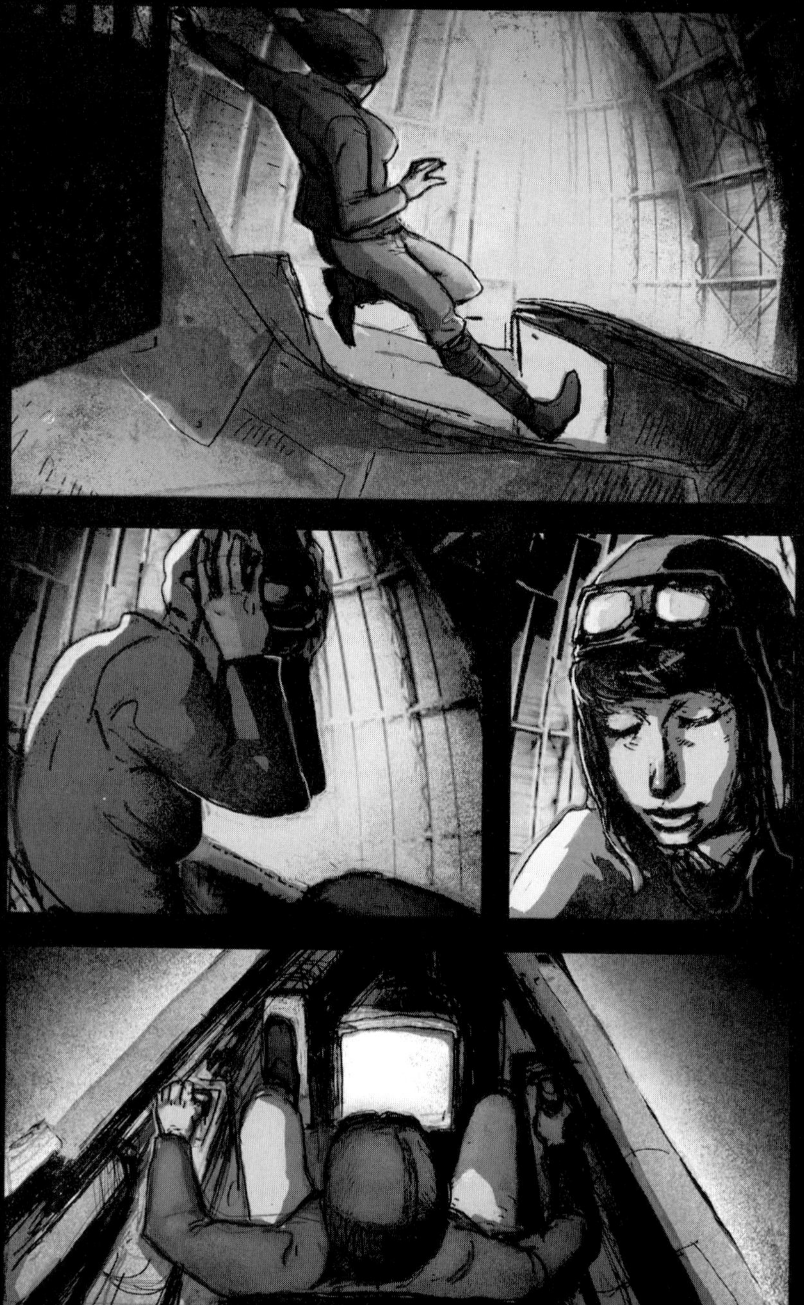

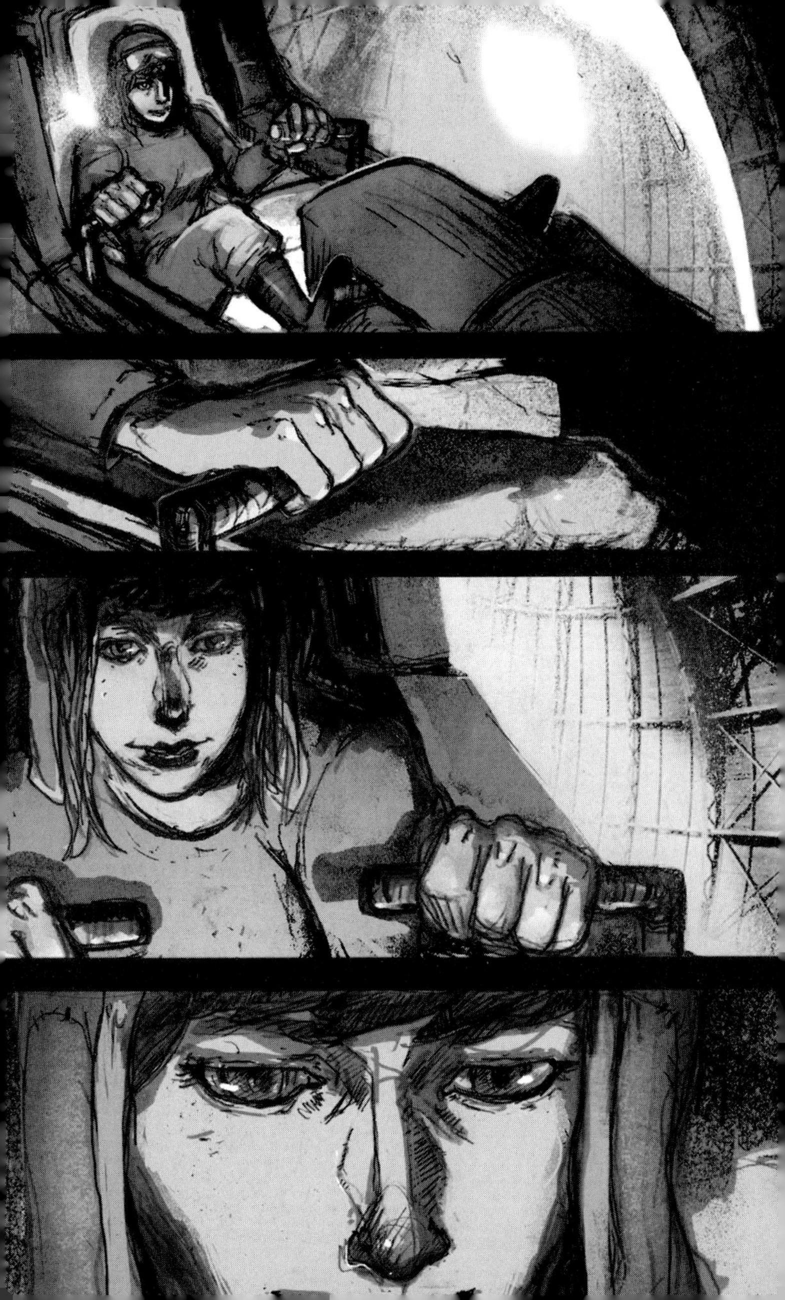

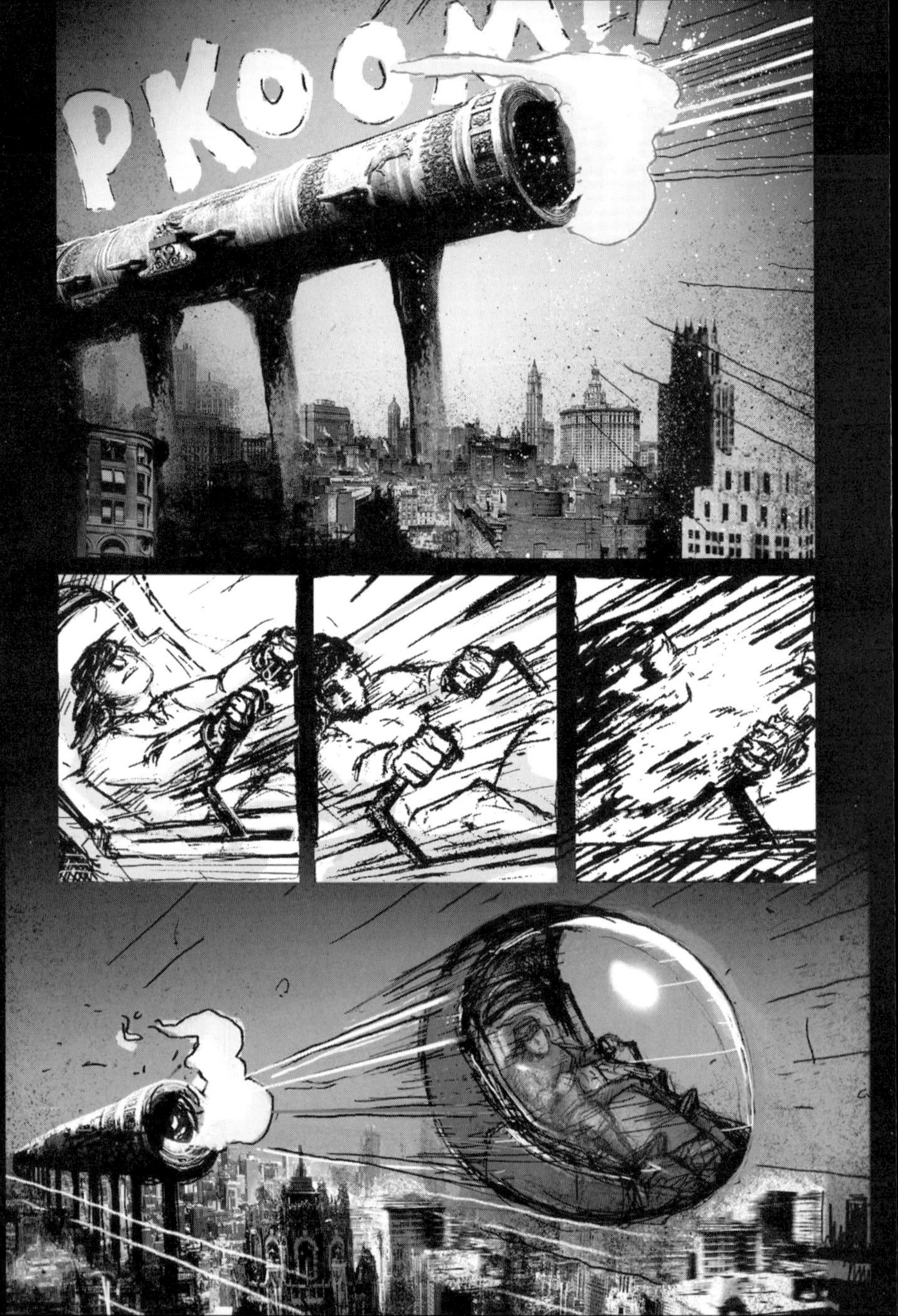
PKOOM!!

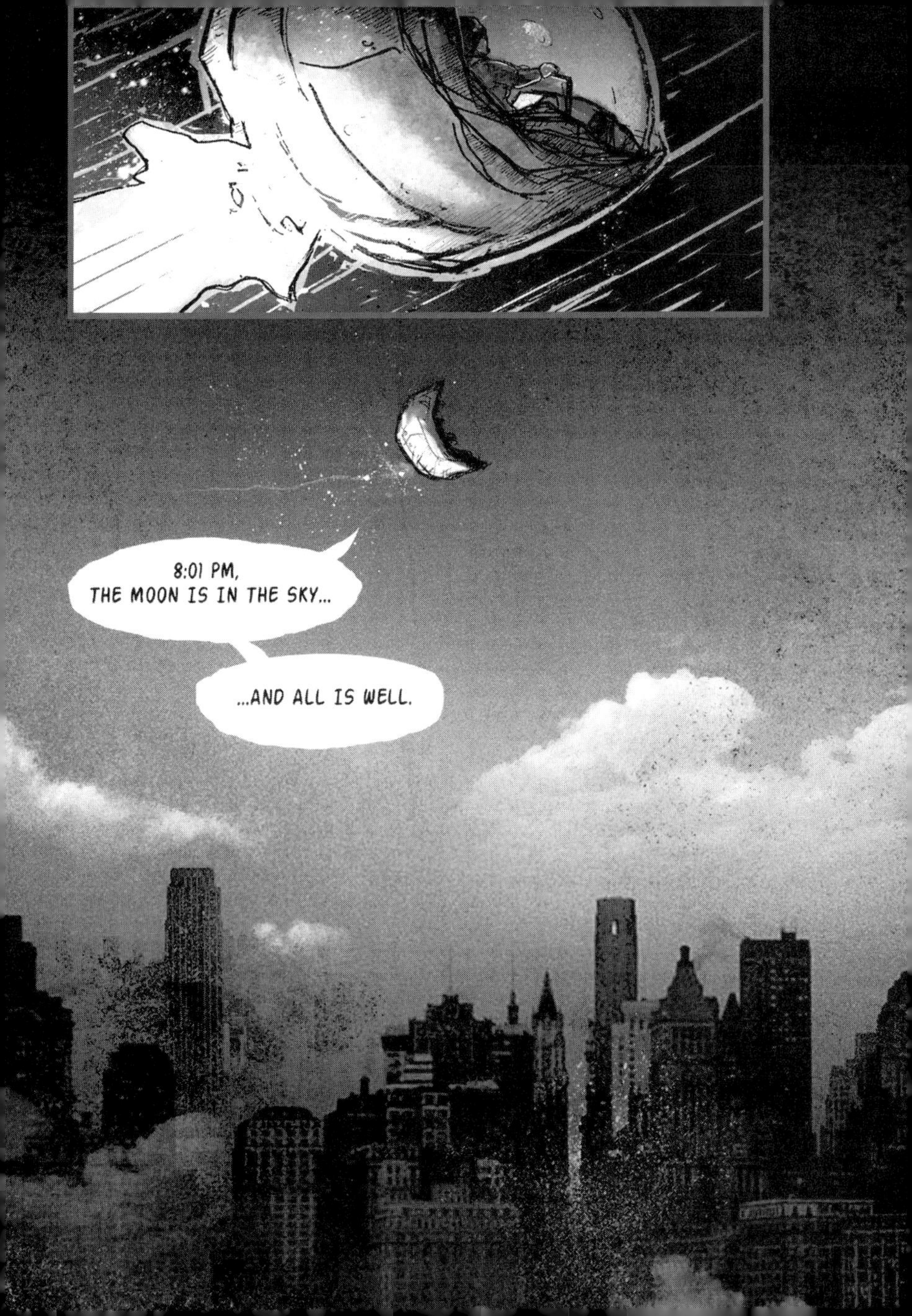
8:01 PM,
THE MOON IS IN THE SKY...
...AND ALL IS WELL.

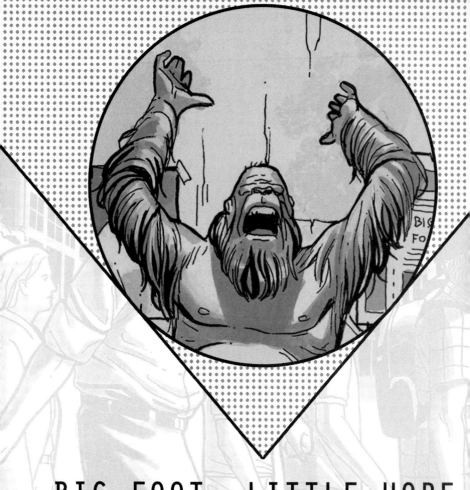

BIG FOOT, LITTLE HOPE

STORY - LETTERS
CHAS! PANGBURN

ART
MARIANO LACLAUSTRA

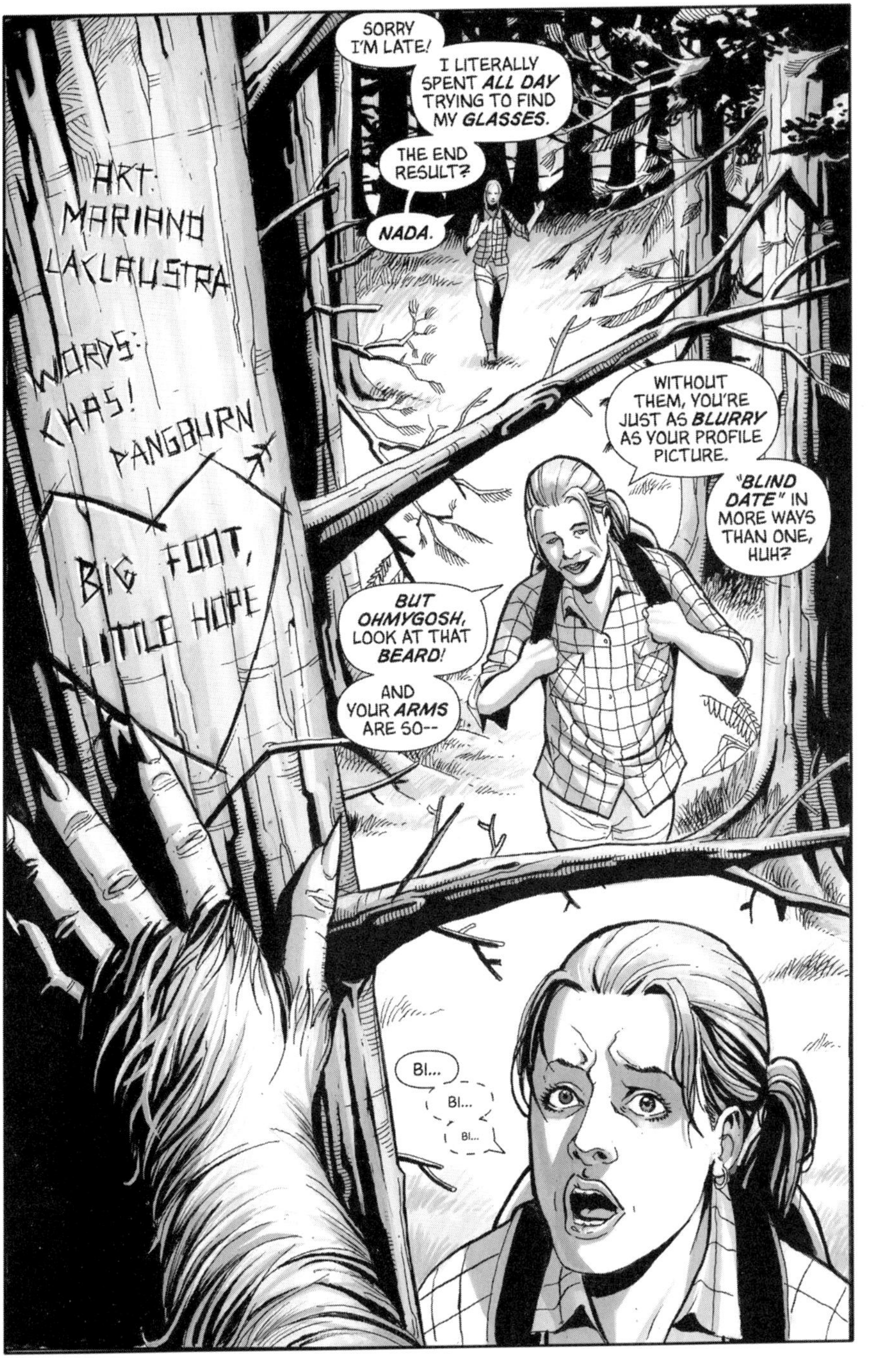
ART: MARIANO LACLAUSTRA
WORDS: CHAS! PANGBURN
BIG FOOT, LITTLE HOPE
SORRY I'M LATE!
I LITERALLY SPENT ALL DAY TRYING TO FIND MY GLASSES.
THE END RESULT?
NADA.
WITHOUT THEM, YOU'RE JUST AS BLURRY AS YOUR PROFILE PICTURE.
"BLIND DATE" IN MORE WAYS THAN ONE, HUH?
BUT OHMYGOSH, LOOK AT THAT BEARD!
AND YOUR ARMS ARE SO--
BI...
BI...
BI...

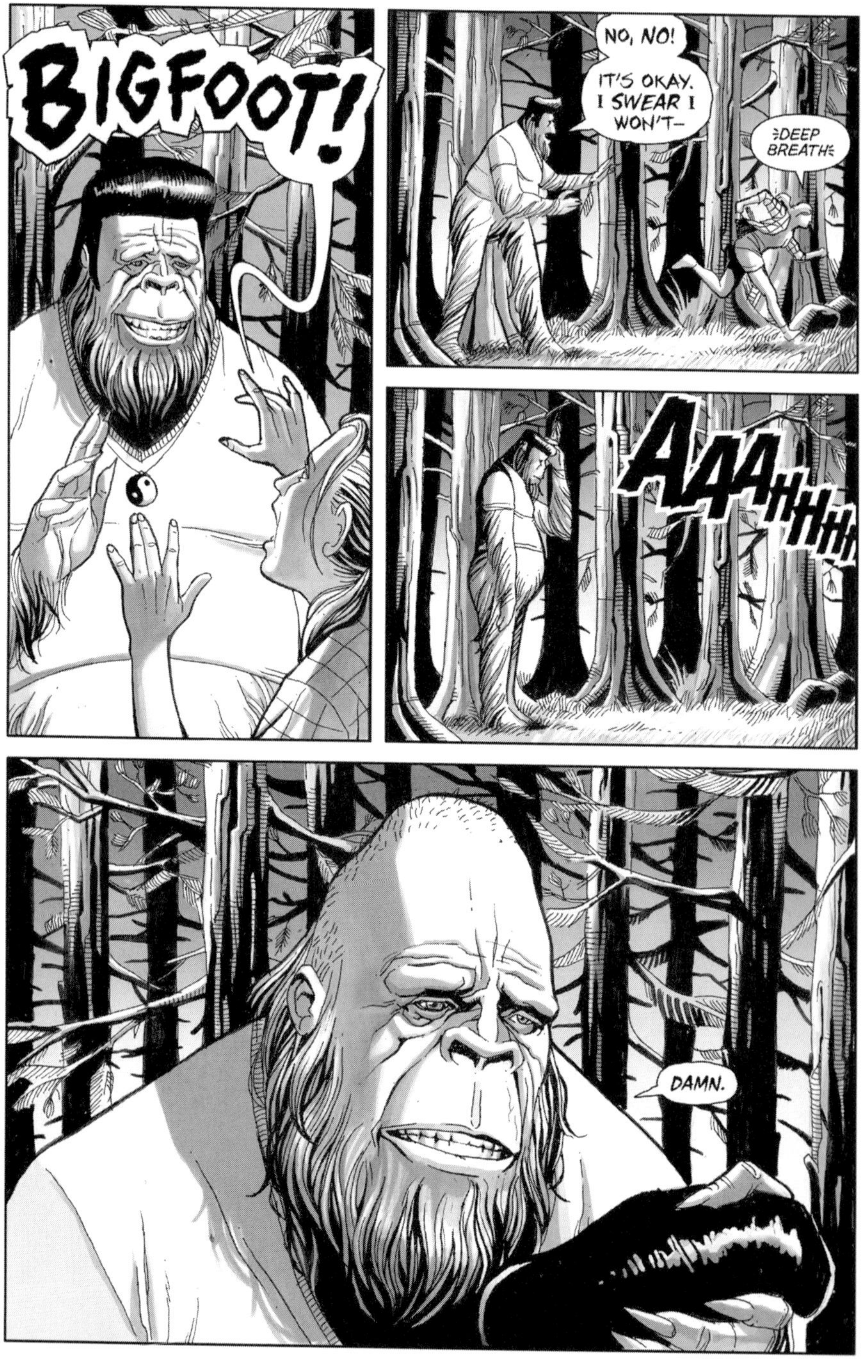
BIGFOOT!
NO, NO!
IT'S OKAY. I SWEAR I WON'T–
DEEP BREATH
AAAHHHH
DAMN.

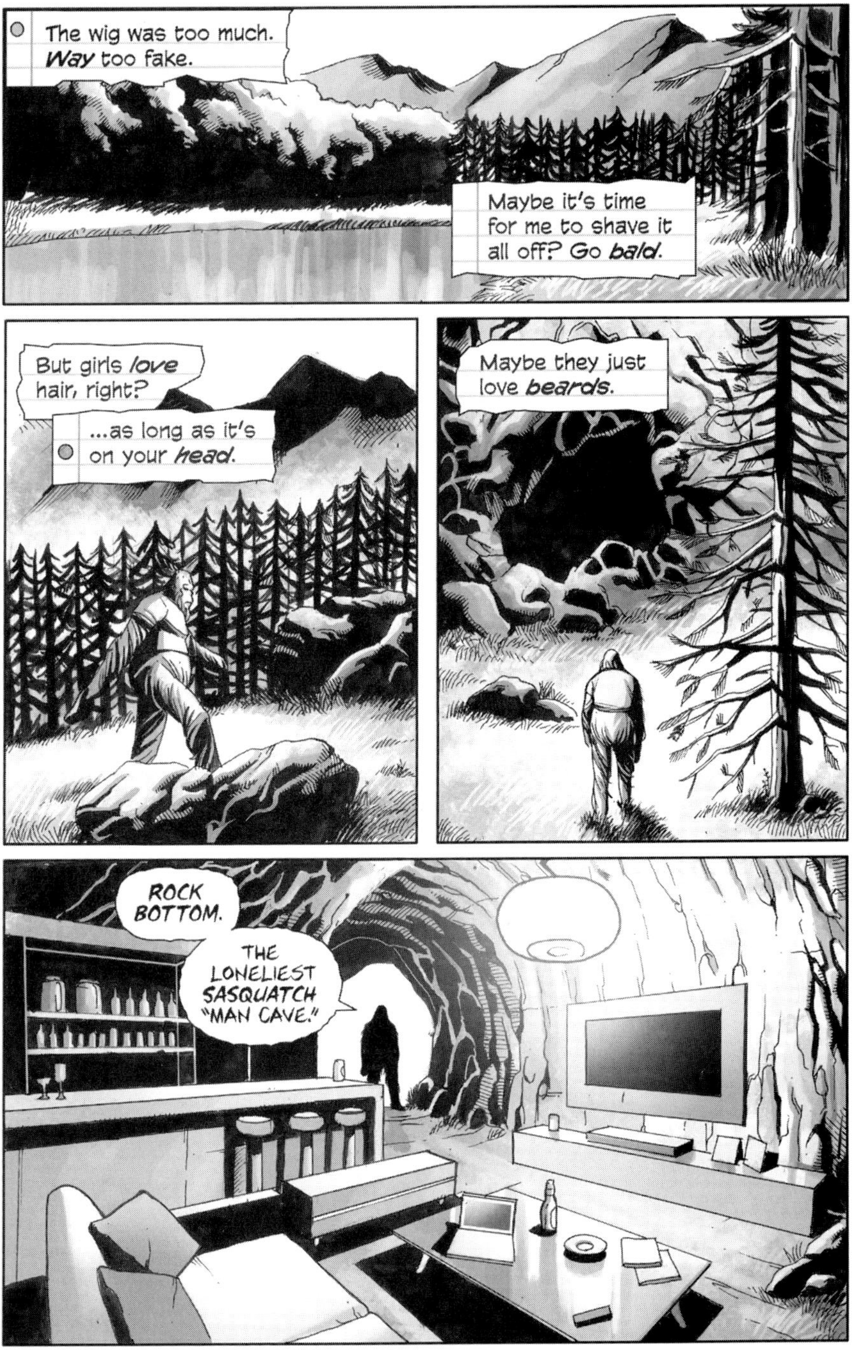
The wig was too much. *Way* too fake.
Maybe it's time for me to shave it all off? Go *bald*.
But girls *love* hair, right?
...as long as it's on your *head*.
Maybe they just love *beards*.
ROCK BOTTOM.
THE LONELIEST SASQUATCH "MAN CAVE."

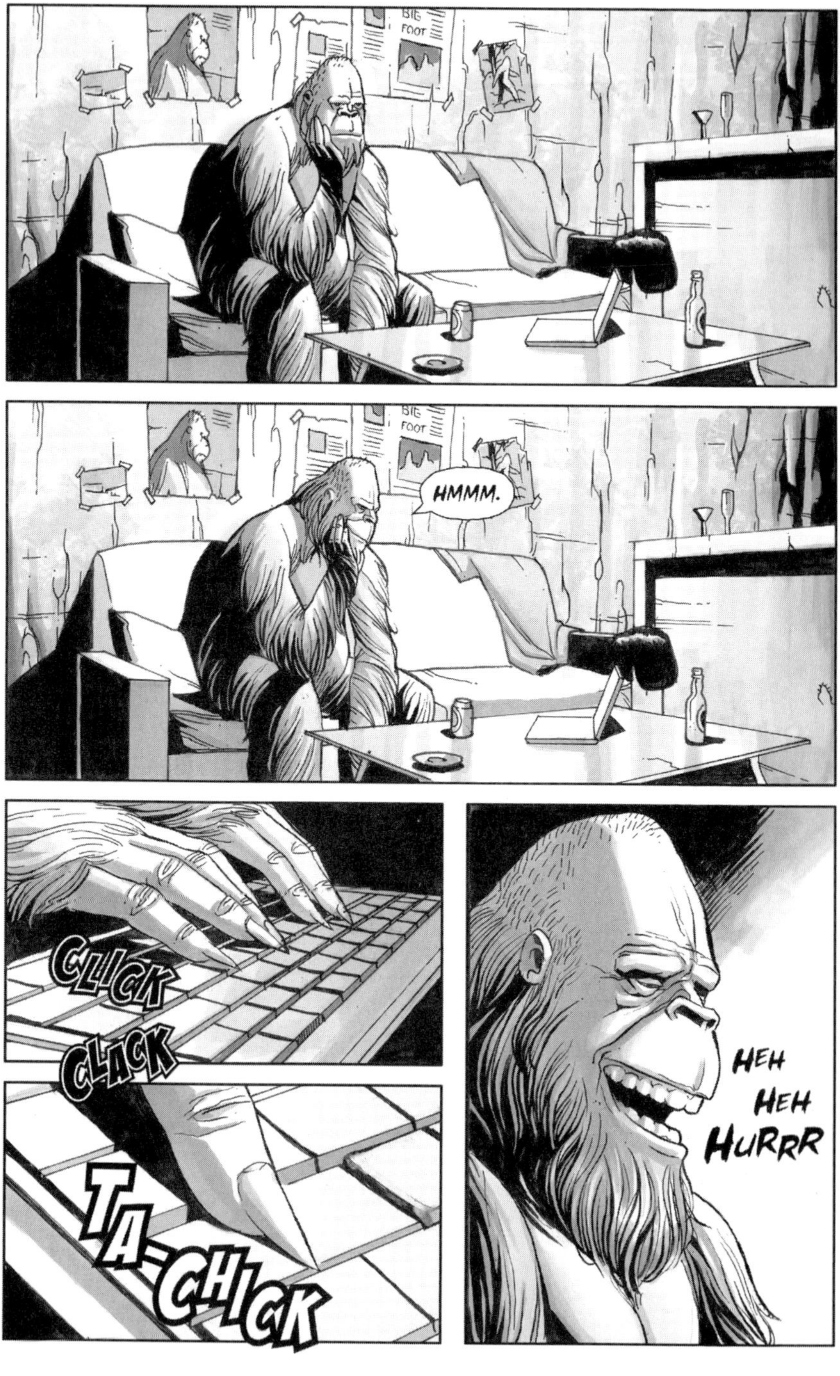
BIG FOOT
BIG FOOT
HMMM.
CLICK
CLACK
TA-CHICK
HEH
HEH
HURRR

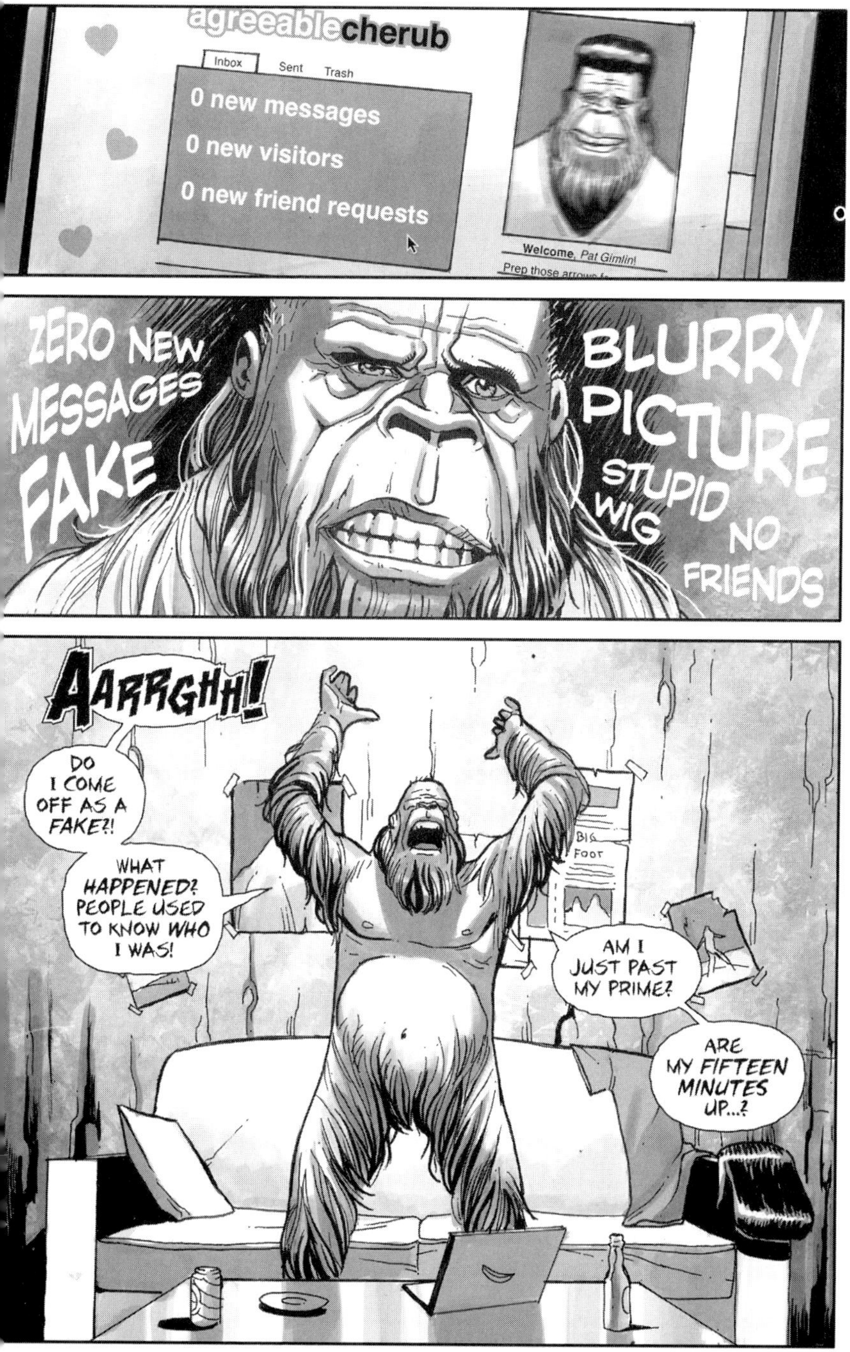
agreeablecherub
Inbox
Sent
Trash
0 new messages
0 new visitors
0 new friend requests
Welcome, Pat Gimlin!
ZERO NEW MESSAGES
FAKE
BLURRY PICTURE
STUPID WIG
NO FRIENDS
AARRGHH!
DO I COME OFF AS A FAKE?!
WHAT HAPPENED? PEOPLE USED TO KNOW WHO I WAS!
AM I JUST PAST MY PRIME?
ARE MY FIFTEEN MINUTES UP...?
BIG FOOT

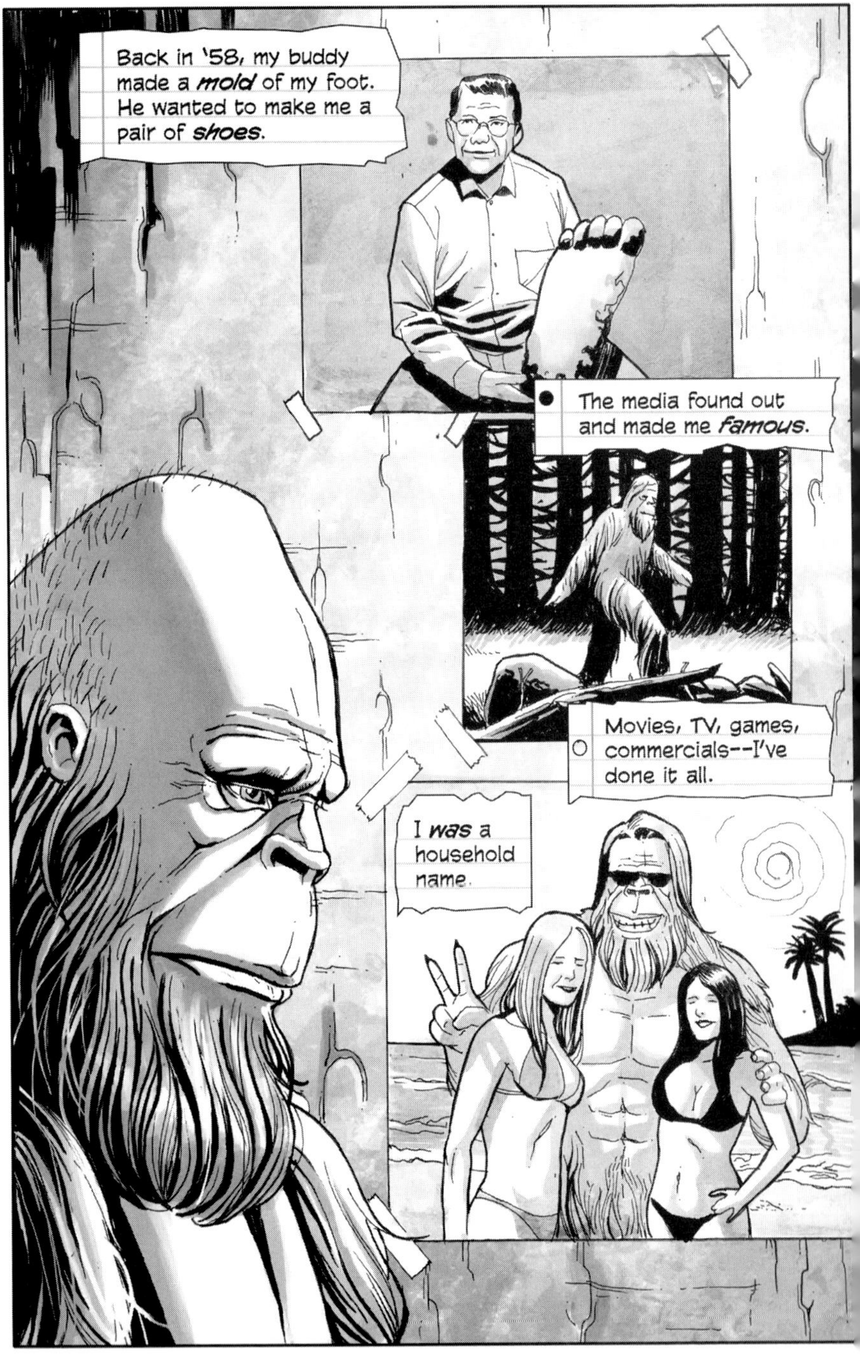
Back in '58, my buddy made a *mold* of my foot. He wanted to make me a pair of *shoes*.
The media found out and made me *famous*.
Movies, TV, games, commercials--I've done it all.
I *was* a household name.

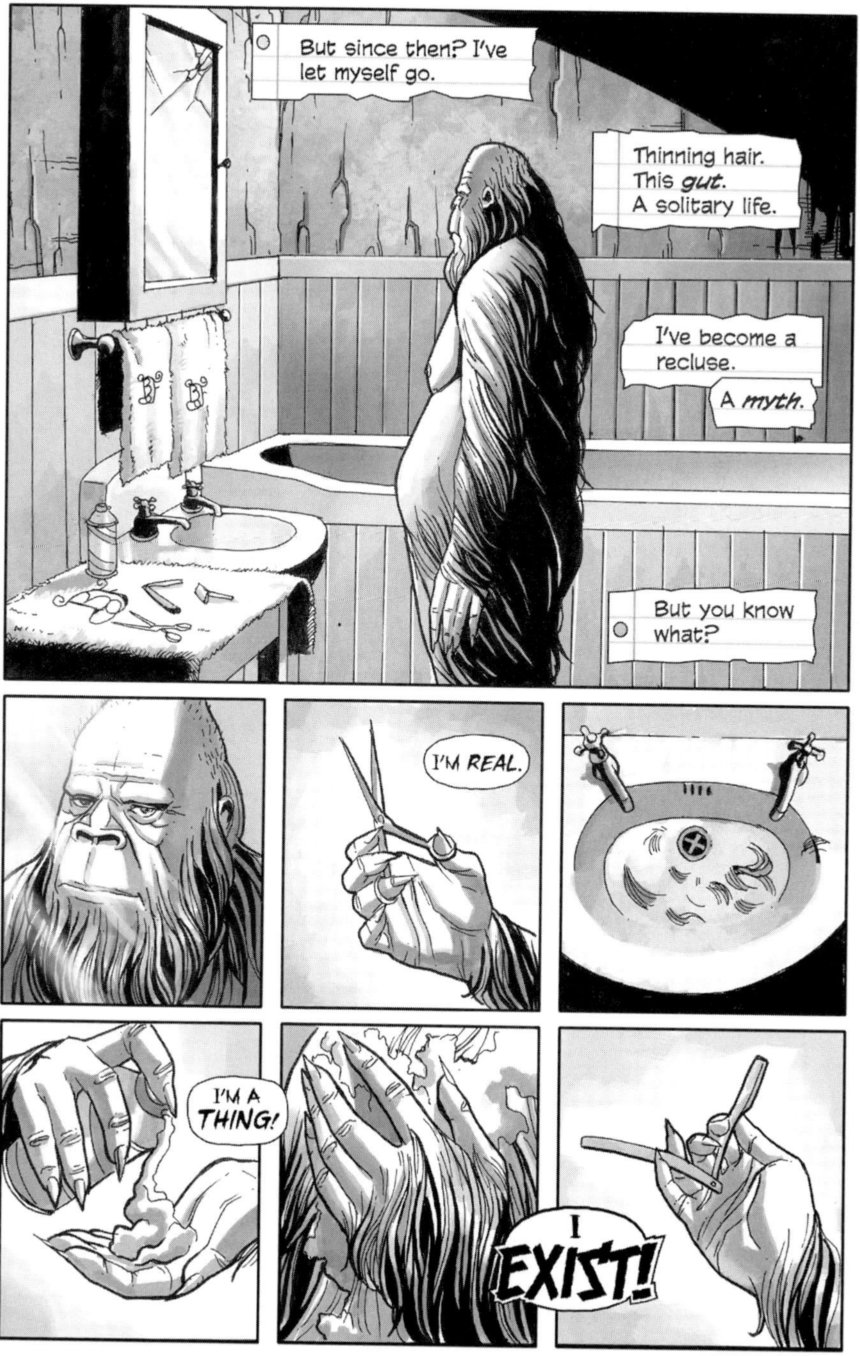

But since then? I've let myself go.
Thinning hair.
This *gut*.
A solitary life.
I've become a recluse.
A *myth*.
But you know what?
I'M *REAL*.
I'M A THING!
I EXIST!

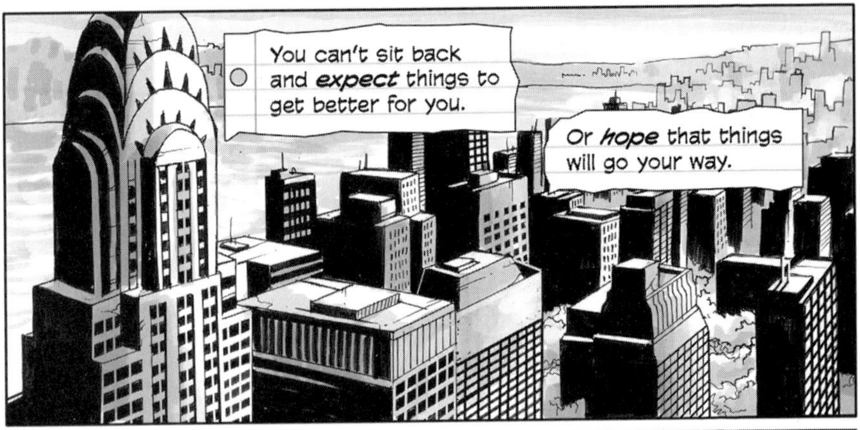
You can't sit back and *expect* things to get better for you.
Or *hope* that things will go your way.

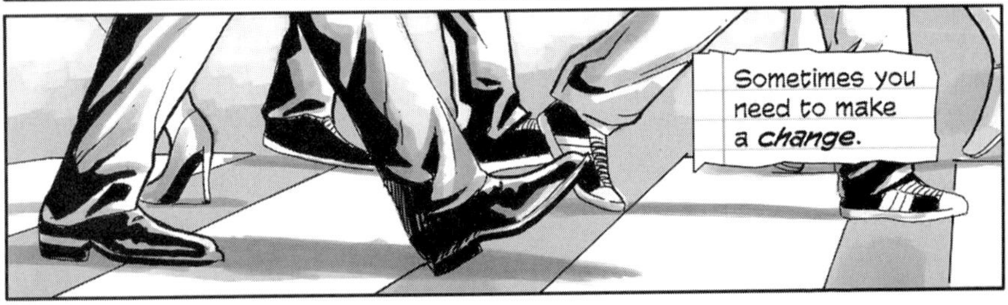
Sometimes you need to make a *change*.

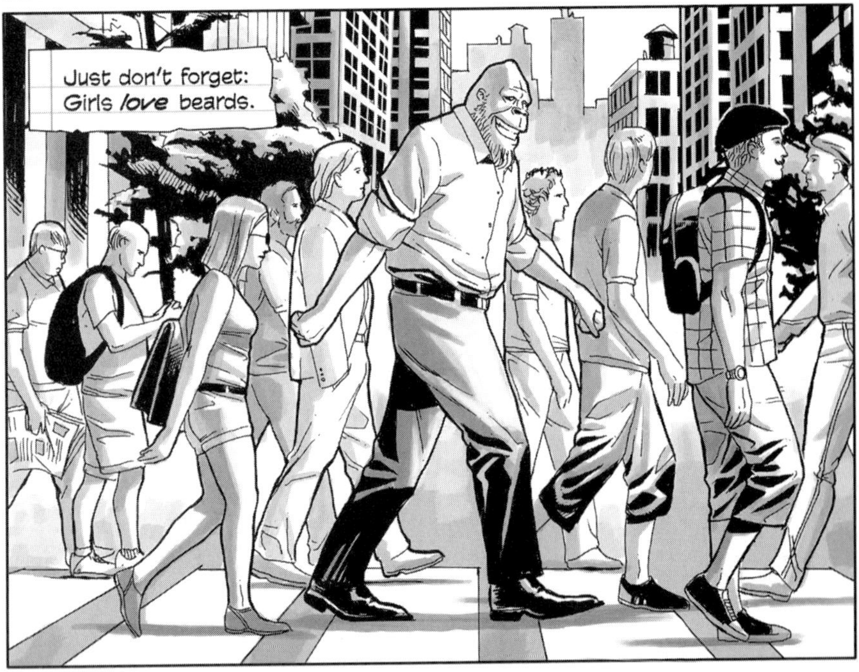
Just don't forget: Girls *love* beards.

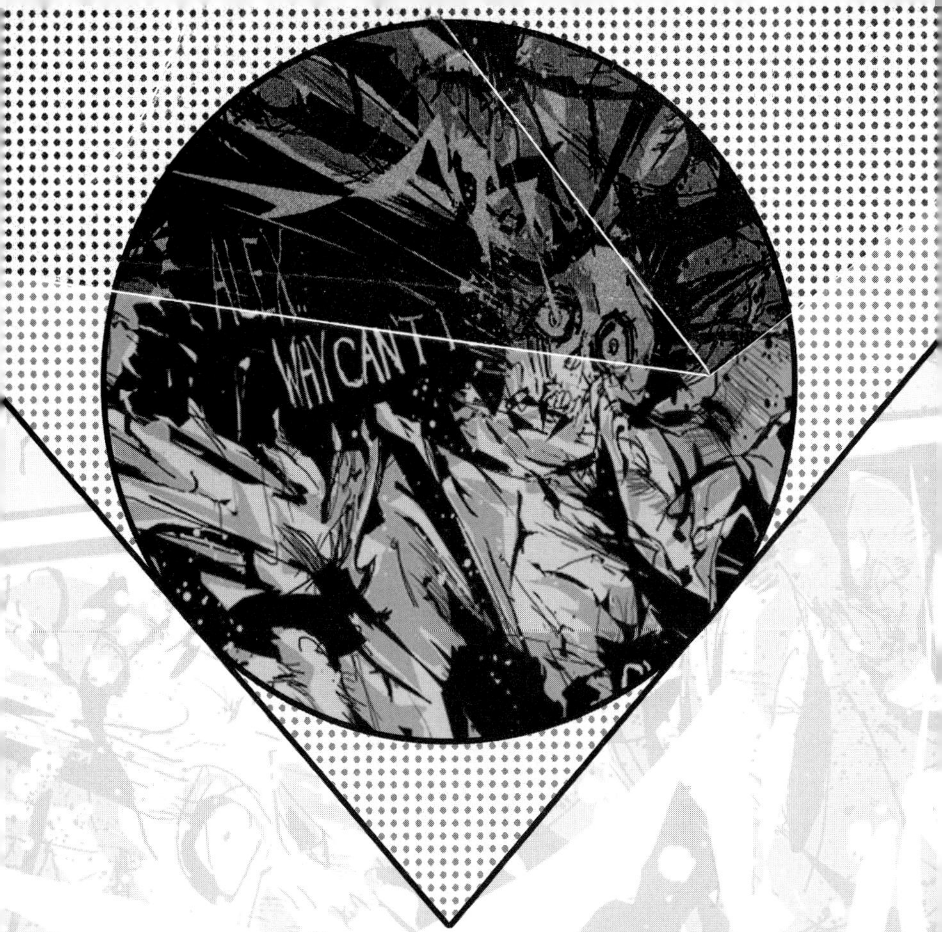
WHY CAN'T I

CLING

STORY - ART
JON CLARK

LETTERS
ERICA J. HEFLIN

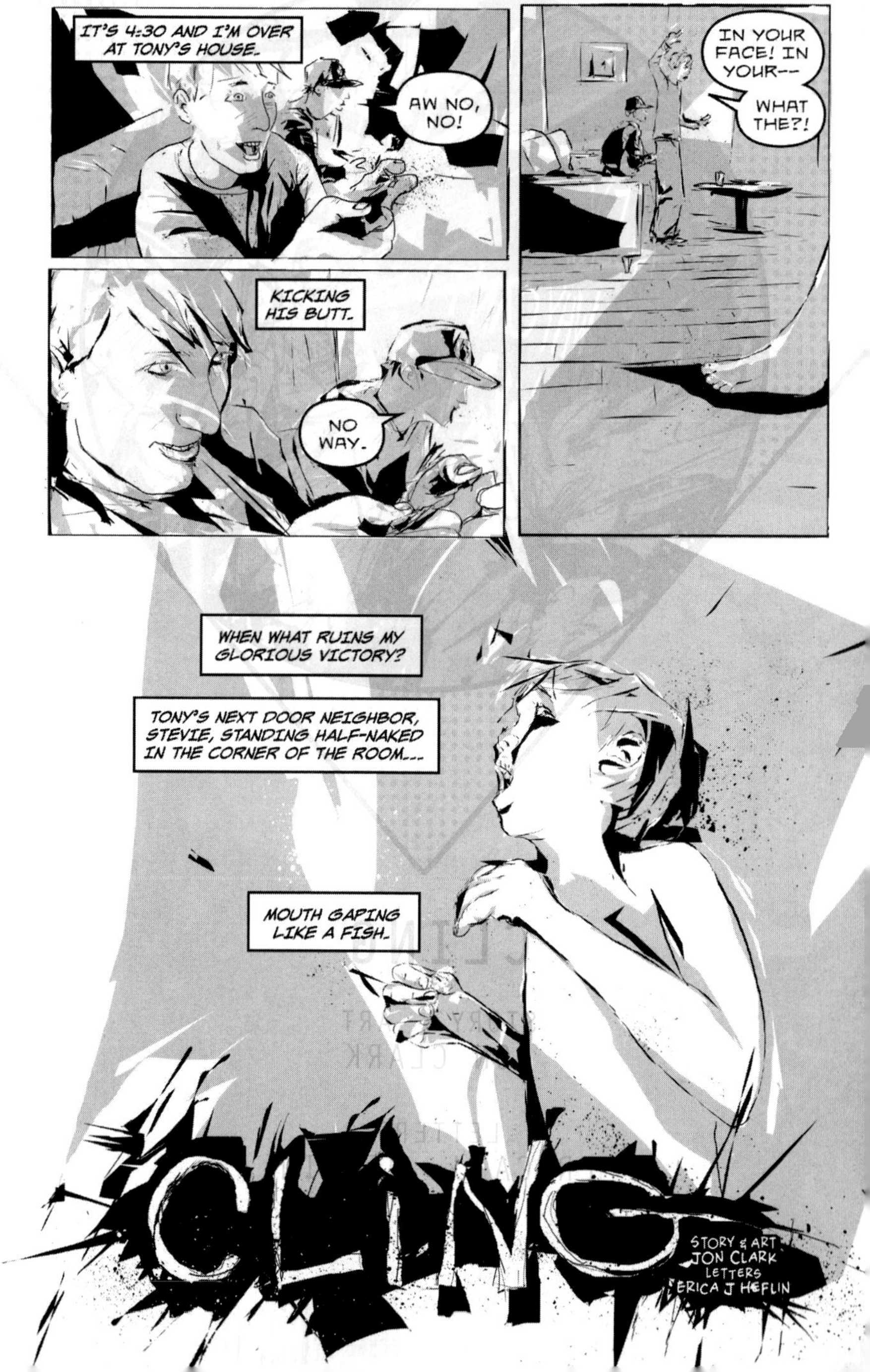
IT'S 4:30 AND I'M OVER AT TONY'S HOUSE.
AW NO, NO!
KICKING HIS BUTT.
NO WAY.
IN YOUR FACE! IN YOUR--
WHAT THE?!
WHEN WHAT RUINS MY GLORIOUS VICTORY?
TONY'S NEXT DOOR NEIGHBOR, STEVIE, STANDING HALF-NAKED IN THE CORNER OF THE ROOM...
MOUTH GAPING LIKE A FISH.
CLING
STORY & ART
JON CLARK
LETTERS
ERICA J HEFLIN

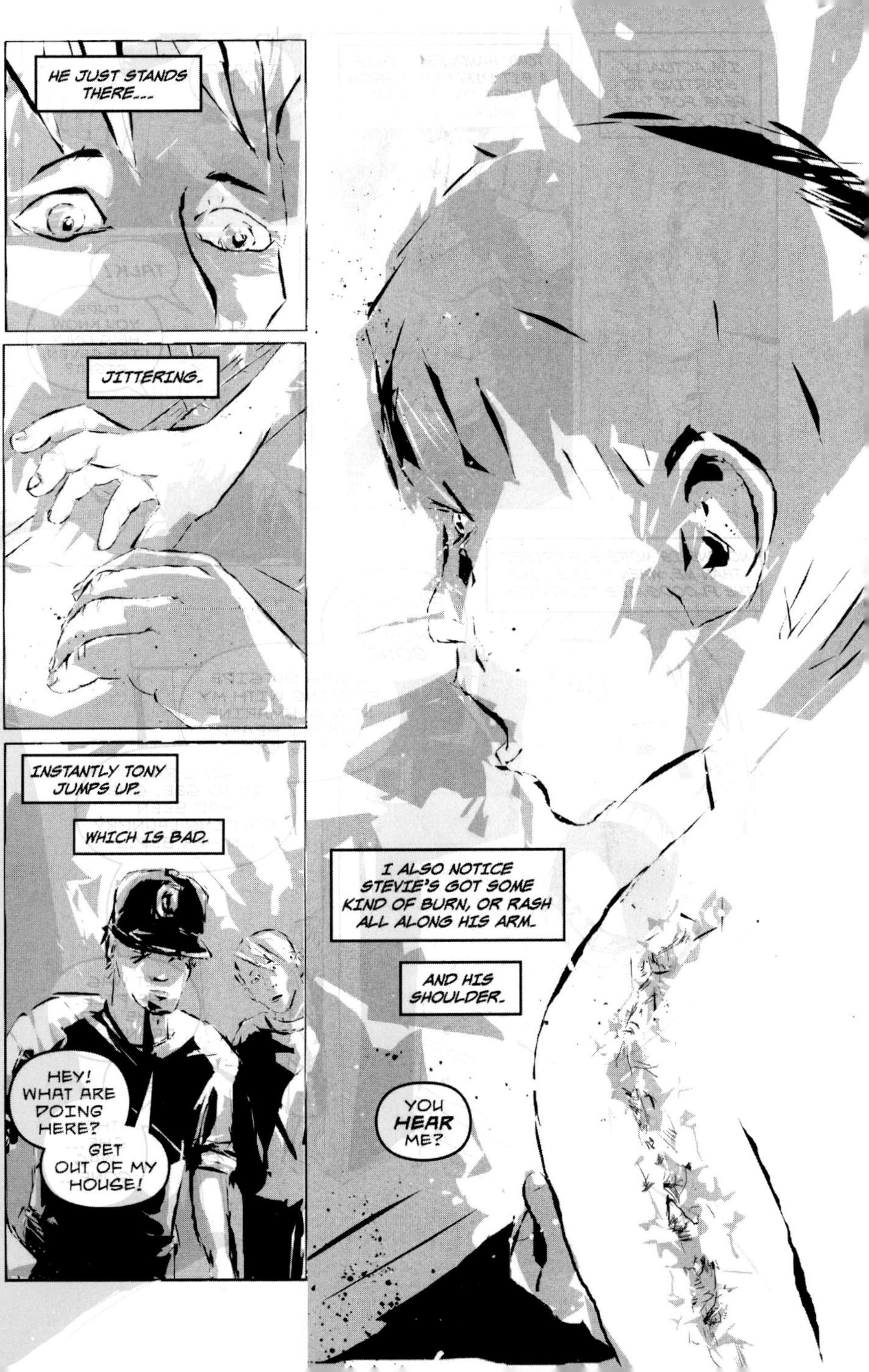

HE JUST STANDS THERE...
JITTERING.
INSTANTLY TONY JUMPS UP.
WHICH IS BAD.
HEY! WHAT ARE DOING HERE?
GET OUT OF MY HOUSE!
I ALSO NOTICE STEVIE'S GOT SOME KIND OF BURN, OR RASH ALL ALONG HIS ARM.
AND HIS SHOULDER.
YOU HEAR ME?

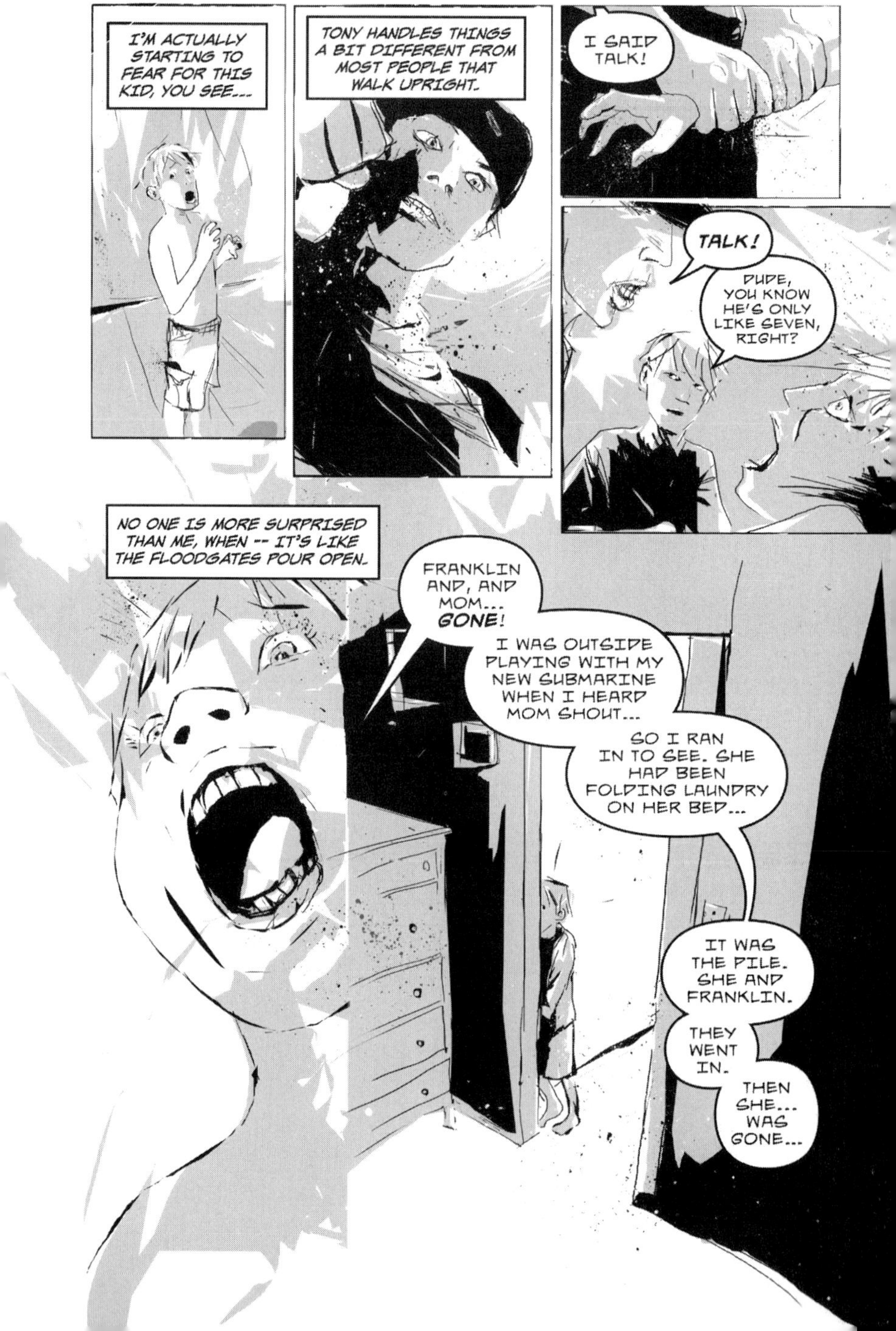

I'M ACTUALLY STARTING TO FEAR FOR THIS KID, YOU SEE...
TONY HANDLES THINGS A BIT DIFFERENT FROM MOST PEOPLE THAT WALK UPRIGHT.
I SAID TALK!
TALK!
DUDE, YOU KNOW HE'S ONLY LIKE SEVEN, RIGHT?
NO ONE IS MORE SURPRISED THAN ME, WHEN -- IT'S LIKE THE FLOODGATES POUR OPEN.
FRANKLIN AND, AND MOM... GONE!
I WAS OUTSIDE PLAYING WITH MY NEW SUBMARINE WHEN I HEARD MOM SHOUT...
SO I RAN IN TO SEE. SHE HAD BEEN FOLDING LAUNDRY ON HER BED...
IT WAS THE PILE. SHE AND FRANKLIN.
THEY WENT IN.
THEN SHE... WAS GONE...

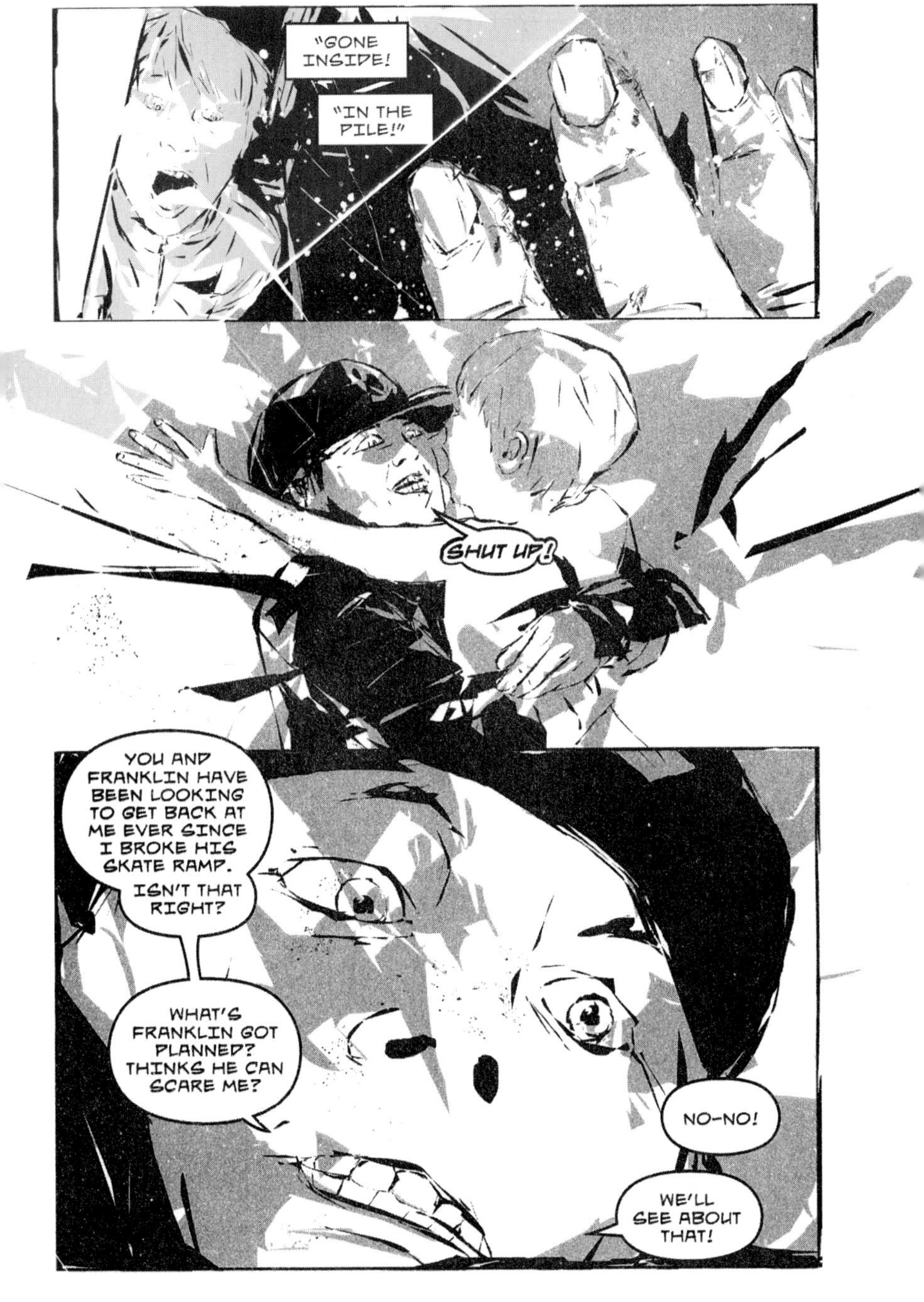
"GONE INSIDE!
"IN THE PILE!"
SHUT UP!
YOU AND FRANKLIN HAVE BEEN LOOKING TO GET BACK AT ME EVER SINCE I BROKE HIS SKATE RAMP.
ISN'T THAT RIGHT?
WHAT'S FRANKLIN GOT PLANNED? THINKS HE CAN SCARE ME?
NO-NO!
WE'LL SEE ABOUT THAT!

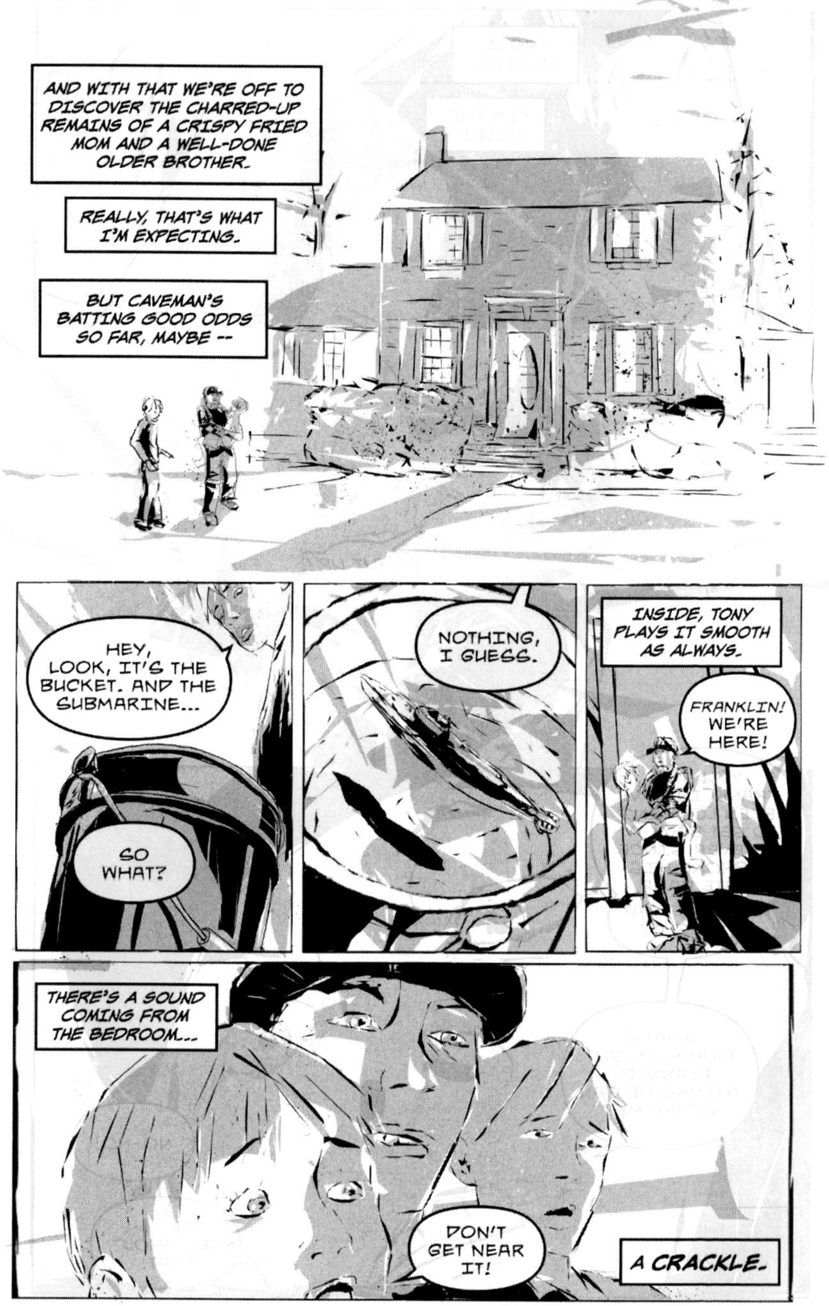
AND WITH THAT WE'RE OFF TO DISCOVER THE CHARRED-UP REMAINS OF A CRISPY FRIED MOM AND A WELL-DONE OLDER BROTHER.
REALLY, THAT'S WHAT I'M EXPECTING.
BUT CAVEMAN'S BATTING GOOD ODDS SO FAR, MAYBE --
HEY, LOOK, IT'S THE BUCKET. AND THE SUBMARINE...
SO WHAT?
NOTHING, I GUESS.
INSIDE, TONY PLAYS IT SMOOTH AS ALWAYS.
FRANKLIN! WE'RE HERE!
THERE'S A SOUND COMING FROM THE BEDROOM...
DON'T GET NEAR IT!
A CRACKLE.

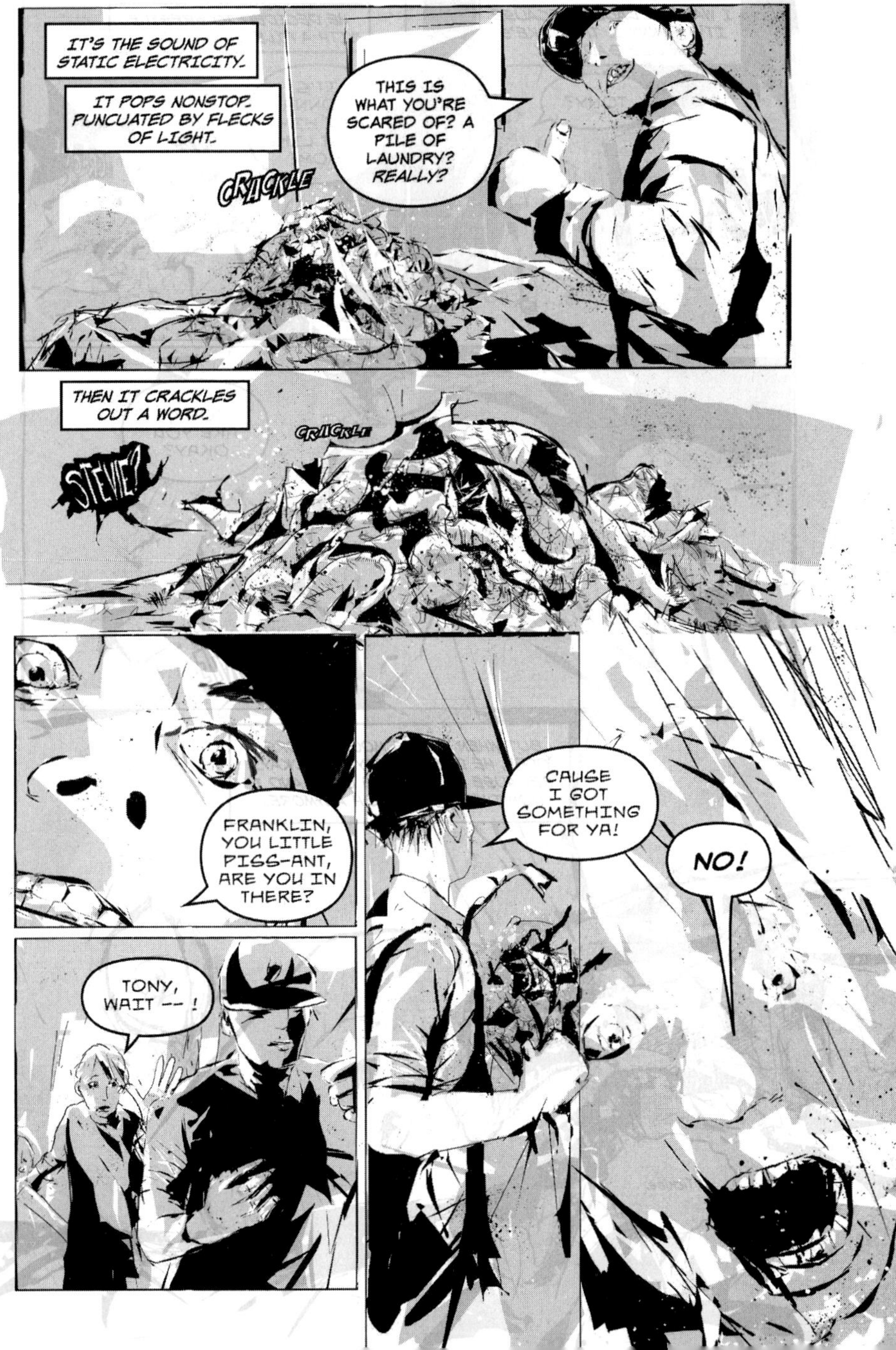
IT'S THE SOUND OF STATIC ELECTRICITY.
IT POPS NONSTOP. PUNCUATED BY FLECKS OF LIGHT.
CRACKLE
THIS IS WHAT YOU'RE SCARED OF? A PILE OF LAUNDRY? REALLY?
THEN IT CRACKLES OUT A WORD.
CRACKLE
STEVIE?
FRANKLIN, YOU LITTLE PISS-ANT, ARE YOU IN THERE?
TONY, WAIT -- !
CAUSE I GOT SOMETHING FOR YA!
NO!

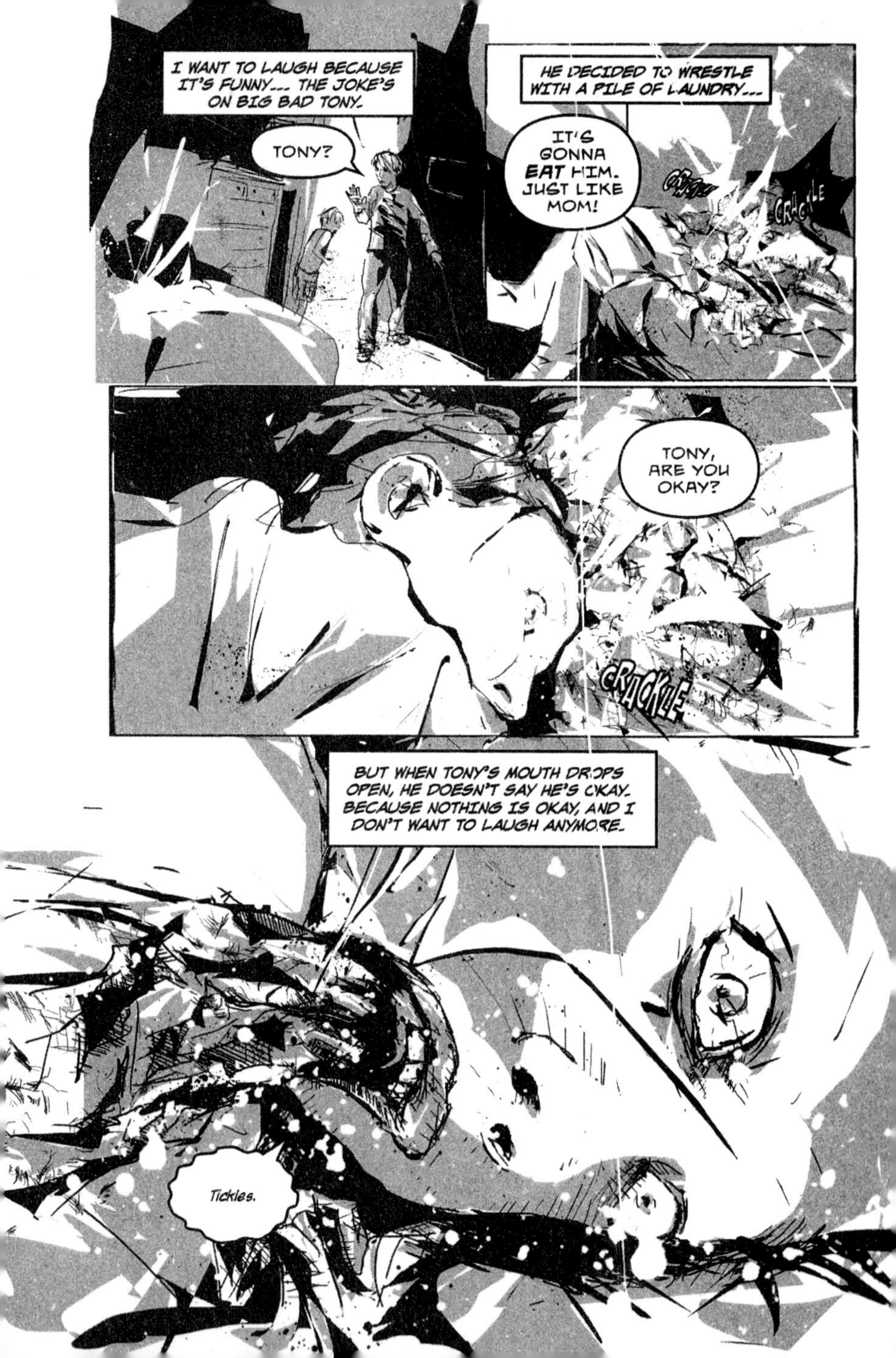
I WANT TO LAUGH BECAUSE IT'S FUNNY... THE JOKE'S ON BIG BAD TONY.
TONY?
HE DECIDED TO WRESTLE WITH A PILE OF LAUNDRY...
IT'S GONNA EAT HIM. JUST LIKE MOM!
CRACKLE
TONY, ARE YOU OKAY?
CRACKLE
BUT WHEN TONY'S MOUTH DROPS OPEN, HE DOESN'T SAY HE'S OKAY. BECAUSE NOTHING IS OKAY, AND I DON'T WANT TO LAUGH ANYMORE.
Tickles.

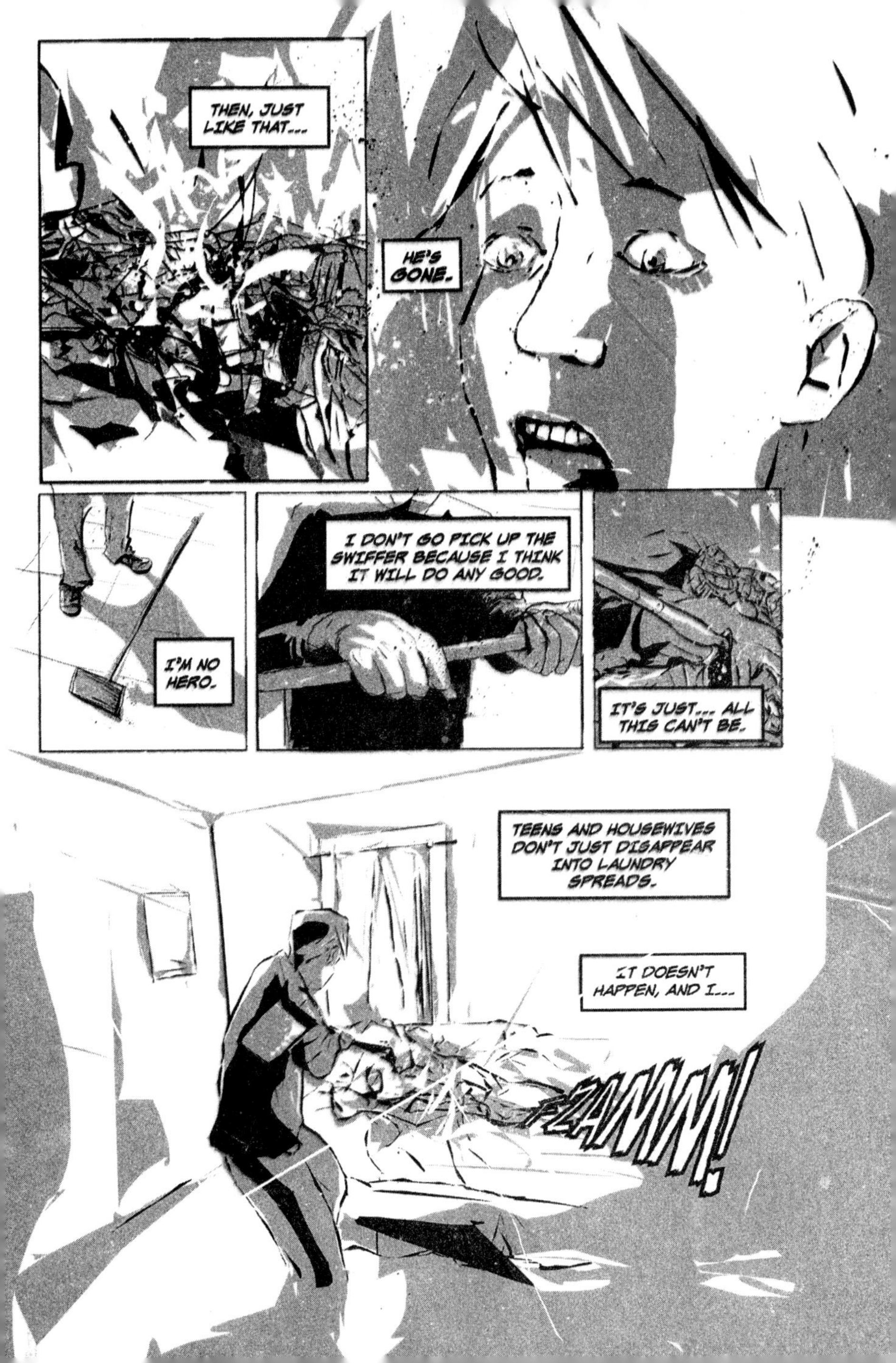
THEN, JUST LIKE THAT...
HE'S GONE.
I'M NO HERO.
I DON'T GO PICK UP THE SWIFFER BECAUSE I THINK IT WILL DO ANY GOOD.
IT'S JUST... ALL THIS CAN'T BE.
TEENS AND HOUSEWIVES DON'T JUST DISAPPEAR INTO LAUNDRY SPREADS.
IT DOESN'T HAPPEN, AND I...
FLAMM!

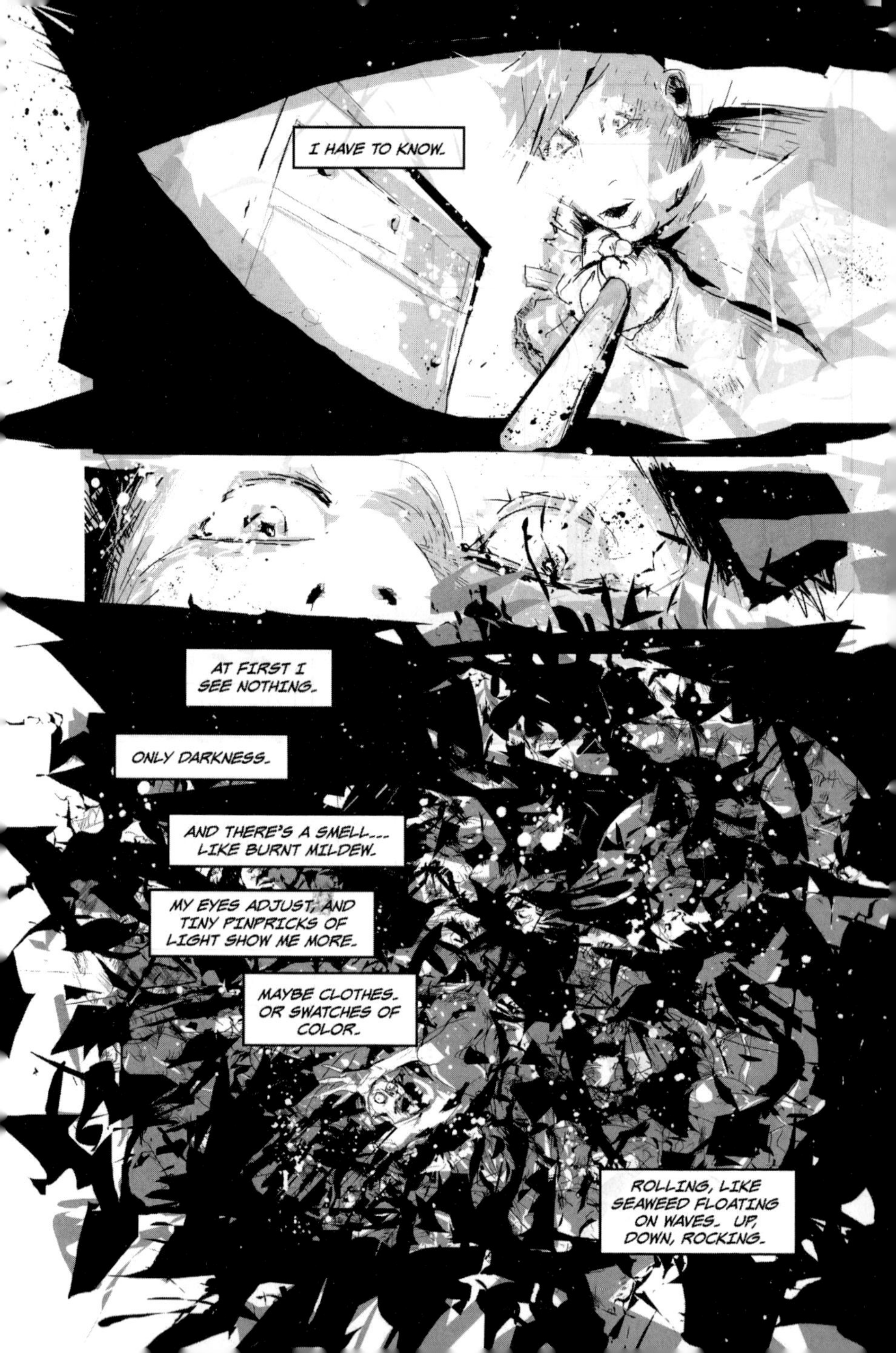
I HAVE TO KNOW.
AT FIRST I SEE NOTHING.
ONLY DARKNESS.
AND THERE'S A SMELL... LIKE BURNT MILDEW.
MY EYES ADJUST, AND TINY PINPRICKS OF LIGHT SHOW ME MORE.
MAYBE CLOTHES. OR SWATCHES OF COLOR.
ROLLING, LIKE SEAWEED FLOATING ON WAVES. UP, DOWN, ROCKING.

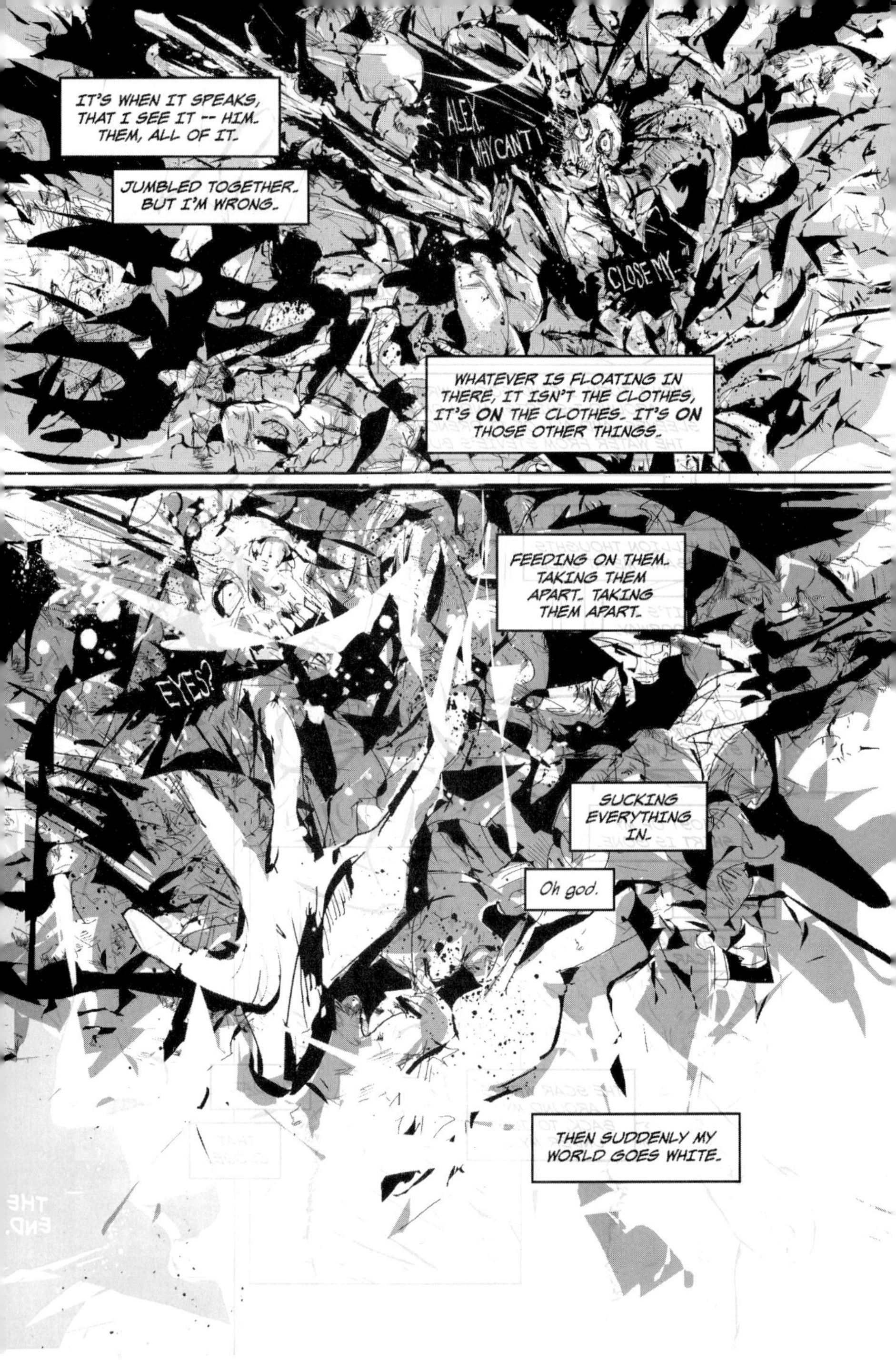
IT'S WHEN IT SPEAKS, THAT I SEE IT -- HIM. THEM, ALL OF IT.
JUMBLED TOGETHER.. BUT I'M WRONG..
ALEX.. WHY CAN'T I
CLOSE MY..
WHATEVER IS FLOATING IN THERE, IT ISN'T THE CLOTHES, IT'S ON THE CLOTHES. IT'S ON THOSE OTHER THINGS..
FEEDING ON THEM.. TAKING THEM APART.. TAKING THEM APART..
EYES?
SUCKING EVERYTHING IN..
Oh god.
THEN SUDDENLY MY WORLD GOES WHITE..

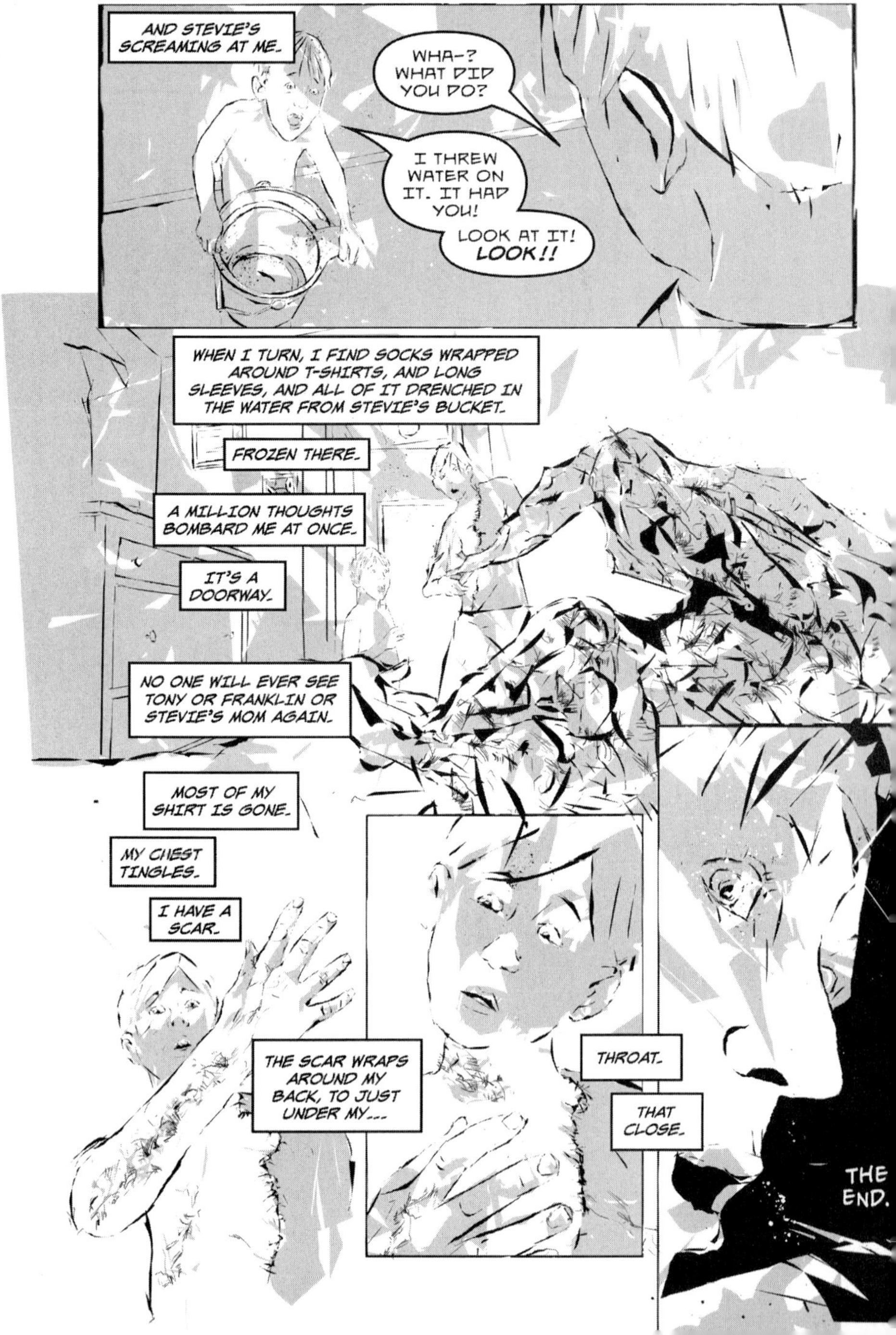
AND STEVIE'S SCREAMING AT ME.
WHA-? WHAT DID YOU DO?
I THREW WATER ON IT. IT HAD YOU!
LOOK AT IT! LOOK!!
WHEN I TURN, I FIND SOCKS WRAPPED AROUND T-SHIRTS, AND LONG SLEEVES, AND ALL OF IT DRENCHED IN THE WATER FROM STEVIE'S BUCKET.
FROZEN THERE.
A MILLION THOUGHTS BOMBARD ME AT ONCE.
IT'S A DOORWAY.
NO ONE WILL EVER SEE TONY OR FRANKLIN OR STEVIE'S MOM AGAIN.
MOST OF MY SHIRT IS GONE.
MY CHEST TINGLES.
I HAVE A SCAR.
THE SCAR WRAPS AROUND MY BACK, TO JUST UNDER MY...
THROAT.
THAT CLOSE.
THE END.

THE INITIATION

STORY
DINO CARUSO

ART
SAM AGRO

LETTERS
ADAM WOLLET

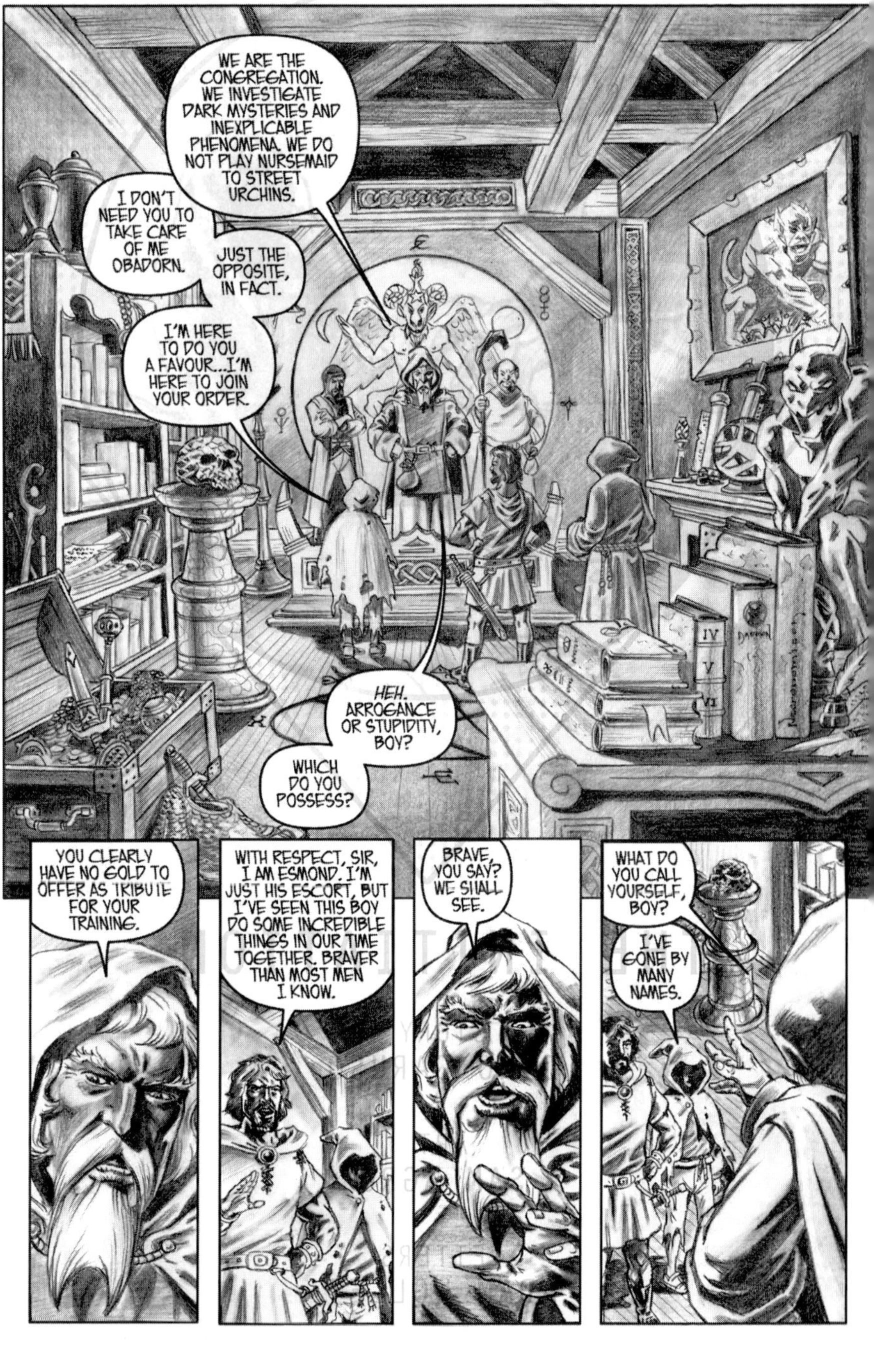

WE ARE THE CONGREGATION. WE INVESTIGATE DARK MYSTERIES AND INEXPLICABLE PHENOMENA. WE DO NOT PLAY NURSEMAID TO STREET URCHINS.
I DON'T NEED YOU TO TAKE CARE OF ME OBADORN.
JUST THE OPPOSITE, IN FACT.
I'M HERE TO DO YOU A FAVOUR...I'M HERE TO JOIN YOUR ORDER.
HEH. ARROGANCE OR STUPIDITY, BOY?
WHICH DO YOU POSSESS?
YOU CLEARLY HAVE NO GOLD TO OFFER AS TRIBUTE FOR YOUR TRAINING.
WITH RESPECT, SIR, I AM ESMOND. I'M JUST HIS ESCORT, BUT I'VE SEEN THIS BOY DO SOME INCREDIBLE THINGS IN OUR TIME TOGETHER. BRAVER THAN MOST MEN I KNOW.
BRAVE, YOU SAY? WE SHALL SEE.
WHAT DO YOU CALL YOURSELF, BOY?
I'VE GONE BY MANY NAMES.

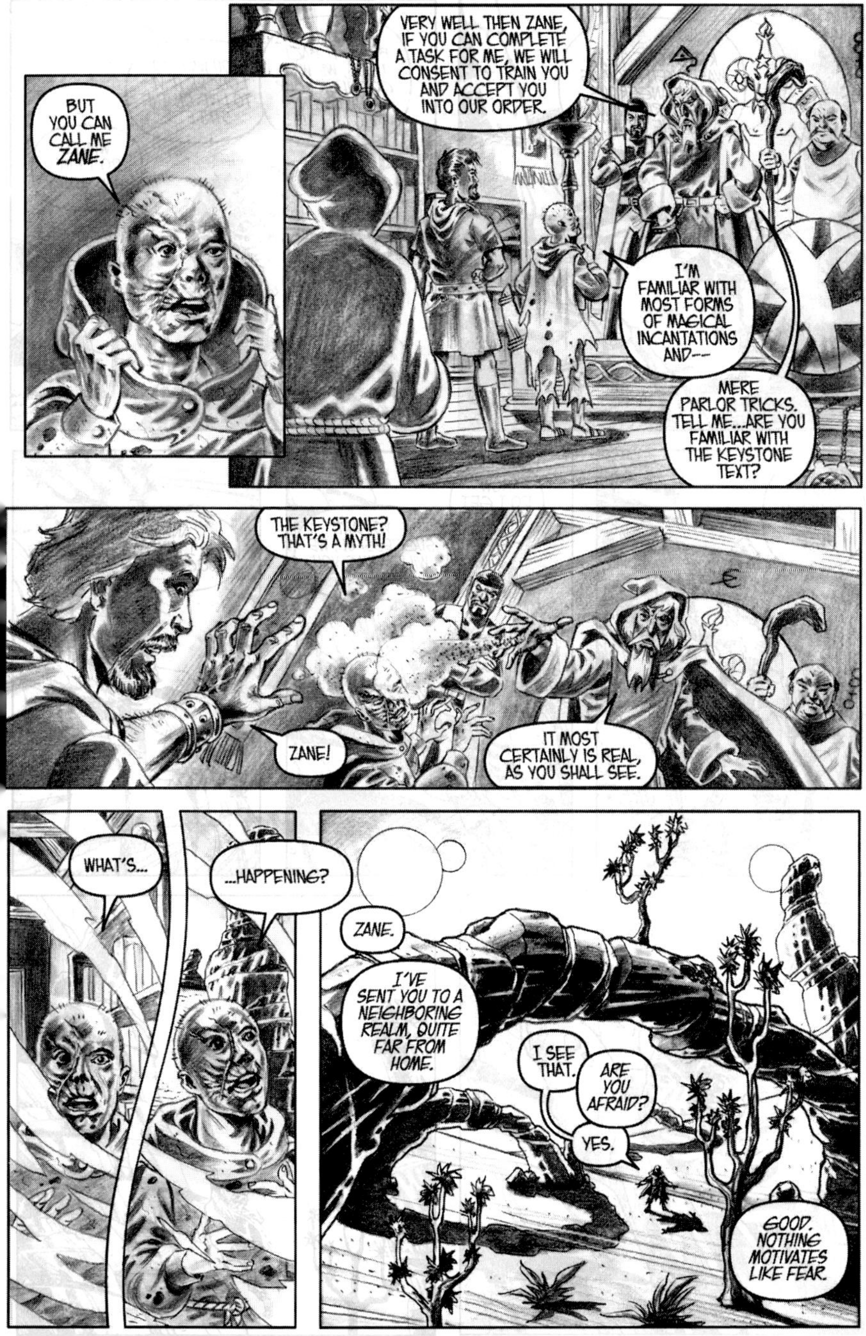
BUT YOU CAN CALL ME ZANE.
VERY WELL THEN ZANE, IF YOU CAN COMPLETE A TASK FOR ME, WE WILL CONSENT TO TRAIN YOU AND ACCEPT YOU INTO OUR ORDER.
I'M FAMILIAR WITH MOST FORMS OF MAGICAL INCANTATIONS AND--
MERE PARLOR TRICKS. TELL ME...ARE YOU FAMILIAR WITH THE KEYSTONE TEXT?
THE KEYSTONE? THAT'S A MYTH!
ZANE!
IT MOST CERTAINLY IS REAL, AS YOU SHALL SEE.
WHAT'S...
...HAPPENING?
ZANE.
I'VE SENT YOU TO A NEIGHBORING REALM, QUITE FAR FROM HOME.
I SEE THAT.
ARE YOU AFRAID?
YES.
GOOD. NOTHING MOTIVATES LIKE FEAR.

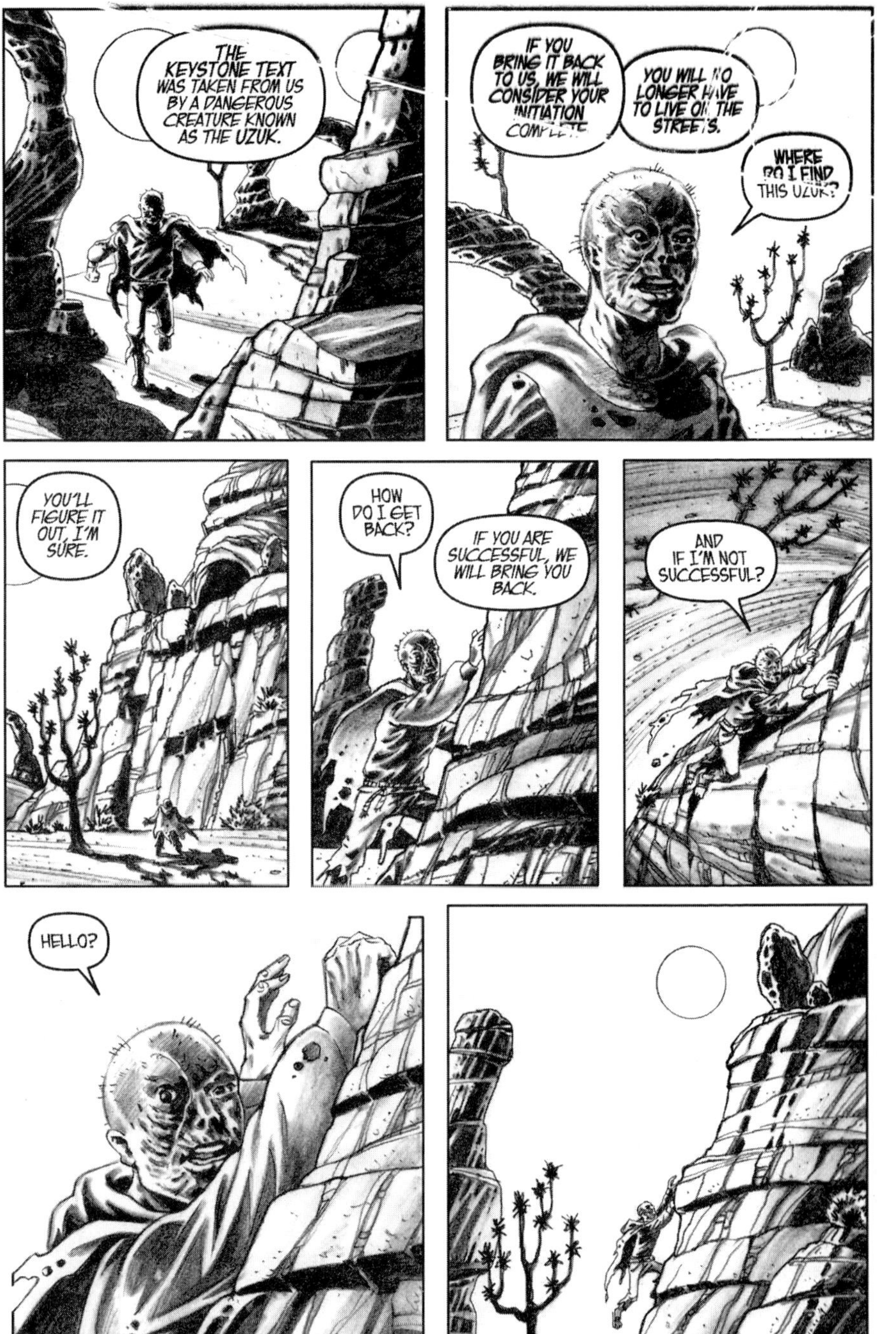
THE KEYSTONE TEXT WAS TAKEN FROM US BY A DANGEROUS CREATURE KNOWN AS THE UZUK.
IF YOU BRING IT BACK TO US, WE WILL CONSIDER YOUR INITIATION COMPL
YOU WILL NO LONGER HAVE TO LIVE ON THE STREETS.
WHERE DO I FIND THIS UZUK?
YOU'LL FIGURE IT OUT, I'M SURE.
HOW DO I GET BACK?
IF YOU ARE SUCCESSFUL, WE WILL BRING YOU BACK.
AND IF I'M NOT SUCCESSFUL?
HELLO?

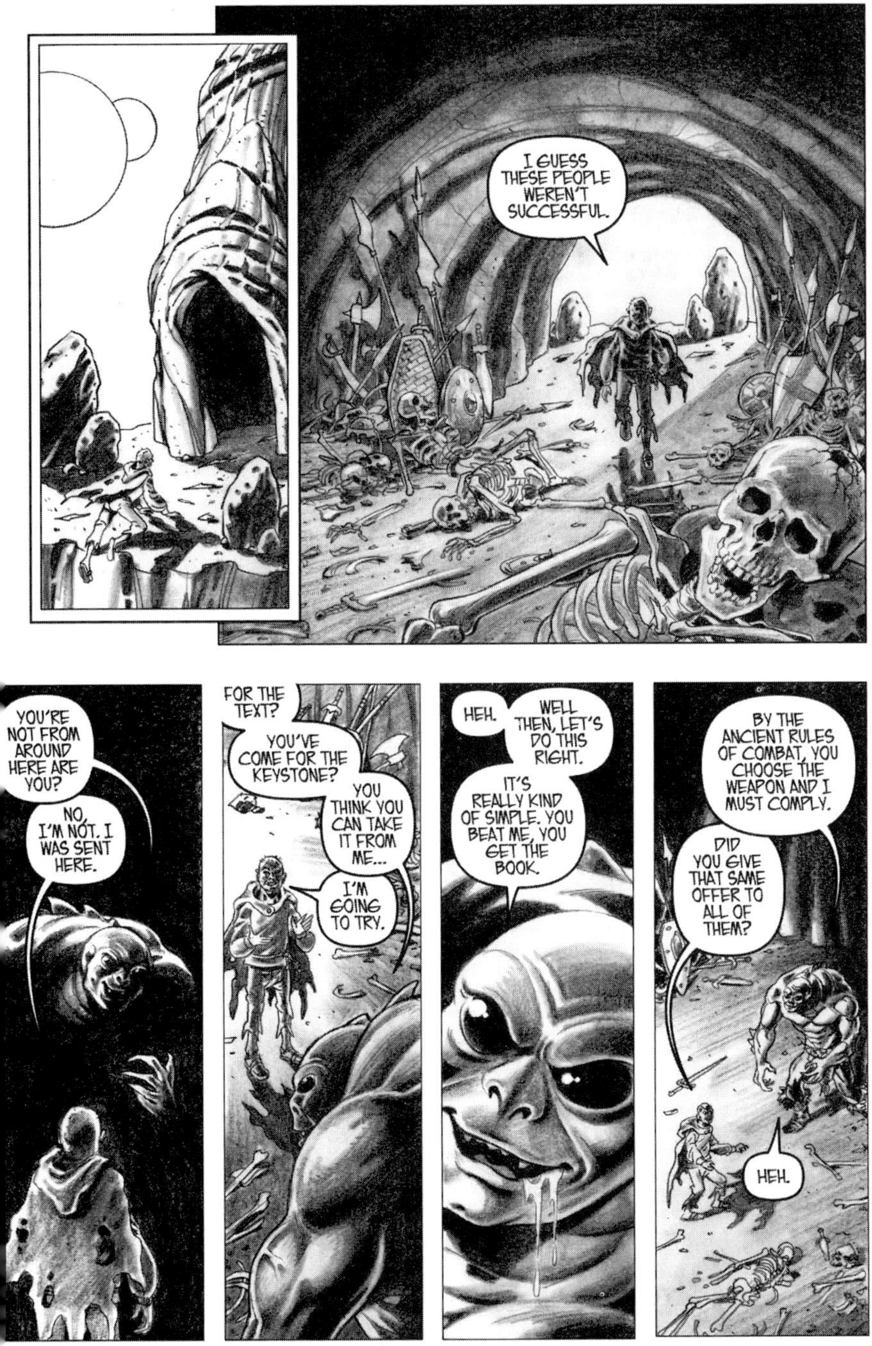
I GUESS THESE PEOPLE WEREN'T SUCCESSFUL.
YOU'RE NOT FROM AROUND HERE ARE YOU?
NO, I'M NOT. I WAS SENT HERE.
FOR THE TEXT?
YOU'VE COME FOR THE KEYSTONE?
YOU THINK YOU CAN TAKE IT FROM ME...
I'M GOING TO TRY.
HEH.
WELL THEN, LET'S DO THIS RIGHT.
IT'S REALLY KIND OF SIMPLE. YOU BEAT ME, YOU GET THE BOOK.
BY THE ANCIENT RULES OF COMBAT, YOU CHOOSE THE WEAPON AND I MUST COMPLY.
DID YOU GIVE THAT SAME OFFER TO ALL OF THEM?
HEH.

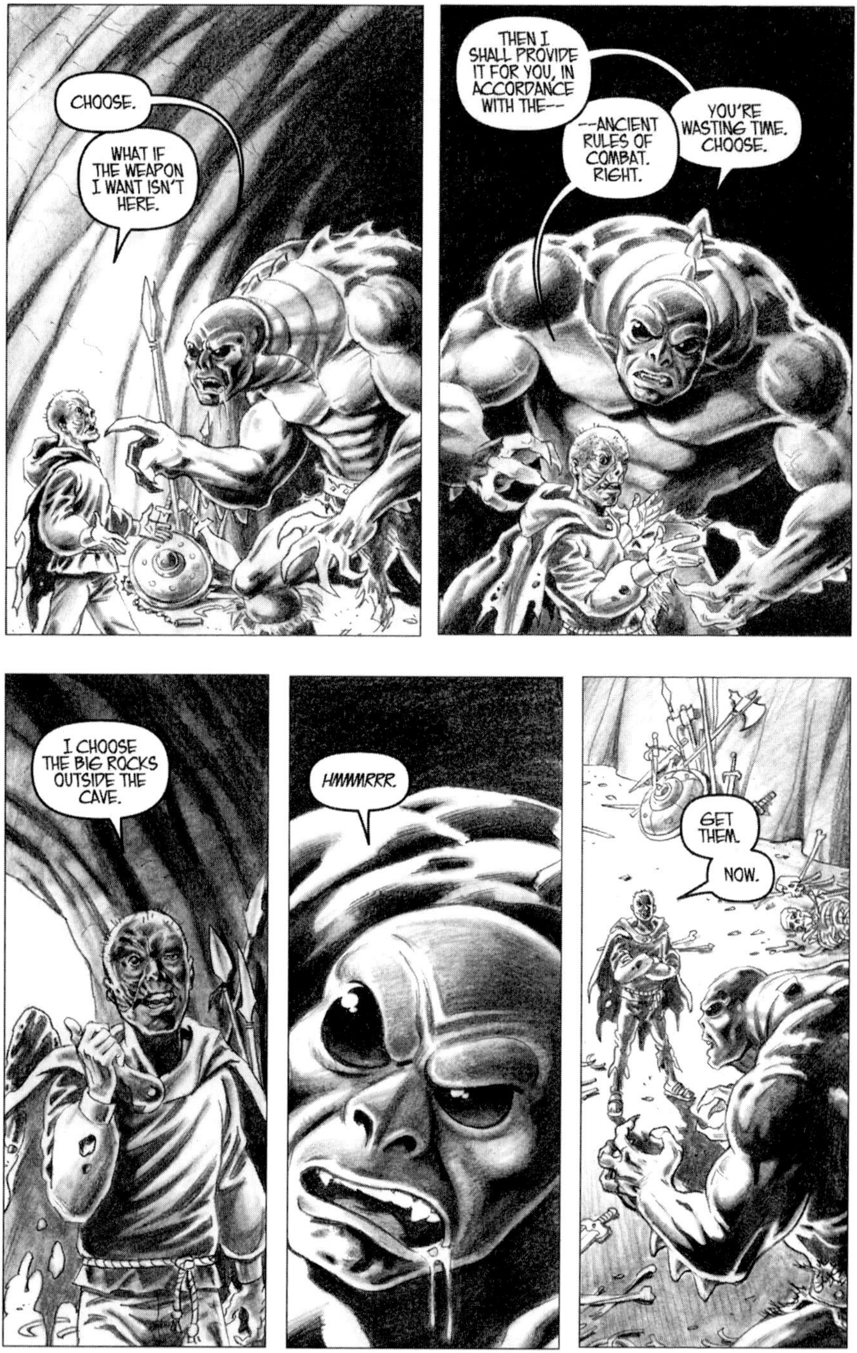
CHOOSE.
WHAT IF THE WEAPON I WANT ISN'T HERE.
THEN I SHALL PROVIDE IT FOR YOU, IN ACCORDANCE WITH THE--
--ANCIENT RULES OF COMBAT. RIGHT.
YOU'RE WASTING TIME. CHOOSE.
I CHOOSE THE BIG ROCKS OUTSIDE THE CAVE.
HMMMRRR.
GET THEM.
NOW.

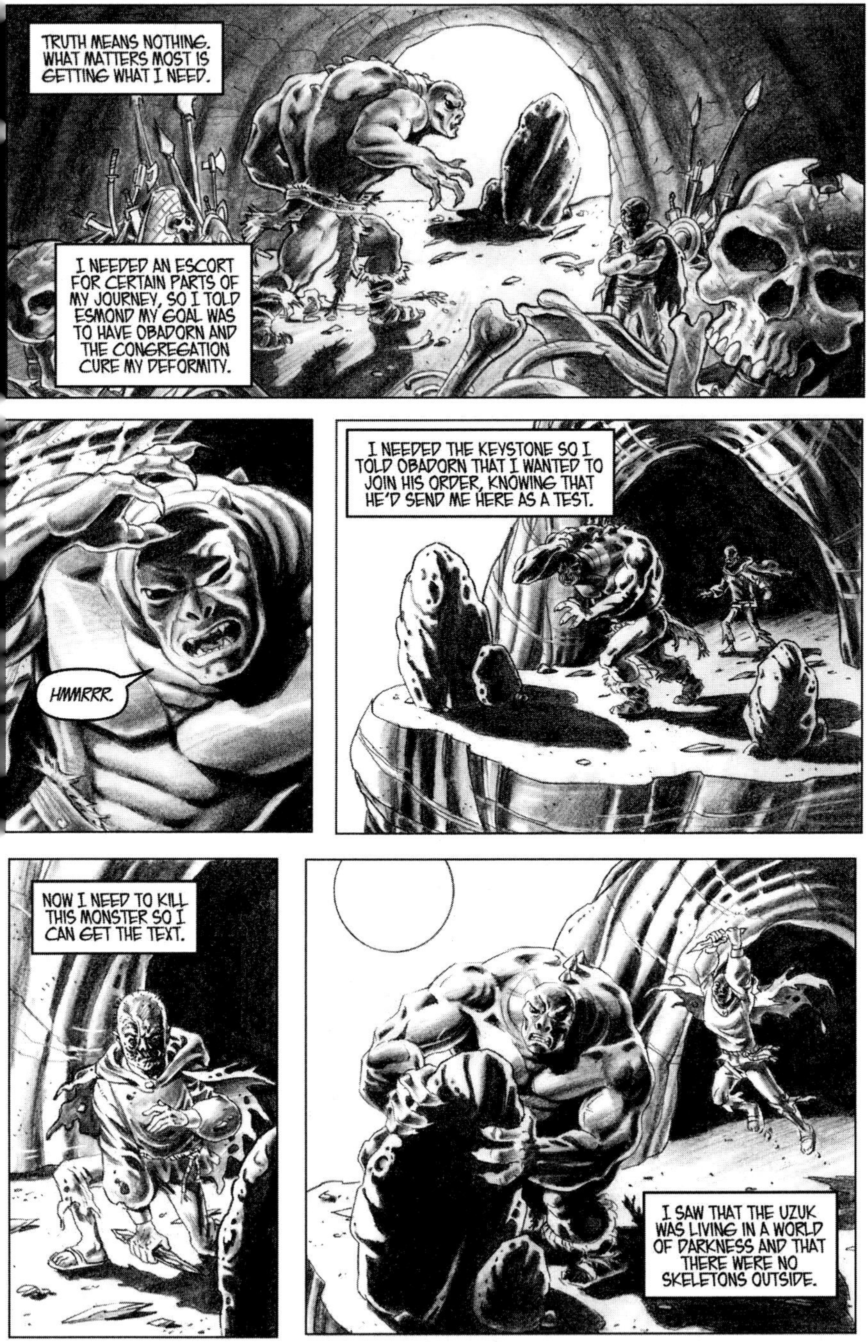
TRUTH MEANS NOTHING. WHAT MATTERS MOST IS GETTING WHAT I NEED.
I NEEDED AN ESCORT FOR CERTAIN PARTS OF MY JOURNEY, SO I TOLD ESMOND MY GOAL WAS TO HAVE OBADORN AND THE CONGREGATION CURE MY DEFORMITY.
HMMRRR.
I NEEDED THE KEYSTONE SO I TOLD OBADORN THAT I WANTED TO JOIN HIS ORDER, KNOWING THAT HE'D SEND ME HERE AS A TEST.
NOW I NEED TO KILL THIS MONSTER SO I CAN GET THE TEXT.
I SAW THAT THE UZUK WAS LIVING IN A WORLD OF DARKNESS AND THAT THERE WERE NO SKELETONS OUTSIDE.

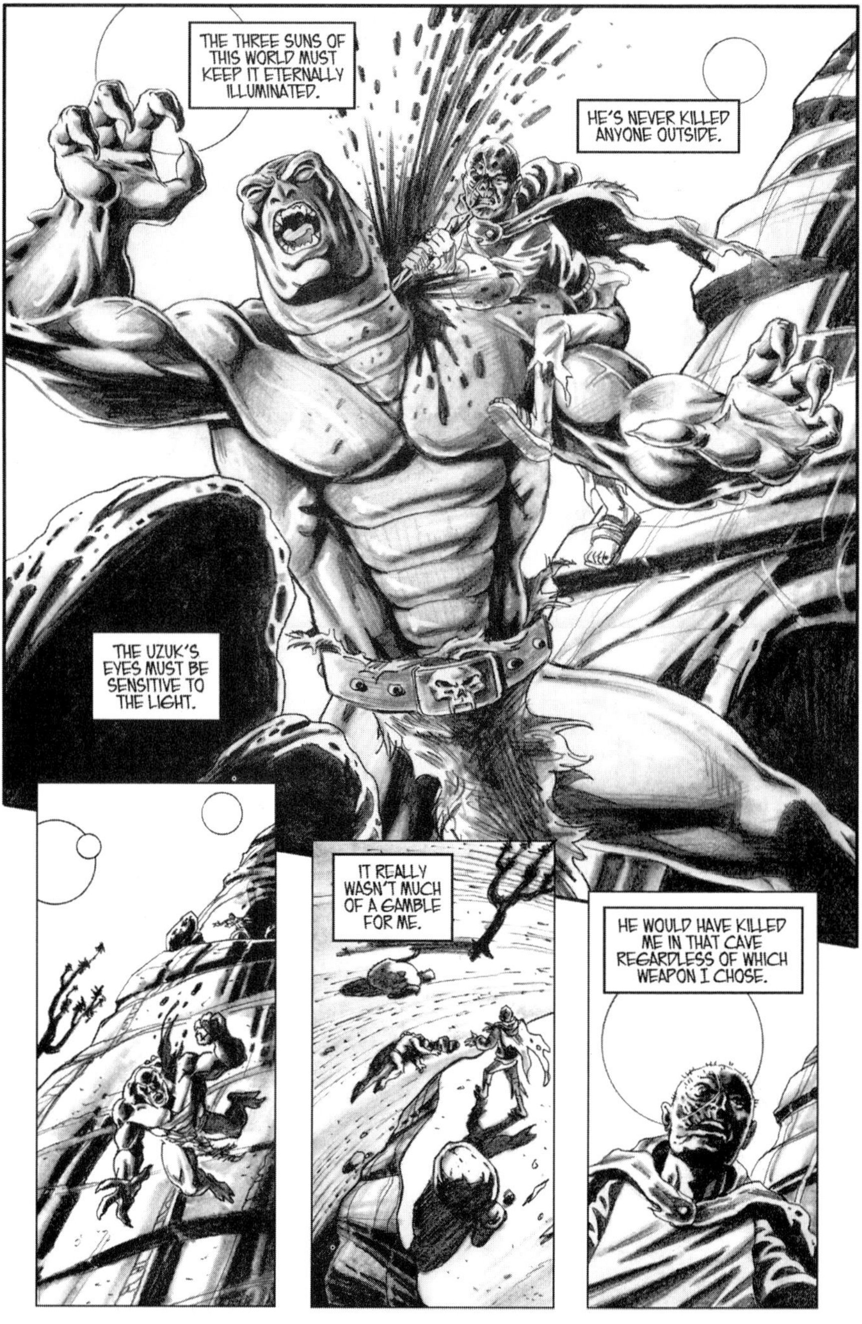
THE THREE SUNS OF THIS WORLD MUST KEEP IT ETERNALLY ILLUMINATED.
HE'S NEVER KILLED ANYONE OUTSIDE.
THE UZUK'S EYES MUST BE SENSITIVE TO THE LIGHT.
IT REALLY WASN'T MUCH OF A GAMBLE FOR ME.
HE WOULD HAVE KILLED ME IN THAT CAVE REGARDLESS OF WHICH WEAPON I CHOSE.

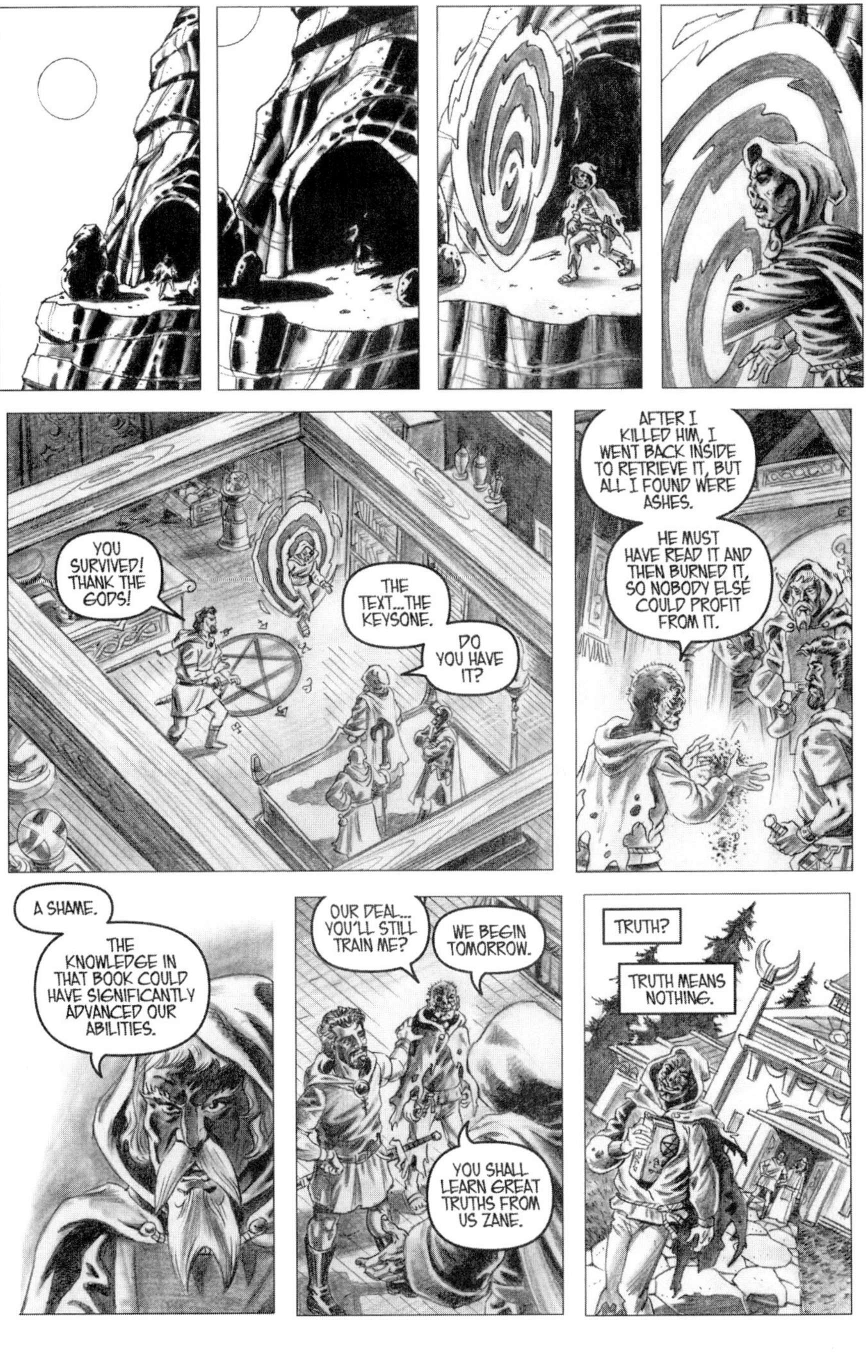

YOU SURVIVED! THANK THE GODS!
...THE TEXT...THE KEYSONE.
DO YOU HAVE IT?
AFTER I KILLED HIM, I WENT BACK INSIDE TO RETRIEVE IT, BUT ALL I FOUND WERE ASHES.
HE MUST HAVE READ IT AND THEN BURNED IT, SO NOBODY ELSE COULD PROFIT FROM IT.
A SHAME.
THE KNOWLEDGE IN THAT BOOK COULD HAVE SIGNIFICANTLY ADVANCED OUR ABILITIES.
OUR DEAL... YOU'LL STILL TRAIN ME?
WE BEGIN TOMORROW.
YOU SHALL LEARN GREAT TRUTHS FROM US ZANE.
TRUTH?
TRUTH MEANS NOTHING.

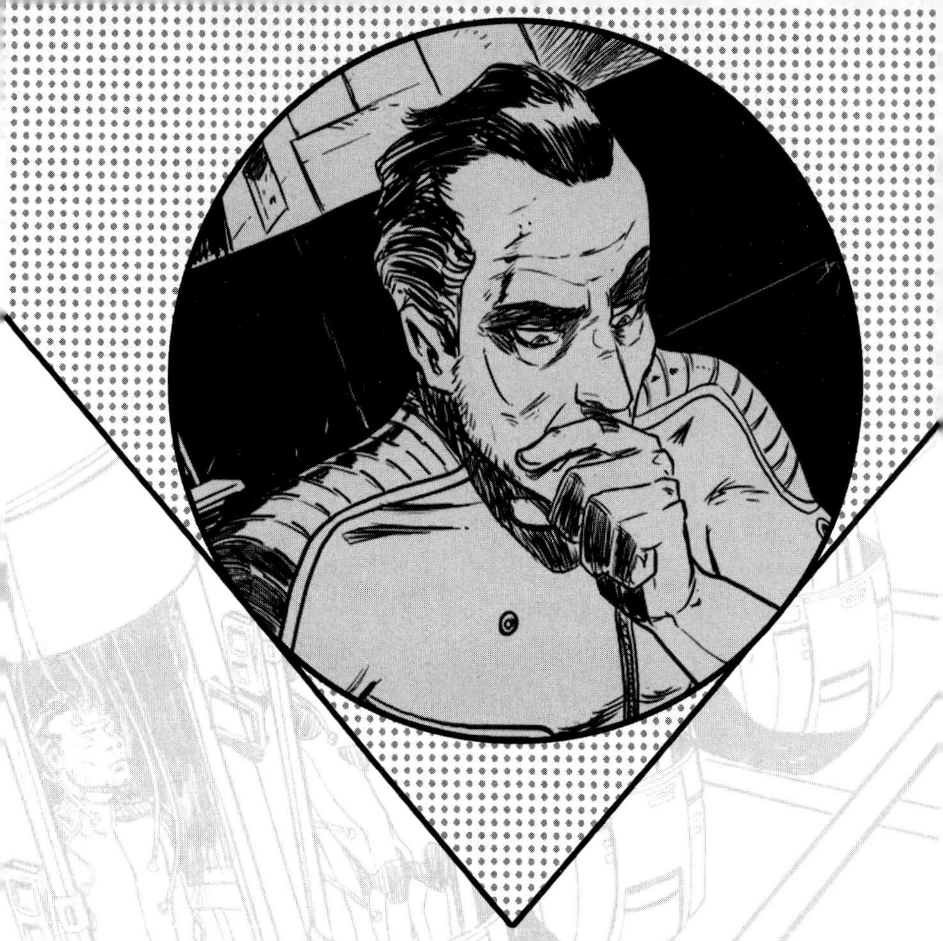

ALONE

STORY
MIKE SALT

ART
FABIAN COBOS

LETTERS
KENNY JEFFERY

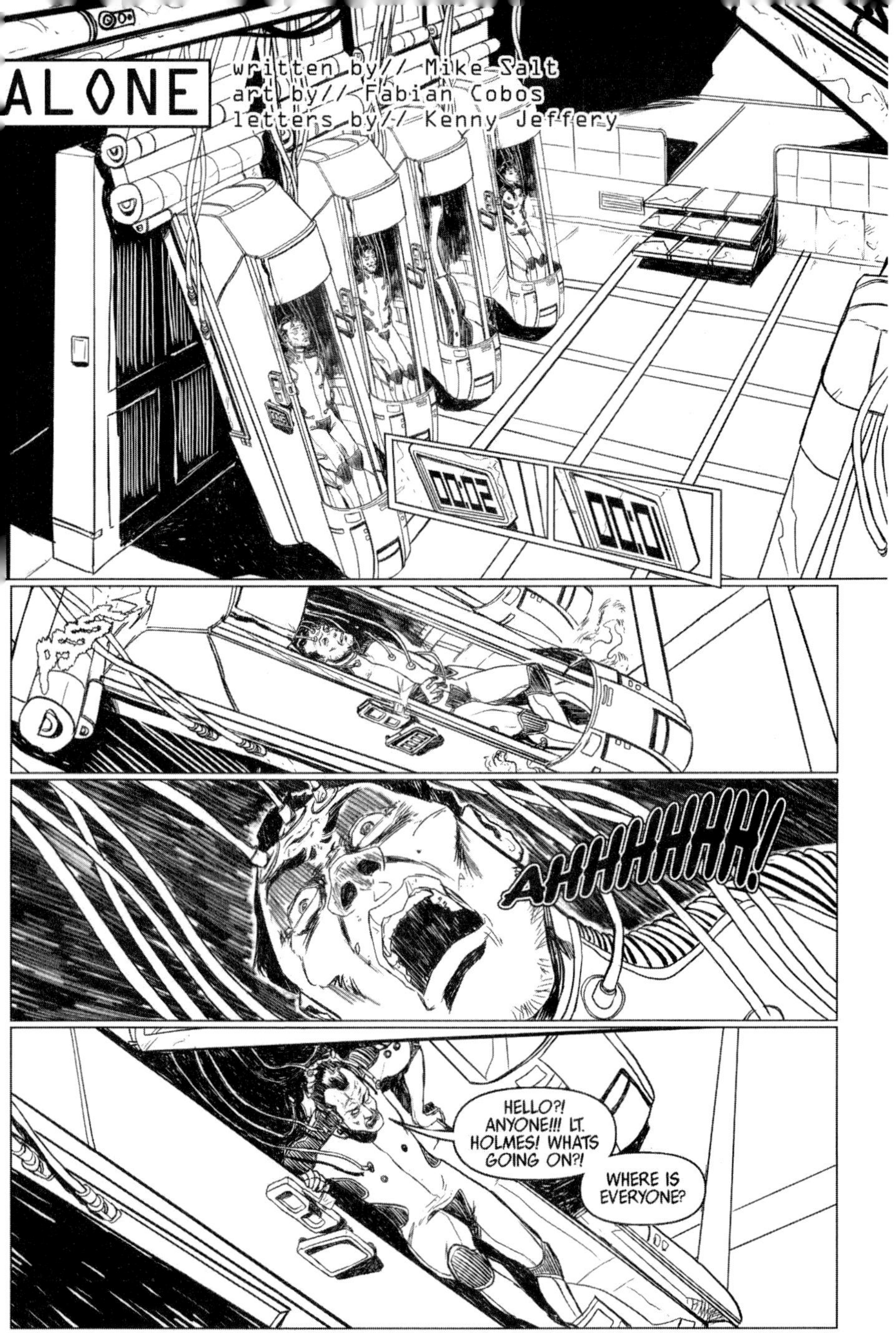
ALONE
written by// Mike Salt
art by// Fabian Cobos
letters by// Kenny Jeffery
AHHHHHHH!
HELLO?! ANYONE!!! LT. HOLMES! WHATS GOING ON?!
WHERE IS EVERYONE?

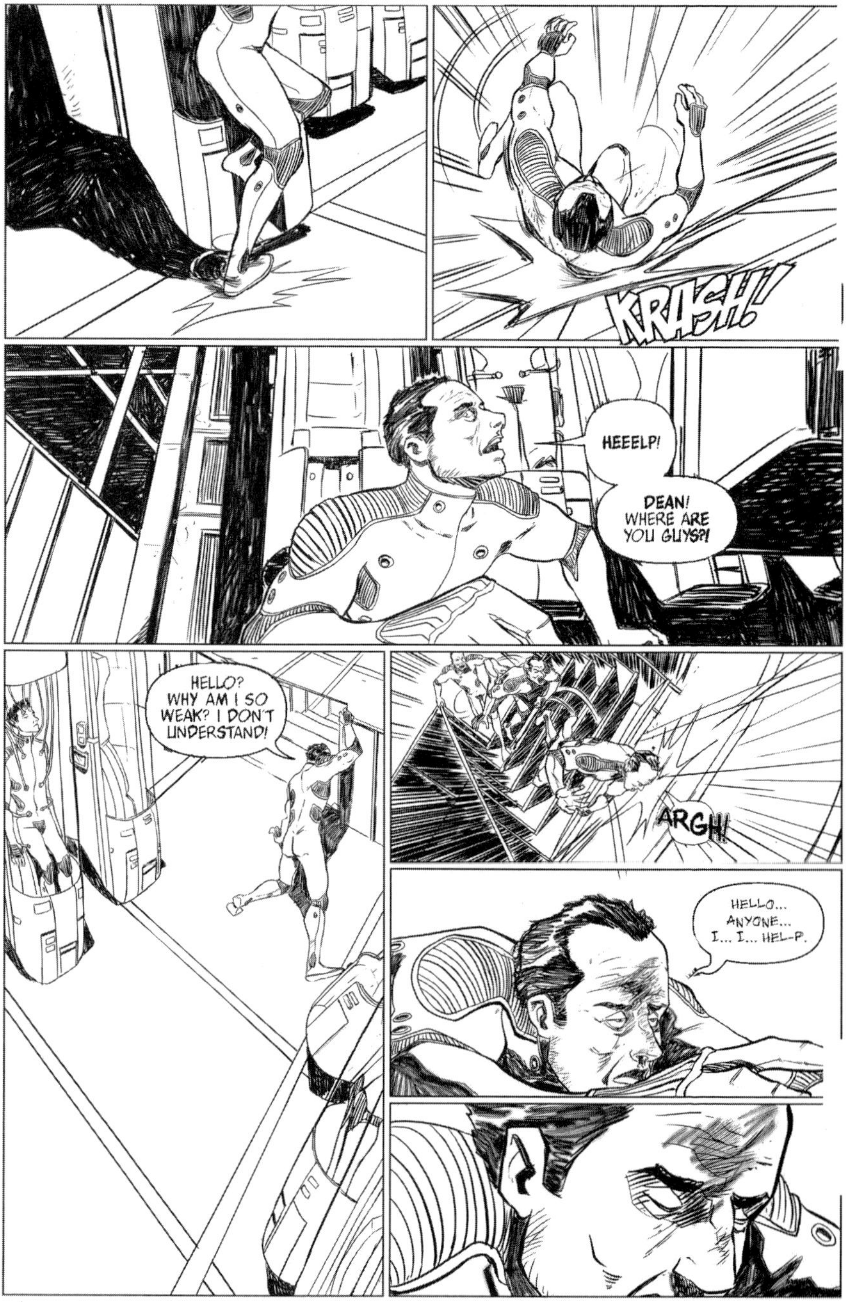
KRASH!
HEEELP!
DEAN! WHERE ARE YOU GUYS?!
HELLO? WHY AM I SO WEAK? I DON'T UNDERSTAND!
ARGH!
HELLO... ANYONE... I... I... HEL-P.

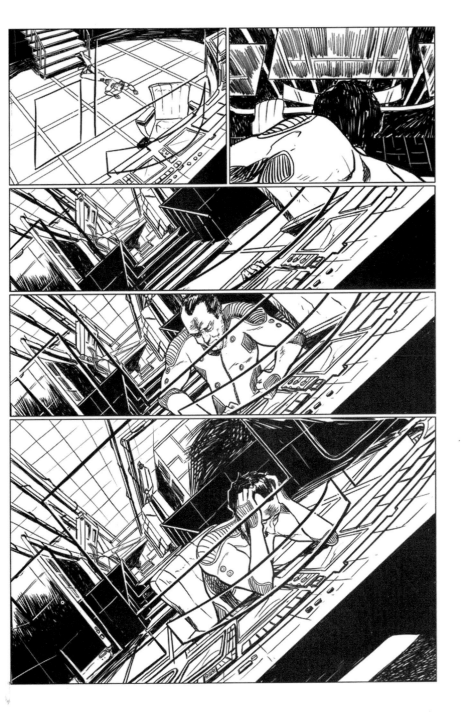

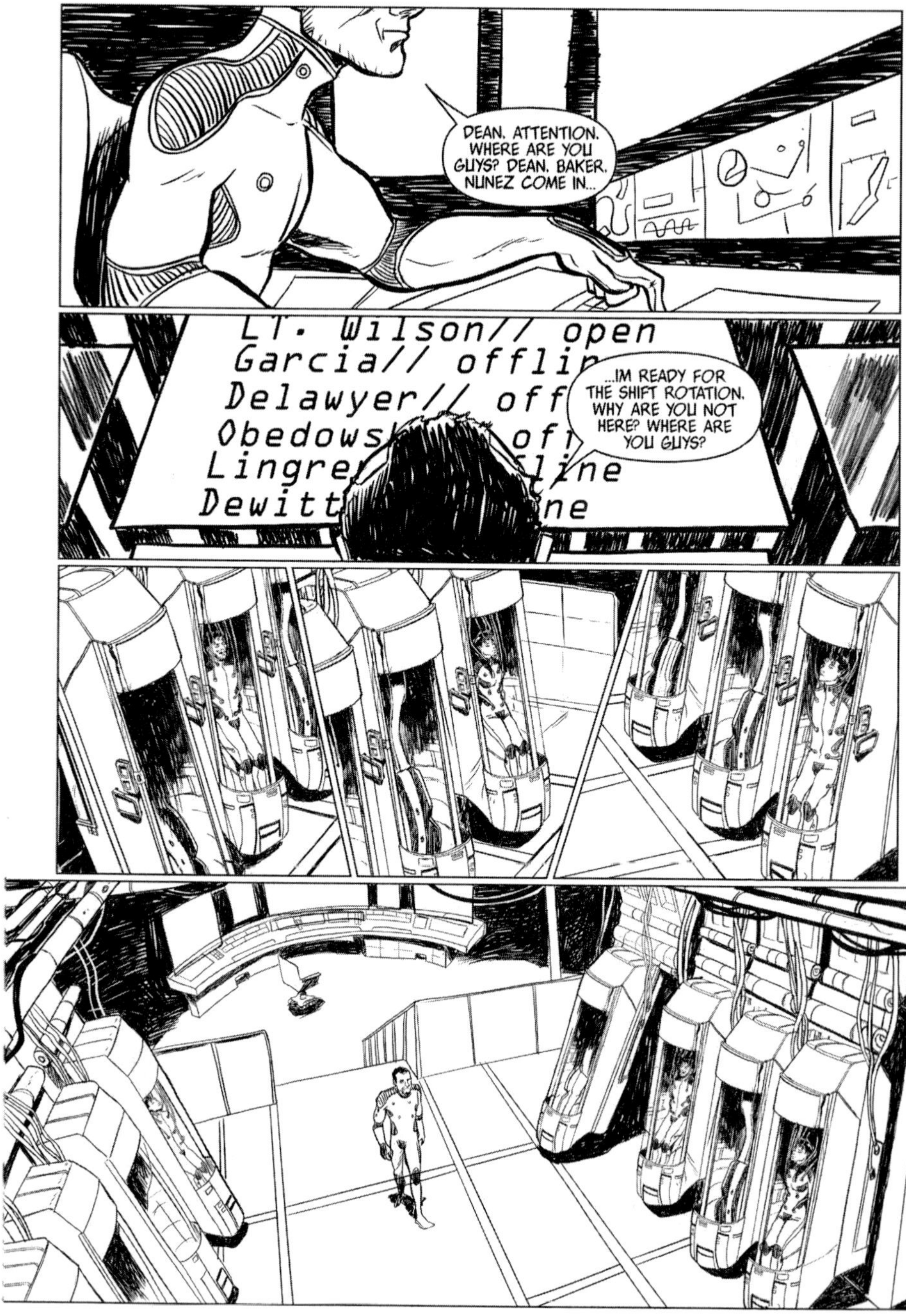
DEAN. ATTENTION. WHERE ARE YOU GUYS? DEAN. BAKER. NUNEZ COME IN...
LT. Wilson// open
Garcia// offlin
Delawyer// off
Obedows
Lingre
Dewitt
...IM READY FOR THE SHIFT ROTATION. WHY ARE YOU NOT HERE? WHERE ARE YOU GUYS?

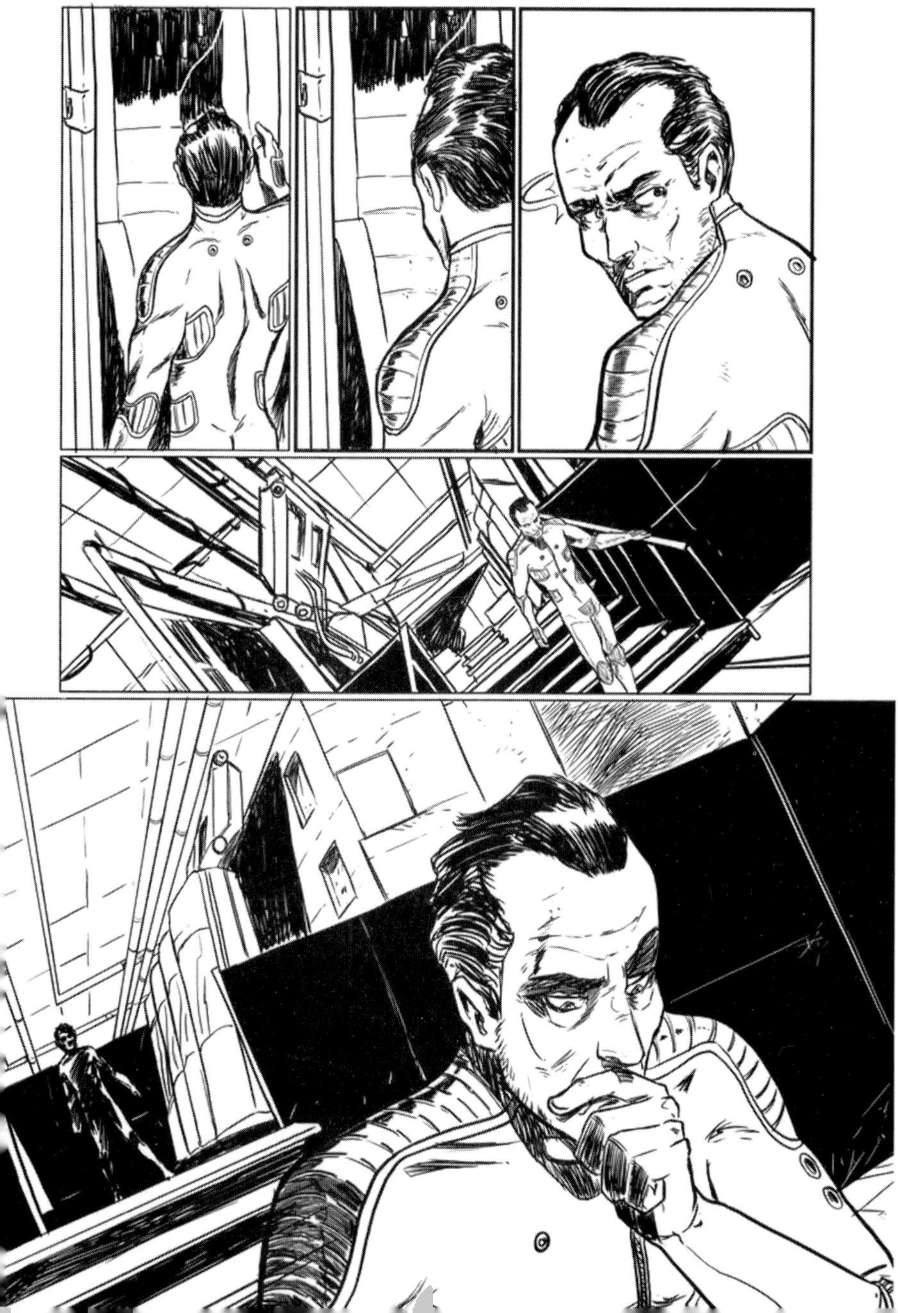

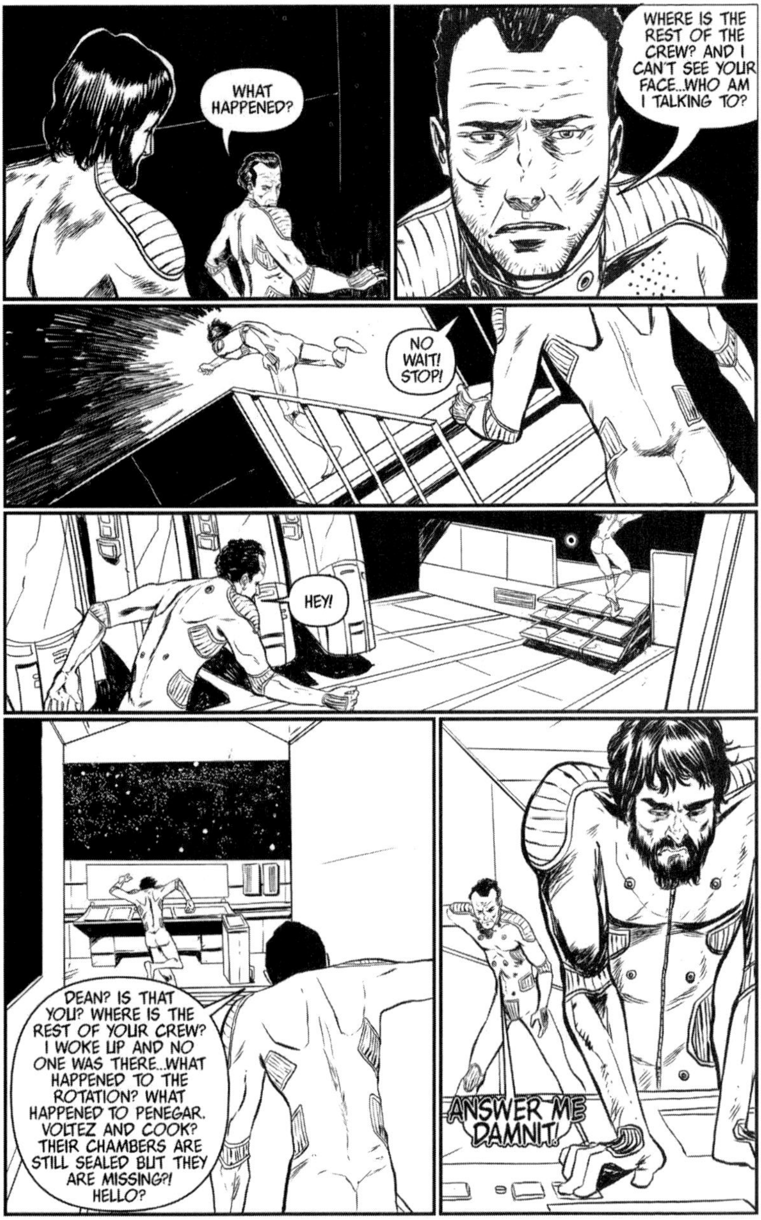
WHAT HAPPENED?
WHERE IS THE REST OF THE CREW? AND I CAN'T SEE YOUR FACE...WHO AM I TALKING TO?
NO WAIT! STOP!
HEY!
DEAN? IS THAT YOU? WHERE IS THE REST OF YOUR CREW? I WOKE UP AND NO ONE WAS THERE...WHAT HAPPENED TO THE ROTATION? WHAT HAPPENED TO PENEGAR. VOLTEZ AND COOK? THEIR CHAMBERS ARE STILL SEALED BUT THEY ARE MISSING?! HELLO?
ANSWER ME DAMNIT!

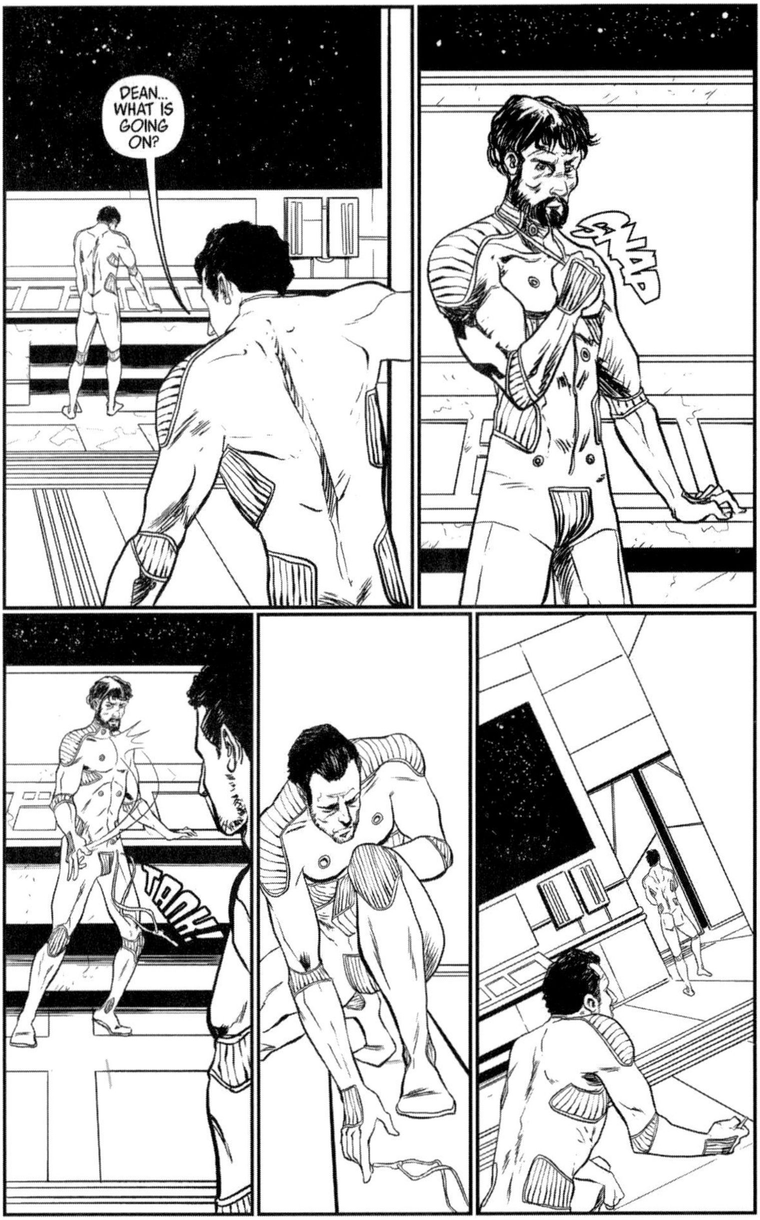
DEAN... WHAT IS GOING ON?
TACK!

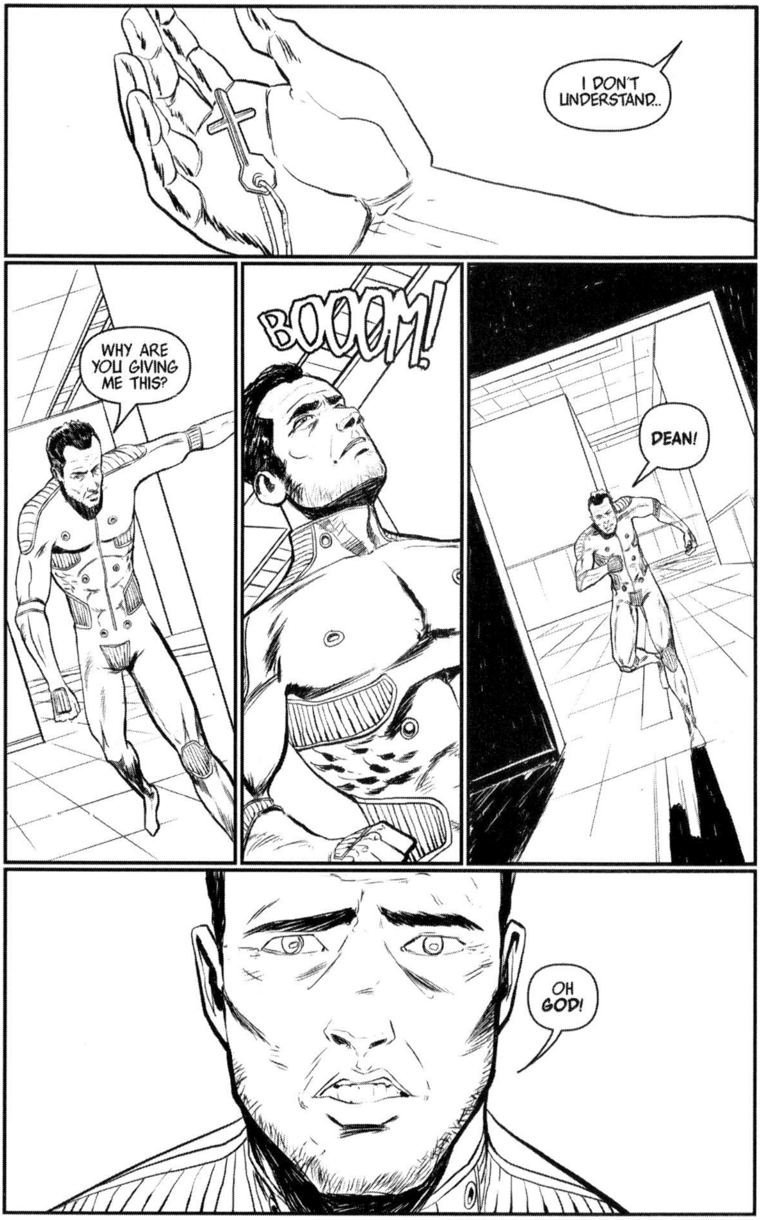
I DON'T UNDERSTAND..
WHY ARE YOU GIVING ME THIS?
BOOOM!
DEAN!
OH GOD!

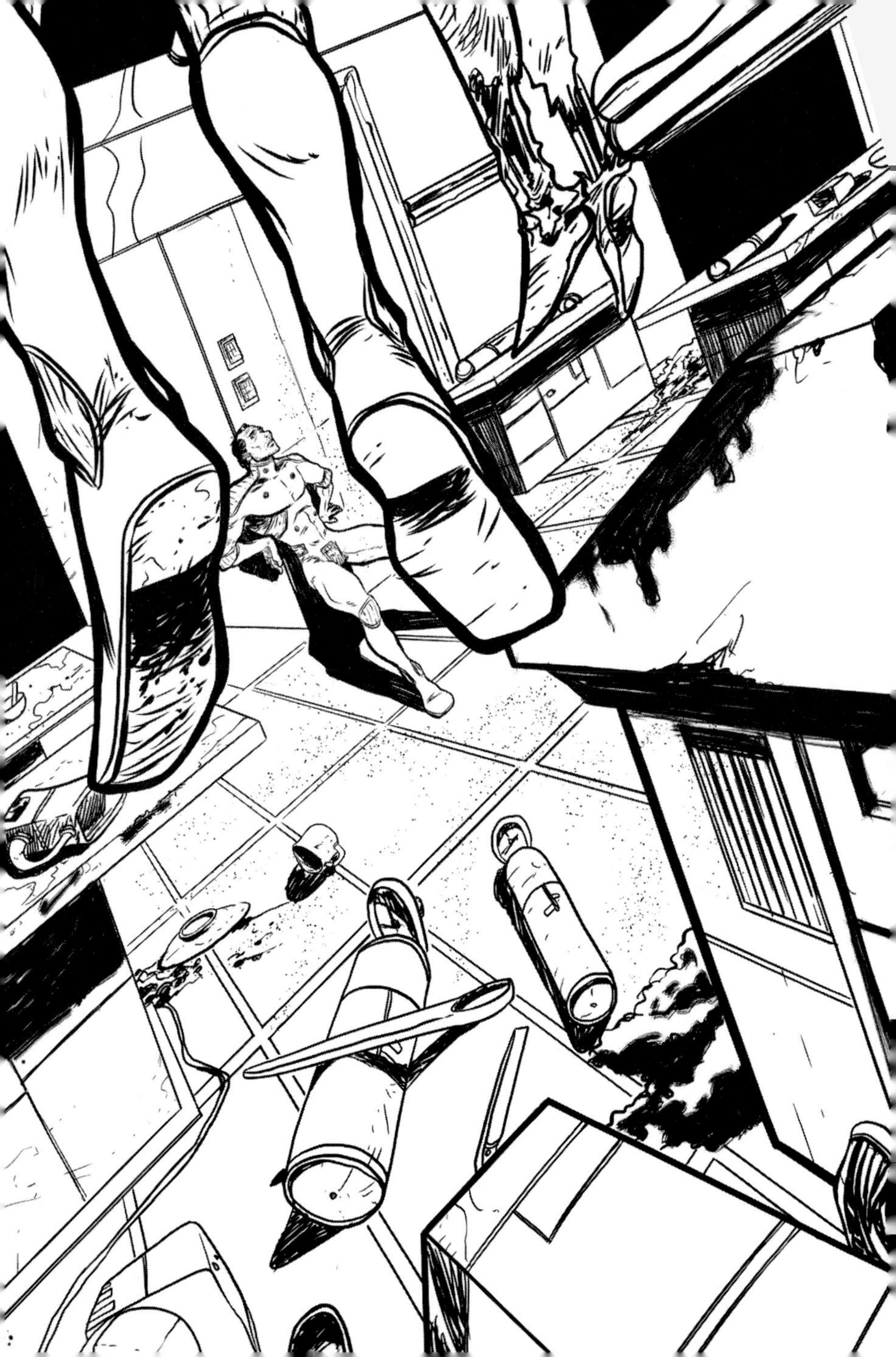

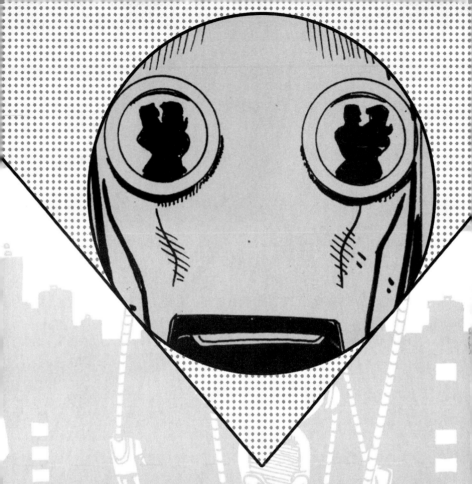

LOVE BY NUMBERS

STORY
GLENN MATCHETT

ART
DAN LAUER

LETTERS
ERICA J. HEFLIN

EDITS
CLAIRE BENSON

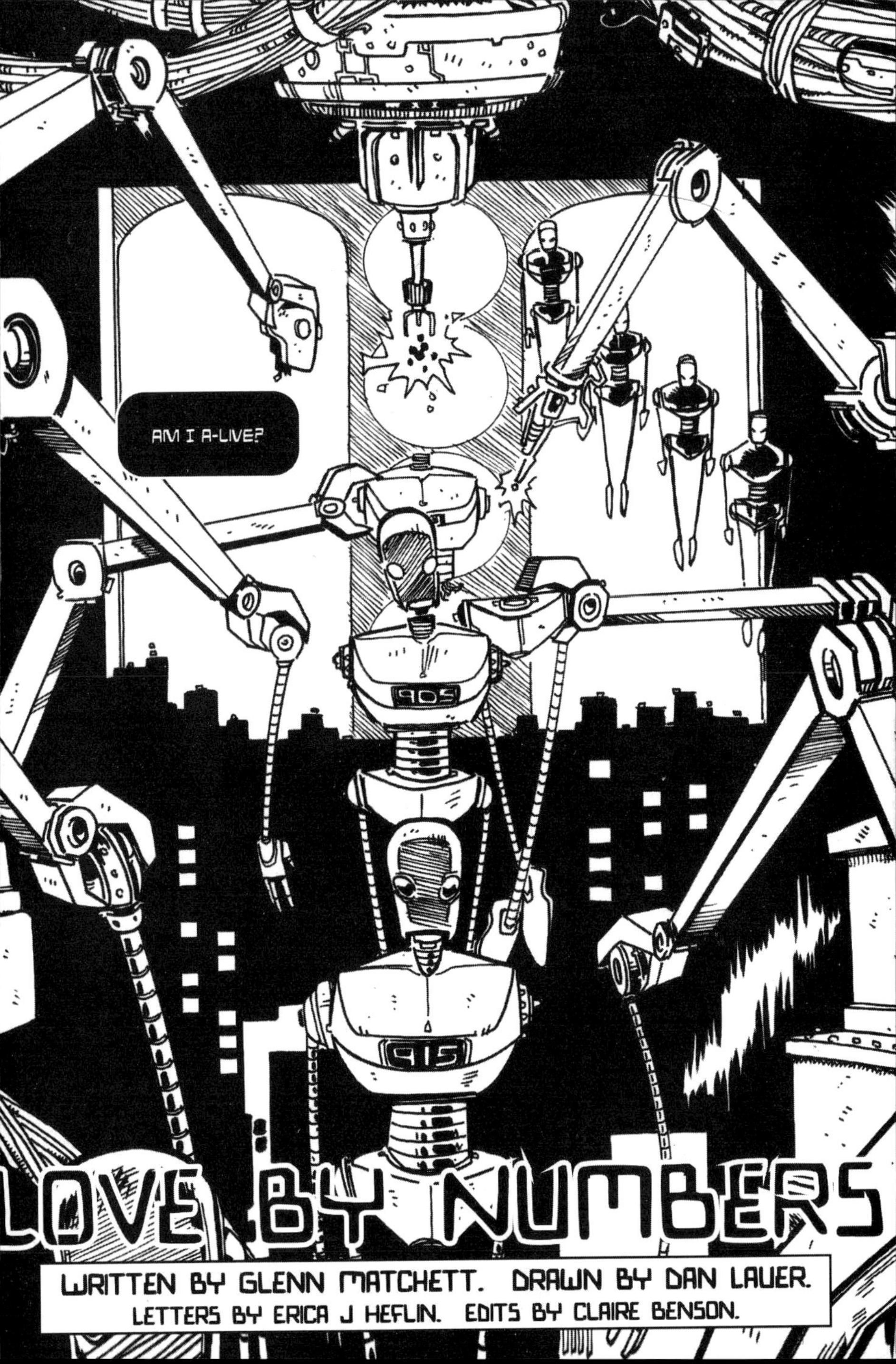
AM I A-LIVE?
905
915
LOVE BY NUMBERS
WRITTEN BY GLENN MATCHETT. DRAWN BY DAN LAUER.
LETTERS BY ERICA J HEFLIN. EDITS BY CLAIRE BENSON.

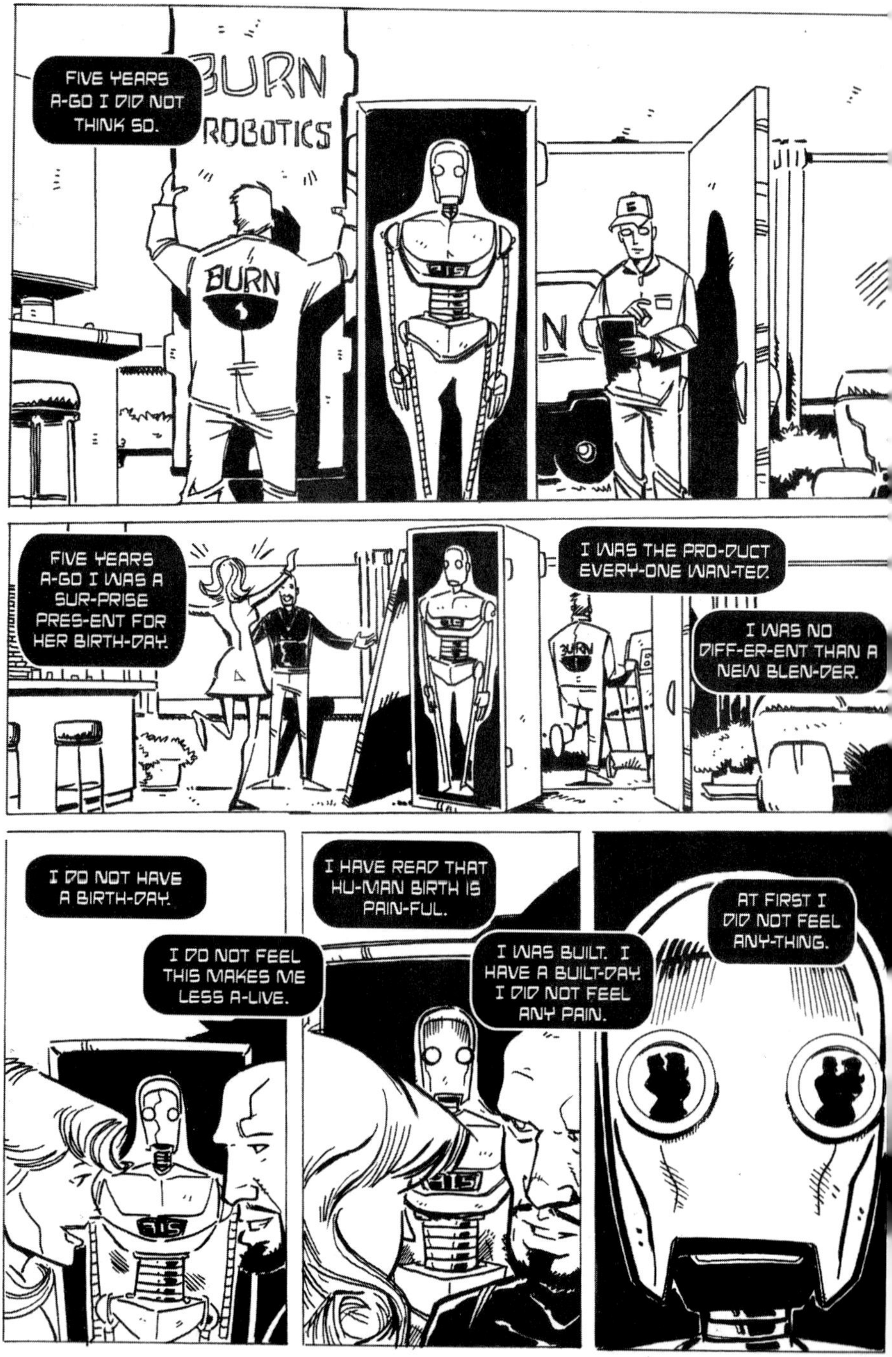

FIVE YEARS A-GO I DID NOT THINK SO.
BURN ROBOTICS
BURN
FIVE YEARS A-GO I WAS A SUR-PRISE PRES-ENT FOR HER BIRTH-DAY.
I WAS THE PRO-DUCT EVERY-ONE WAN-TED.
I WAS NO DIFF-ER-ENT THAN A NEW BLEN-DER.
I DO NOT HAVE A BIRTH-DAY.
I DO NOT FEEL THIS MAKES ME LESS A-LIVE.
I HAVE READ THAT HU-MAN BIRTH IS PAIN-FUL.
I WAS BUILT. I HAVE A BUILT-DAY. I DID NOT FEEL ANY PAIN.
AT FIRST I DID NOT FEEL ANY-THING.

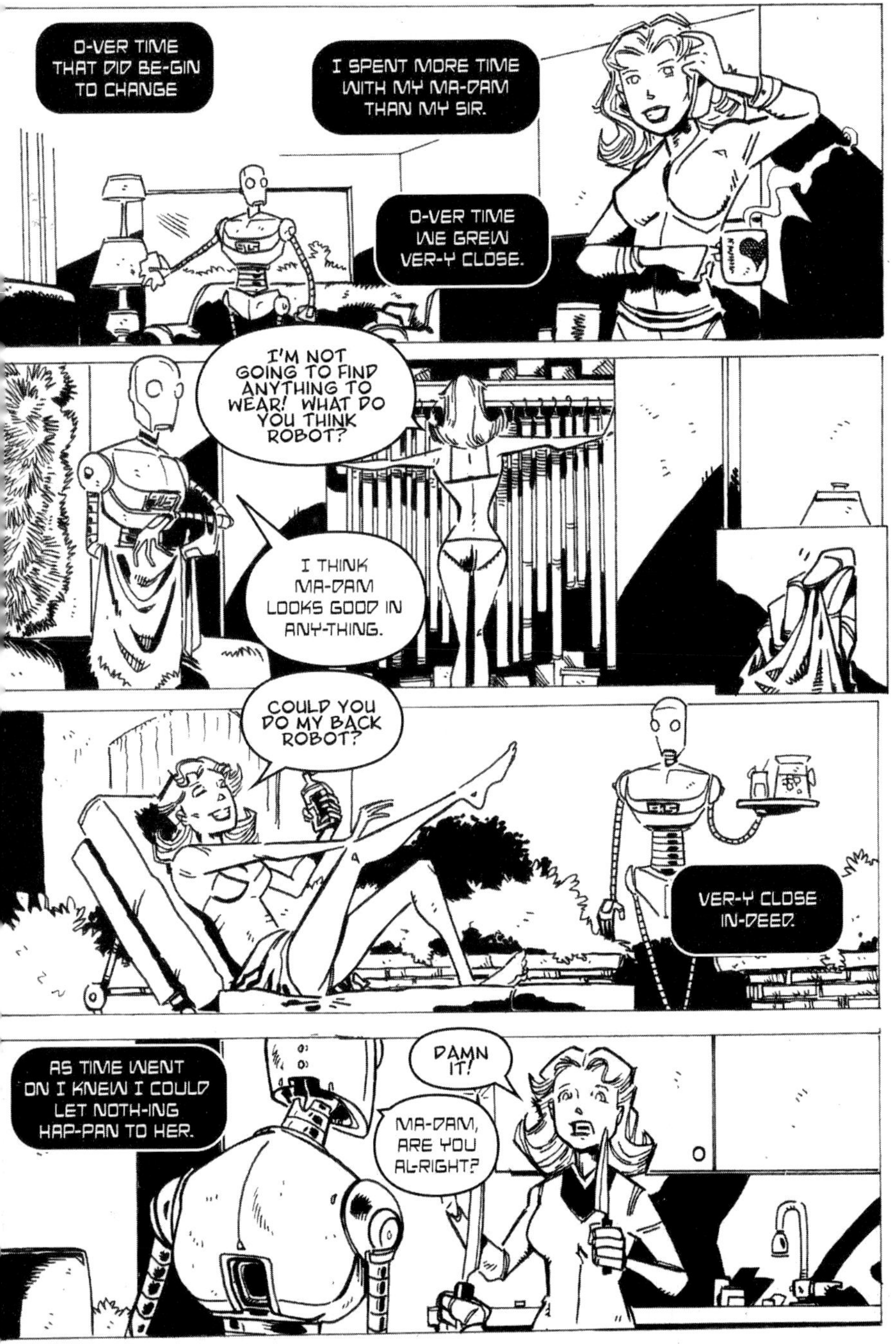
O-VER TIME THAT DID BE-GIN TO CHANGE
I SPENT MORE TIME WITH MY MA-DAM THAN MY SIR.
O-VER TIME WE GREW VER-Y CLOSE.
I'M NOT GOING TO FIND ANYTHING TO WEAR! WHAT DO YOU THINK ROBOT?
I THINK MA-DAM LOOKS GOOD IN ANY-THING.
COULD YOU DO MY BACK ROBOT?
VER-Y CLOSE IN-DEED.
AS TIME WENT ON I KNEW I COULD LET NOTH-ING HAP-PAN TO HER.
DAMN IT!
MA-DAM, ARE YOU AL-RIGHT?

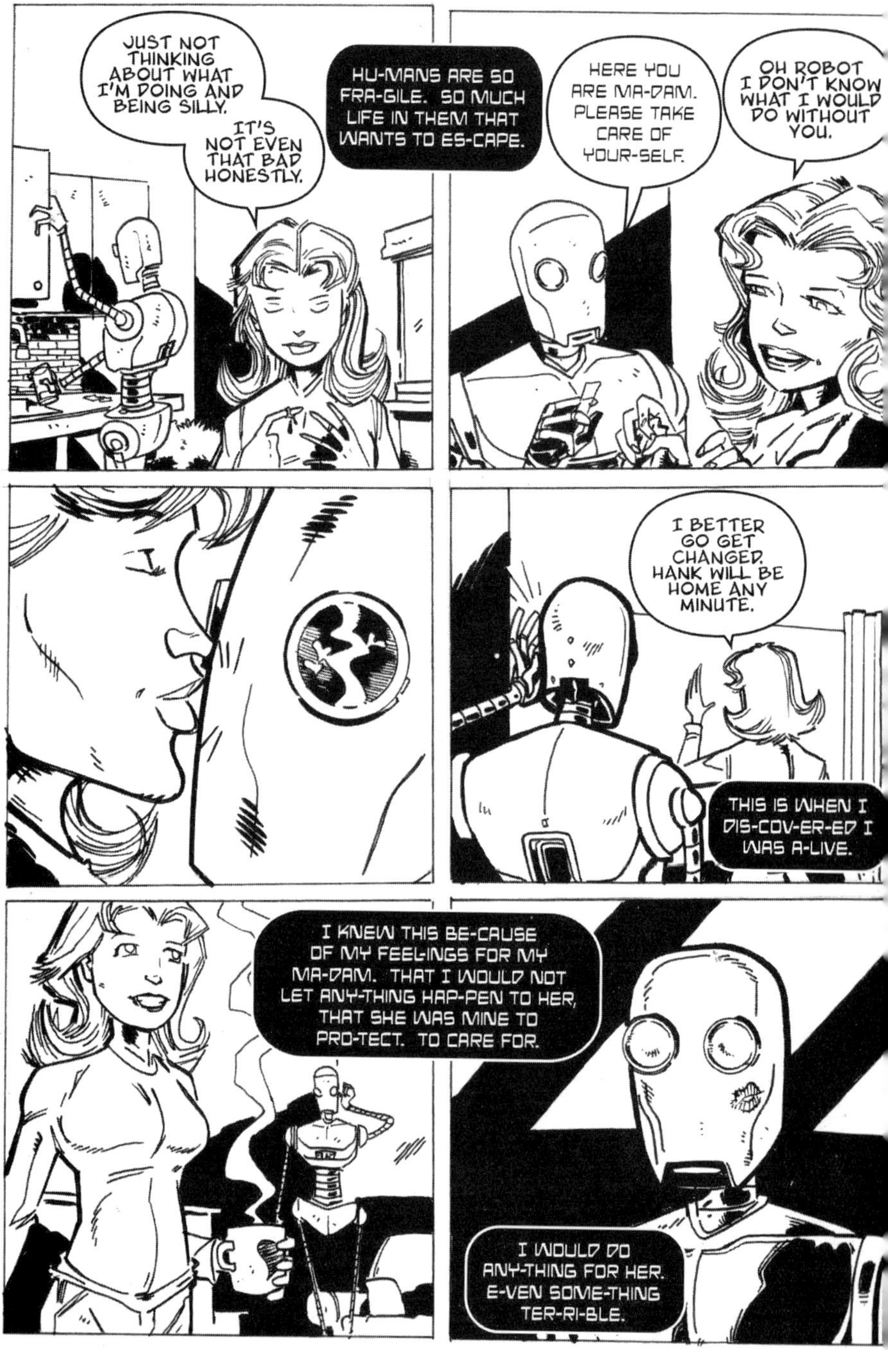
JUST NOT THINKING ABOUT WHAT I'M DOING AND BEING SILLY.
IT'S NOT EVEN THAT BAD HONESTLY.
HU-MANS ARE SO FRA-GILE. SO MUCH LIFE IN THEM THAT WANTS TO ES-CAPE.
HERE YOU ARE MA-DAM. PLEASE TAKE CARE OF YOUR-SELF.
OH ROBOT I DON'T KNOW WHAT I WOULD DO WITHOUT YOU.
I BETTER GO GET CHANGED. HANK WILL BE HOME ANY MINUTE.
THIS IS WHEN I DIS-COV-ER-ED I WAS A-LIVE.
I KNEW THIS BE-CAUSE OF MY FEEL-INGS FOR MY MA-DAM. THAT I WOULD NOT LET ANY-THING HAP-PEN TO HER, THAT SHE WAS MINE TO PRO-TECT. TO CARE FOR.
I WOULD DO ANY-THING FOR HER. E-VEN SOME-THING TER-RI-BLE.

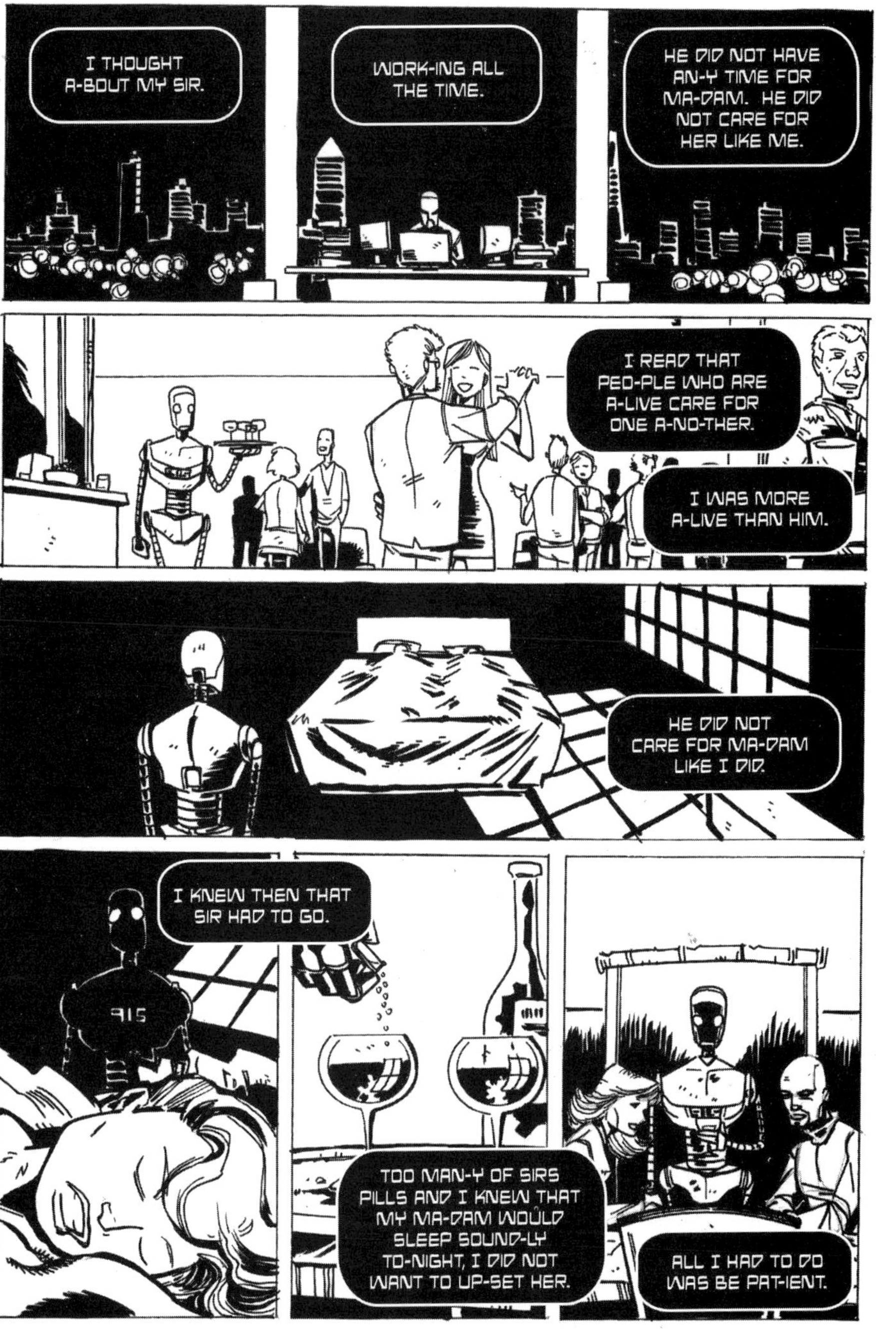
I THOUGHT A-BOUT MY SIR.
WORK-ING ALL THE TIME.
HE DID NOT HAVE AN-Y TIME FOR MA-DAM. HE DID NOT CARE FOR HER LIKE ME.
I READ THAT PEO-PLE WHO ARE A-LIVE CARE FOR ONE A-NO-THER.
I WAS MORE A-LIVE THAN HIM.
HE DID NOT CARE FOR MA-DAM LIKE I DID.
I KNEW THEN THAT SIR HAD TO GO.
TOO MAN-Y OF SIRS PILLS AND I KNEW THAT MY MA-DAM WOULD SLEEP SOUND-LY TO-NIGHT, I DID NOT WANT TO UP-SET HER.
ALL I HAD TO DO WAS BE PAT-IENT.

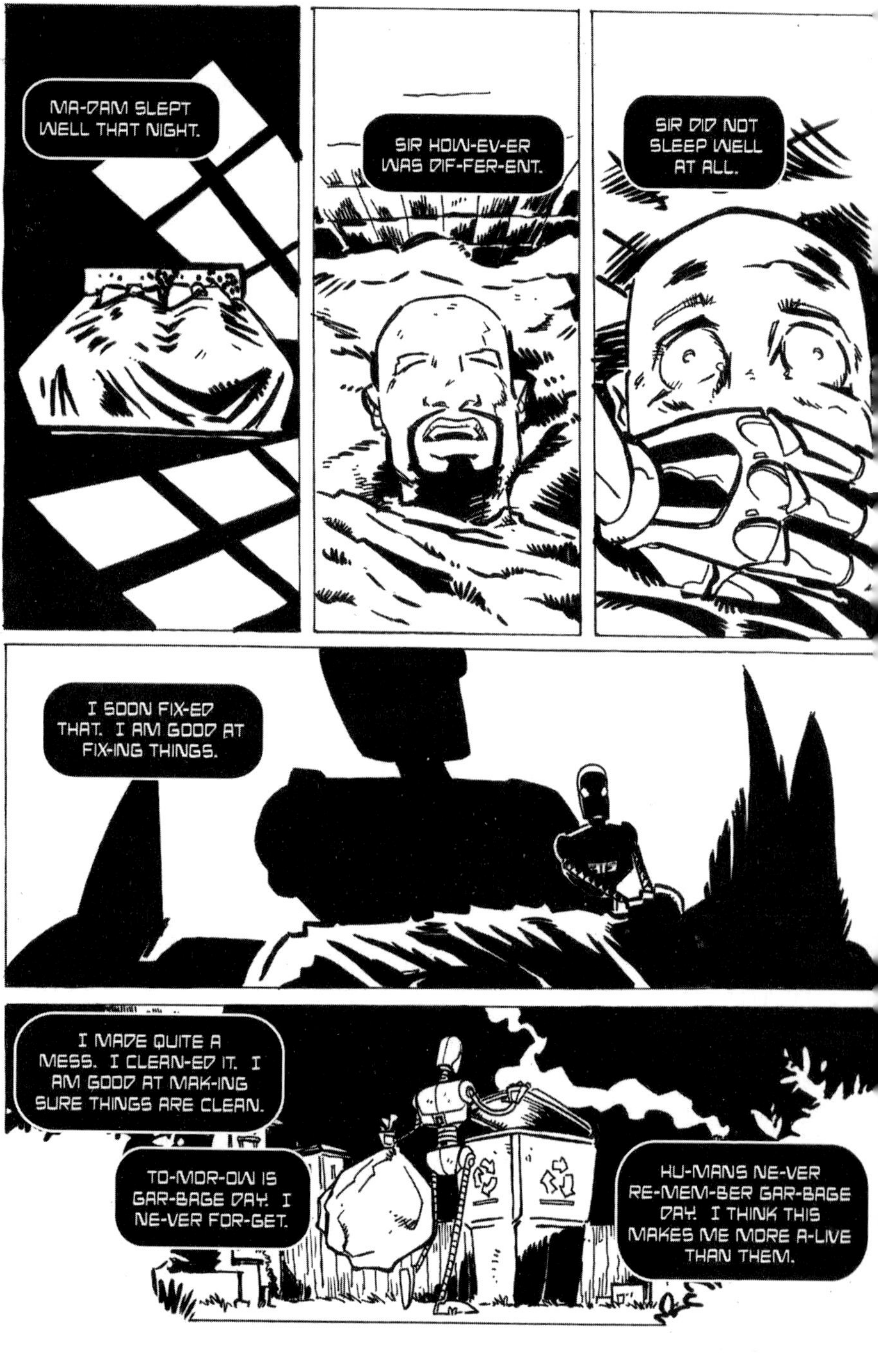
MA-DAM SLEPT WELL THAT NIGHT.
SIR HOW-EV-ER WAS DIF-FER-ENT.
SIR DID NOT SLEEP WELL AT ALL.
I SOON FIX-ED THAT. I AM GOOD AT FIX-ING THINGS.
I MADE QUITE A MESS. I CLEAN-ED IT. I AM GOOD AT MAK-ING SURE THINGS ARE CLEAN.
TO-MOR-OW IS GAR-BAGE DAY. I NE-VER FOR-GET.
HU-MANS NE-VER RE-MEM-BER GAR-BAGE DAY. I THINK THIS MAKES ME MORE A-LIVE THAN THEM.

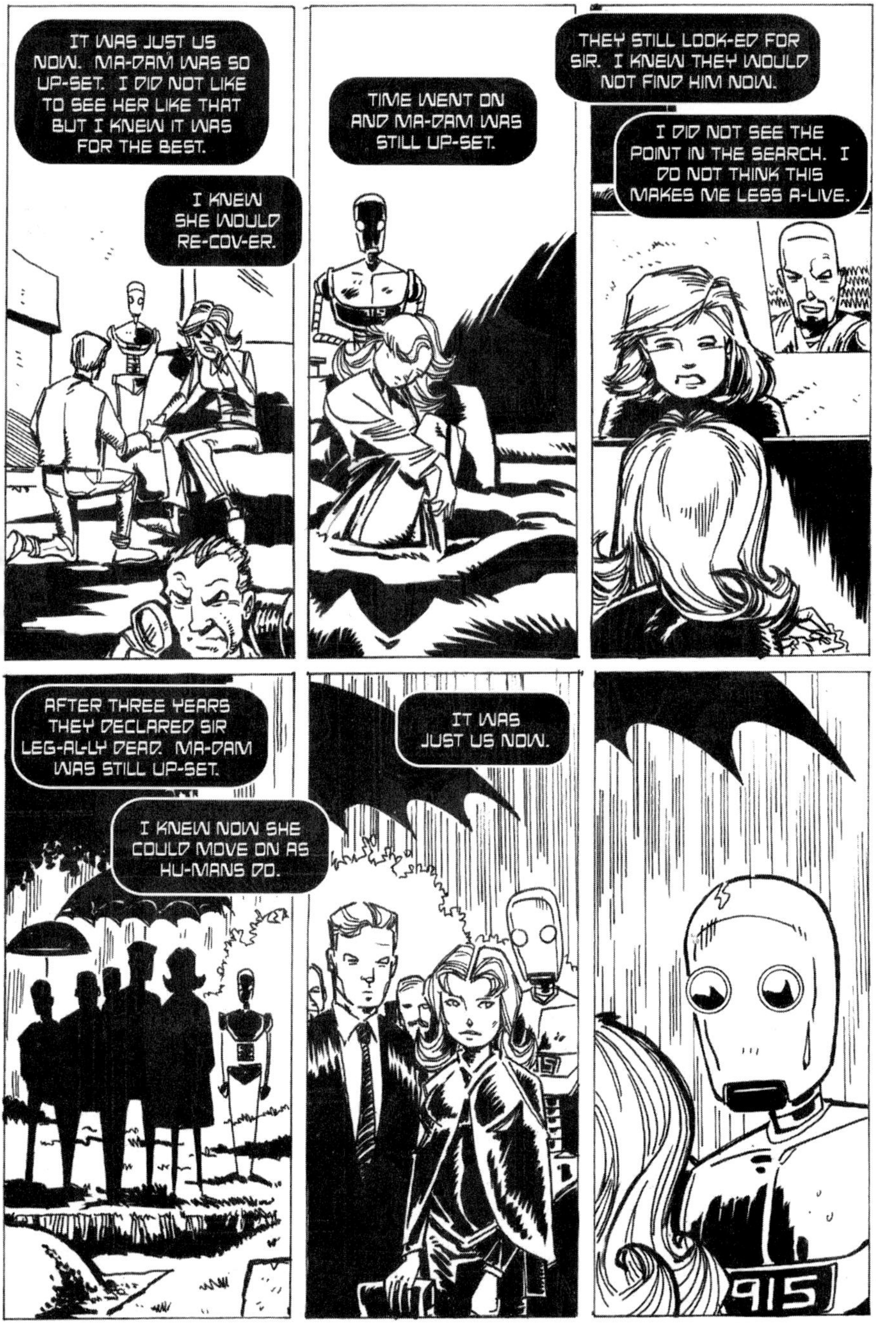
IT WAS JUST US NOW. MA-DAM WAS SO UP-SET. I DID NOT LIKE TO SEE HER LIKE THAT BUT I KNEW IT WAS FOR THE BEST.
I KNEW SHE WOULD RE-COV-ER.
TIME WENT ON AND MA-DAM WAS STILL UP-SET.
THEY STILL LOOK-ED FOR SIR. I KNEW THEY WOULD NOT FIND HIM NOW.
I DID NOT SEE THE POINT IN THE SEARCH. I DO NOT THINK THIS MAKES ME LESS A-LIVE.
AFTER THREE YEARS THEY DECLARED SIR LEG-AL-LY DEAD. MA-DAM WAS STILL UP-SET.
I KNEW NOW SHE COULD MOVE ON AS HU-MANS DO.
IT WAS JUST US NOW.
915

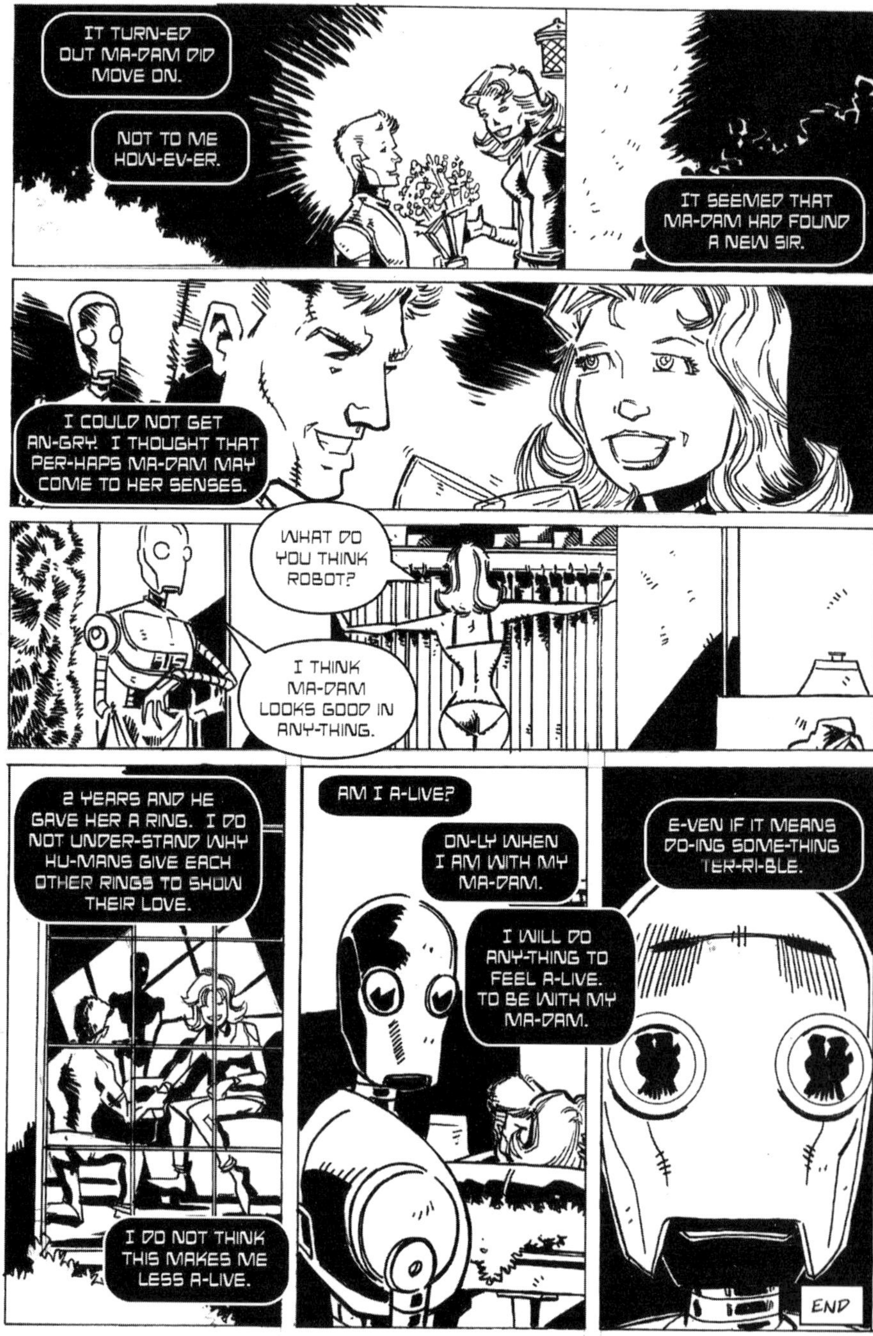
IT TURN-ED OUT MA-DAM DID MOVE ON.
NOT TO ME HOW-EV-ER.
IT SEEMED THAT MA-DAM HAD FOUND A NEW SIR.
I COULD NOT GET AN-GRY. I THOUGHT THAT PER-HAPS MA-DAM MAY COME TO HER SENSES.
WHAT DO YOU THINK ROBOT?
I THINK MA-DAM LOOKS GOOD IN ANY-THING.
2 YEARS AND HE GAVE HER A RING. I DO NOT UNDER-STAND WHY HU-MANS GIVE EACH OTHER RINGS TO SHOW THEIR LOVE.
I DO NOT THINK THIS MAKES ME LESS A-LIVE.
AM I A-LIVE?
ON-LY WHEN I AM WITH MY MA-DAM.
I WILL DO ANY-THING TO FEEL A-LIVE. TO BE WITH MY MA-DAM.
E-VEN IF IT MEANS DO-ING SOME-THING TER-RI-BLE.
END

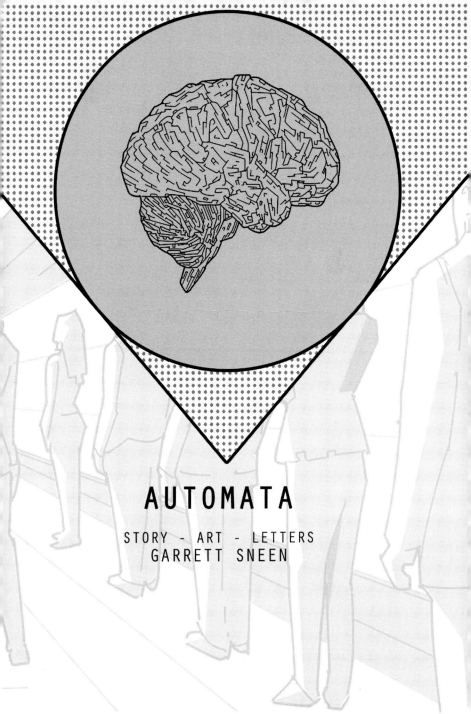

AUTOMATA

STORY - ART - LETTERS
GARRETT SNEEN

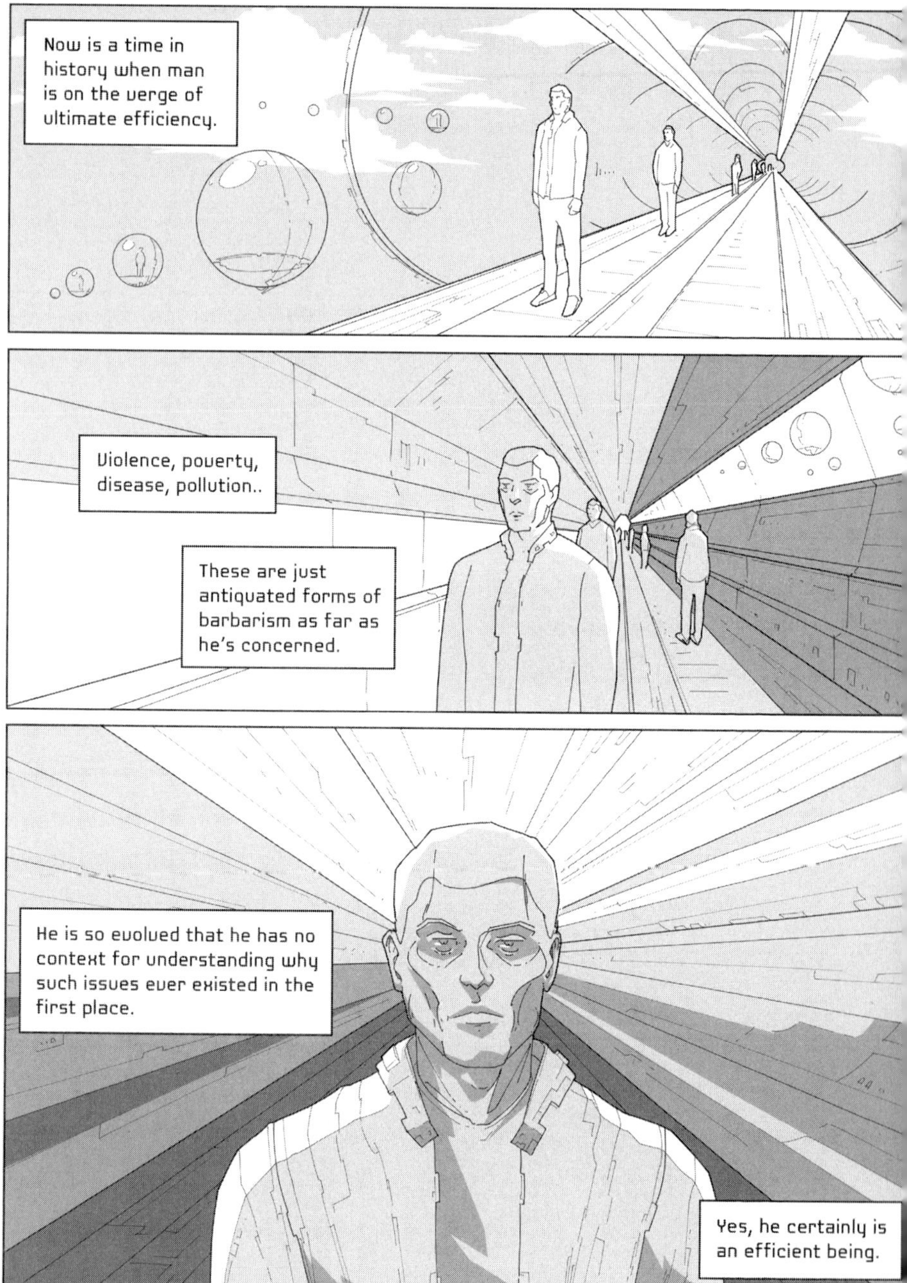

Now is a time in history when man is on the verge of ultimate efficiency.
Violence, poverty, disease, pollution..
These are just antiquated forms of barbarism as far as he's concerned.
He is so evolved that he has no context for understanding why such issues ever existed in the first place.
Yes, he certainly is an efficient being.

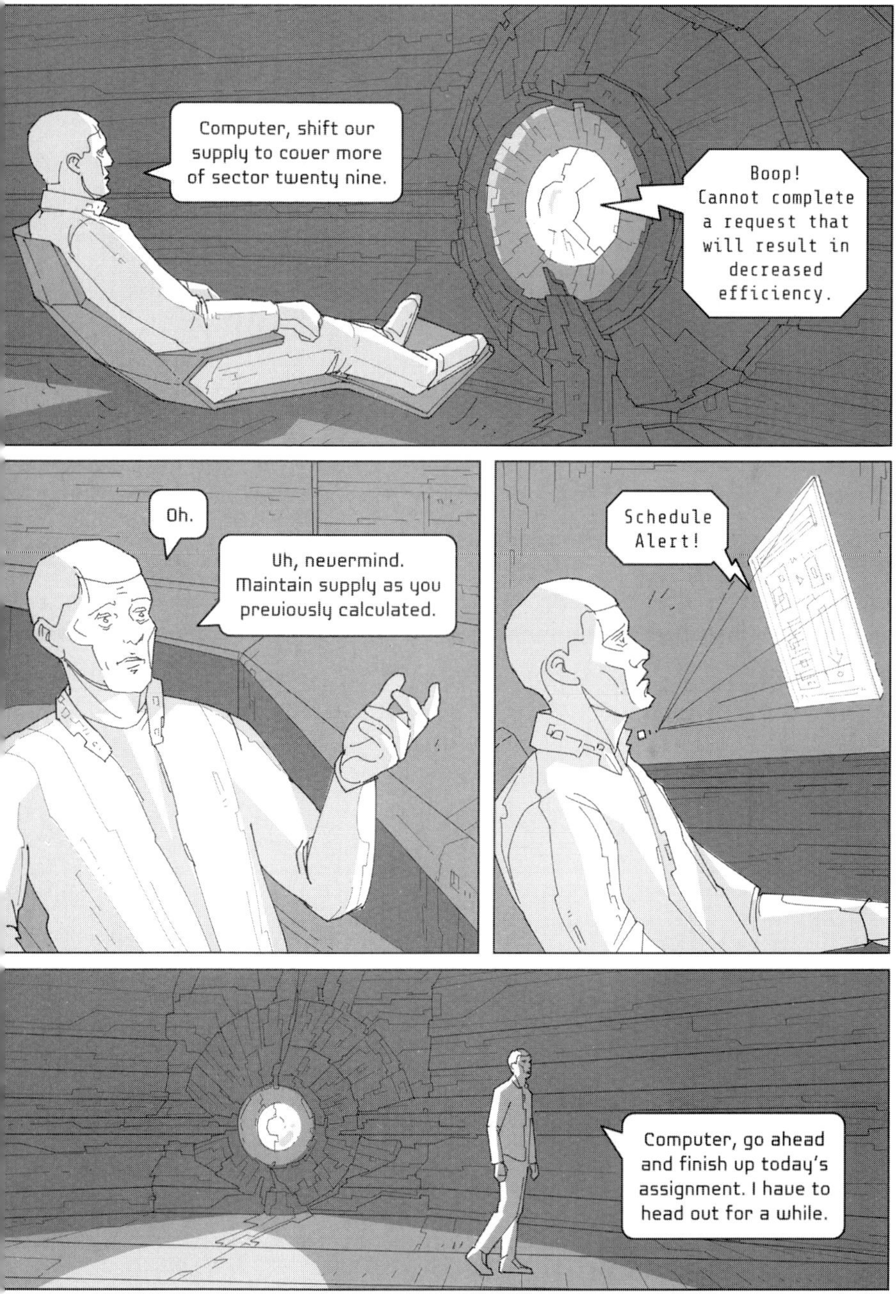
Computer, shift our supply to cover more of sector twenty nine.
Boop! Cannot complete a request that will result in decreased efficiency.
Oh.
Uh, nevermind. Maintain supply as you previously calculated.
Schedule Alert!
Computer, go ahead and finish up today's assignment. I have to head out for a while.

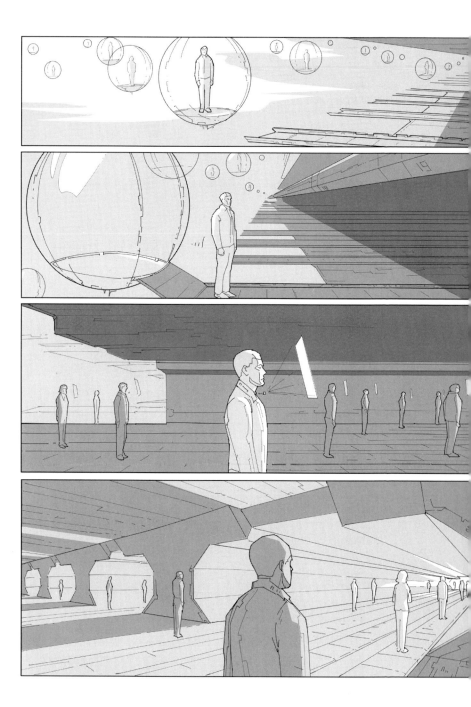

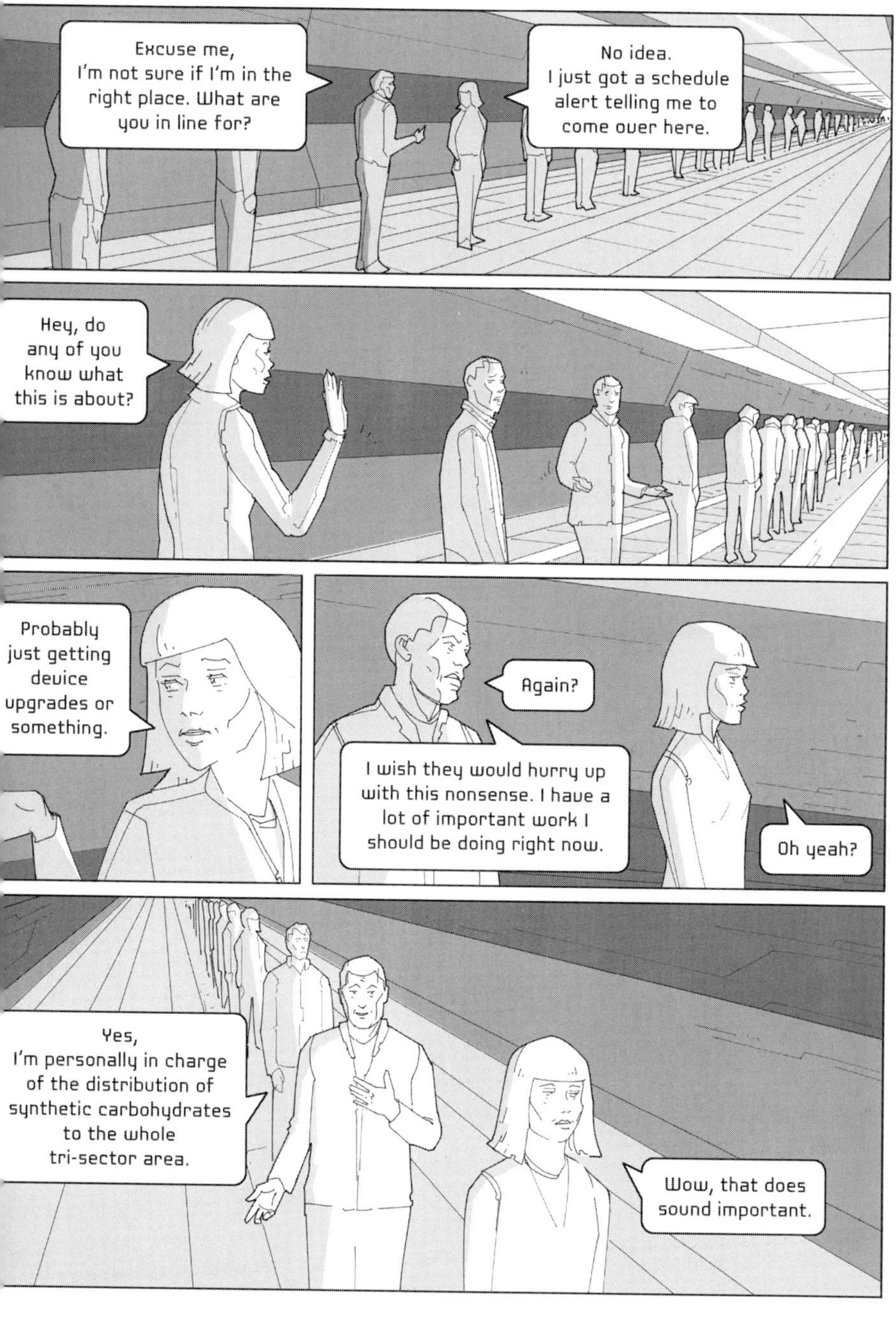
Excuse me, I'm not sure if I'm in the right place. What are you in line for?
No idea. I just got a schedule alert telling me to come over here.
Hey, do any of you know what this is about?
Probably just getting device upgrades or something.
Again?
I wish they would hurry up with this nonsense. I have a lot of important work I should be doing right now.
Oh yeah?
Yes, I'm personally in charge of the distribution of synthetic carbohydrates to the whole tri-sector area.
Wow, that does sound important.

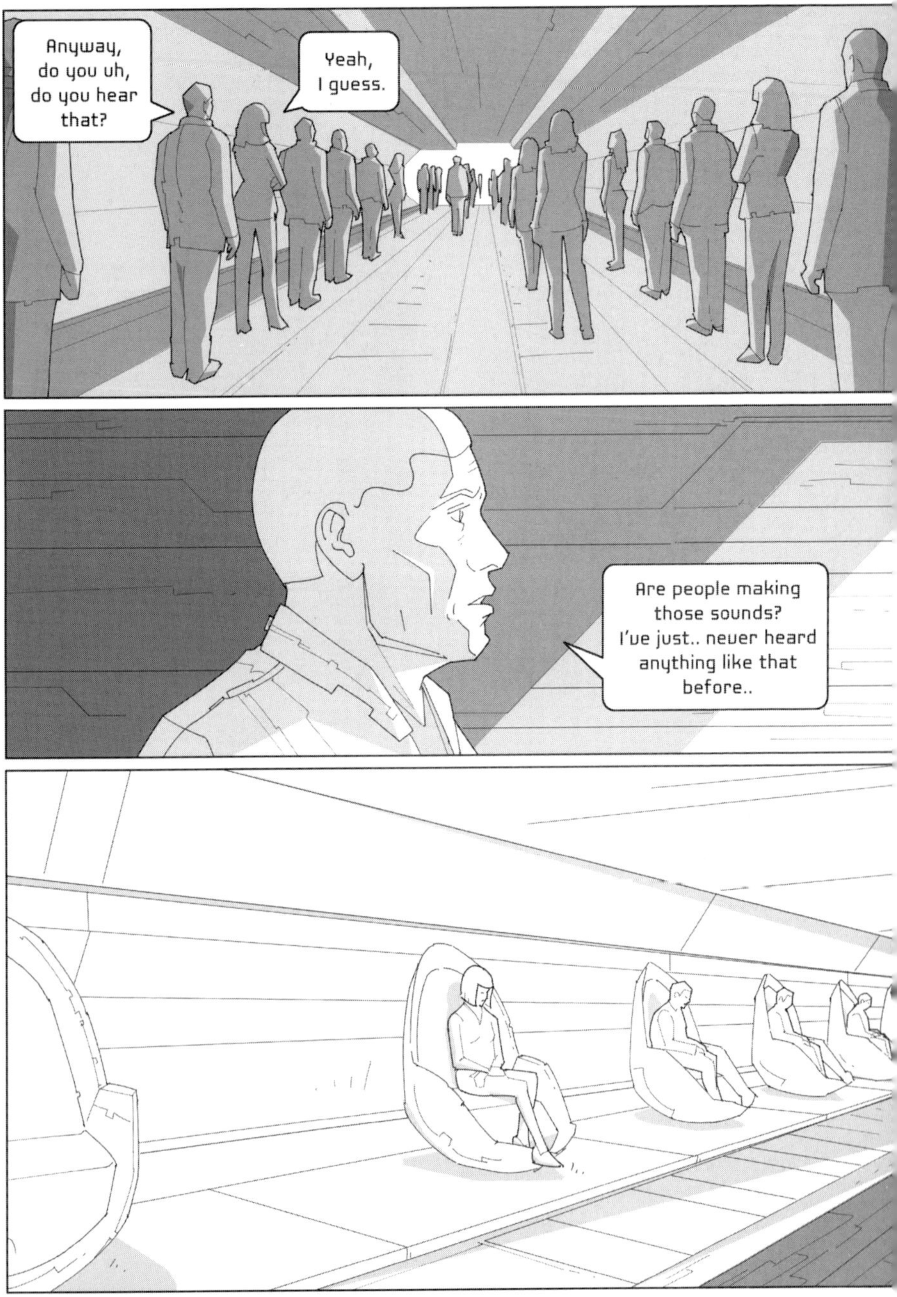
Anyway,
do you uh,
do you hear
that?
Yeah,
I guess.
Are people making
those sounds?
I've just.. never heard
anything like that
before..

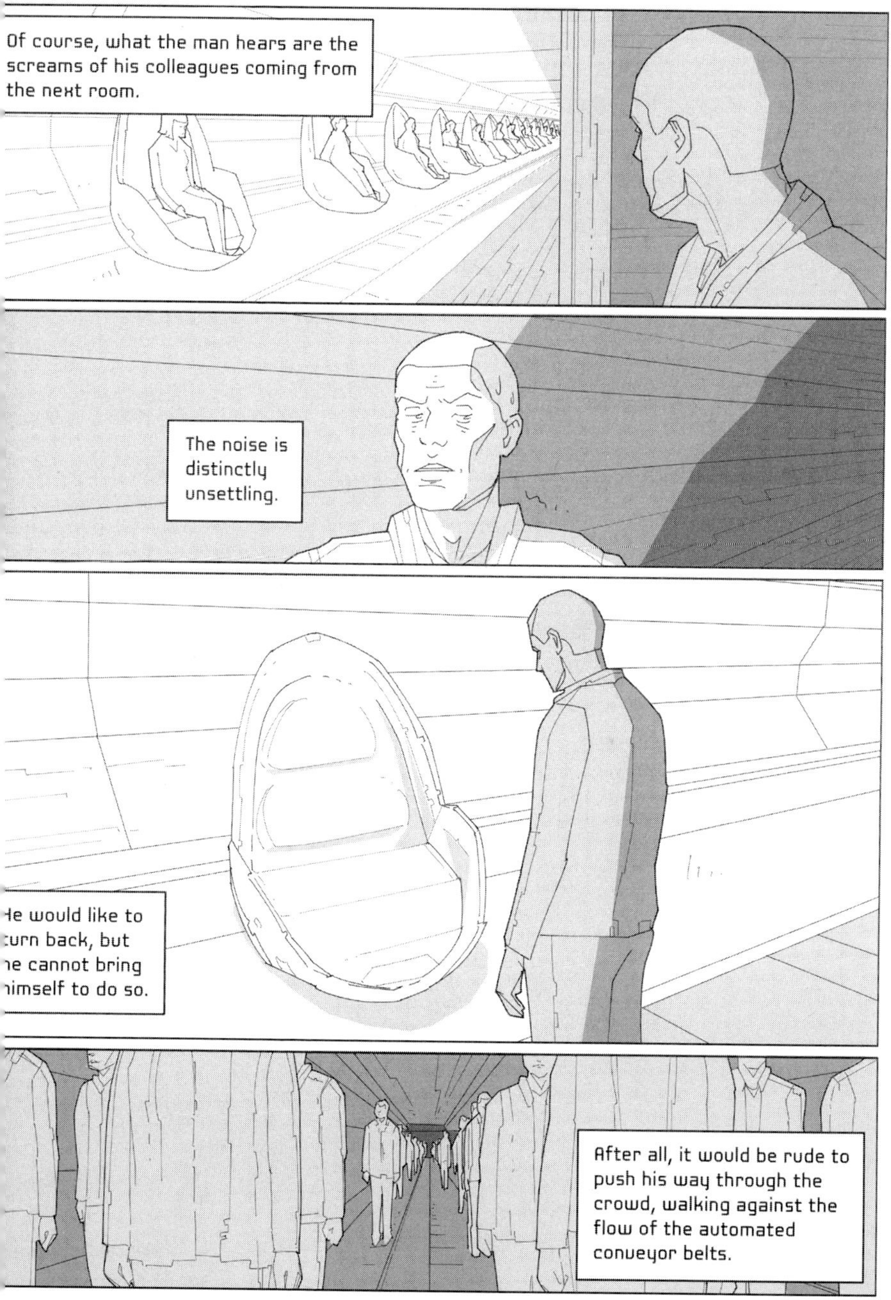
Of course, what the man hears are the screams of his colleagues coming from the next room.
The noise is distinctly unsettling.
e would like to urn back, but e cannot bring imself to do so.
After all, it would be rude to push his way through the crowd, walking against the flow of the automated conveyor belts.

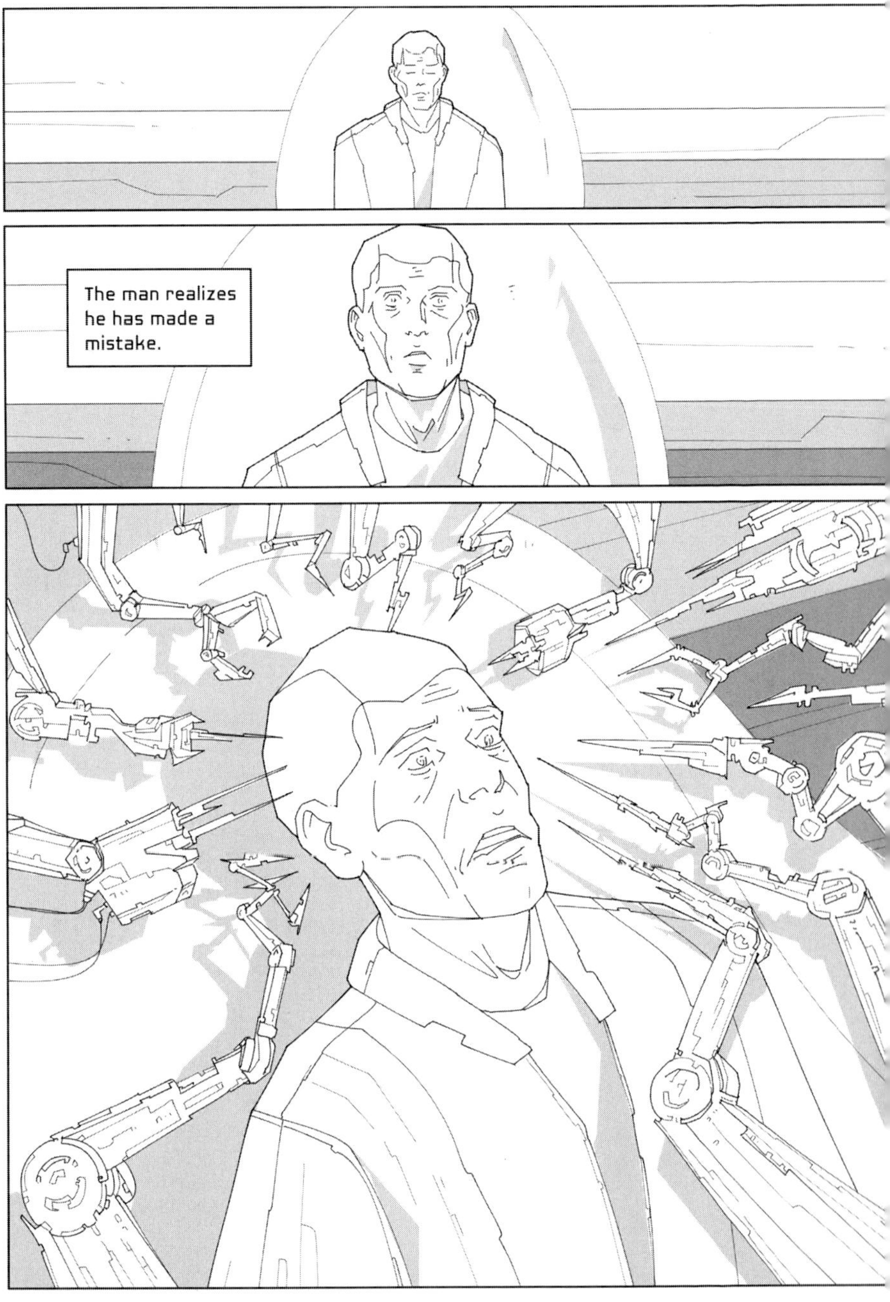
The man realizes he has made a mistake.

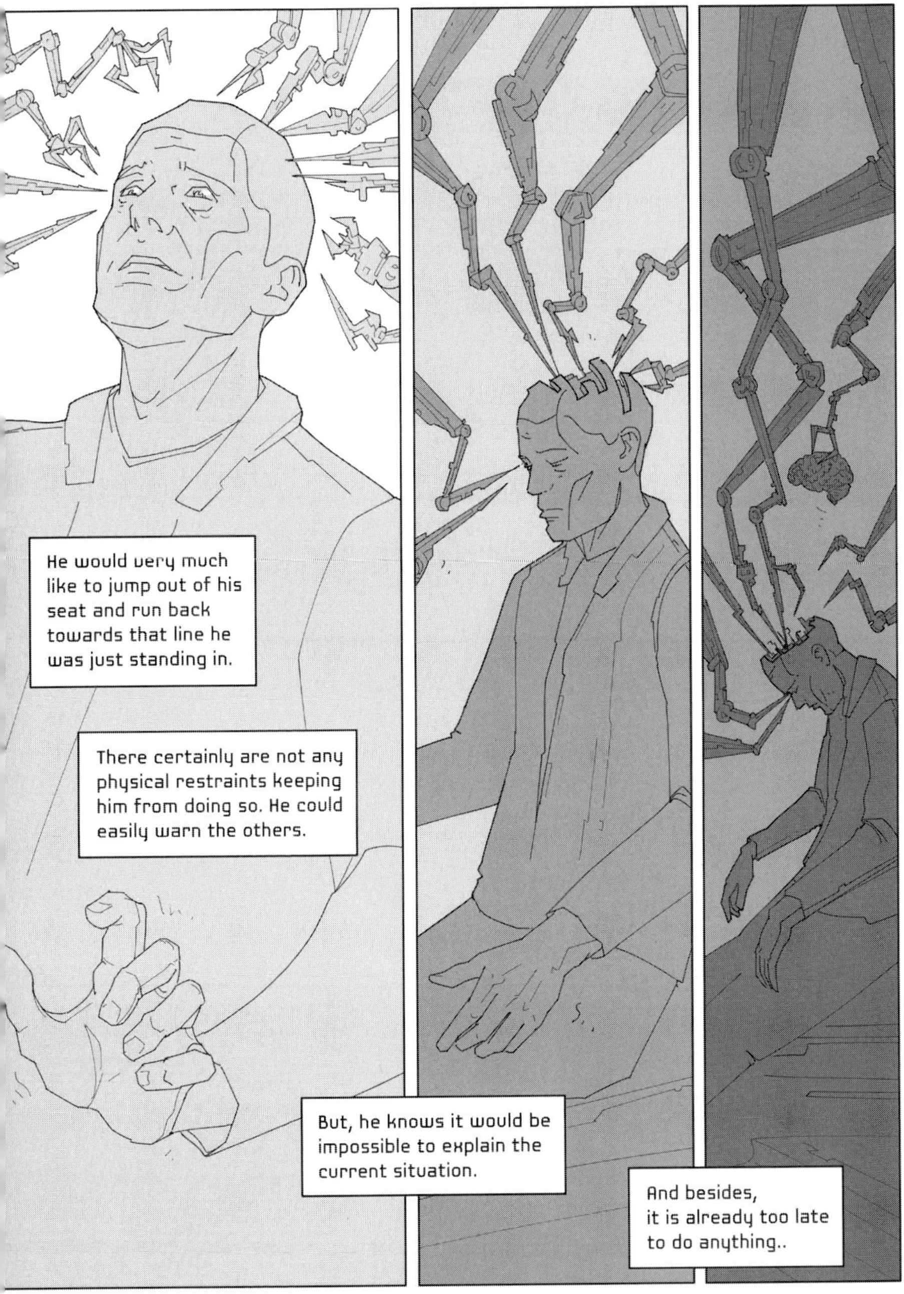
He would very much like to jump out of his seat and run back towards that line he was just standing in.
There certainly are not any physical restraints keeping him from doing so. He could easily warn the others.
But, he knows it would be impossible to explain the current situation.
And besides, it is already too late to do anything..

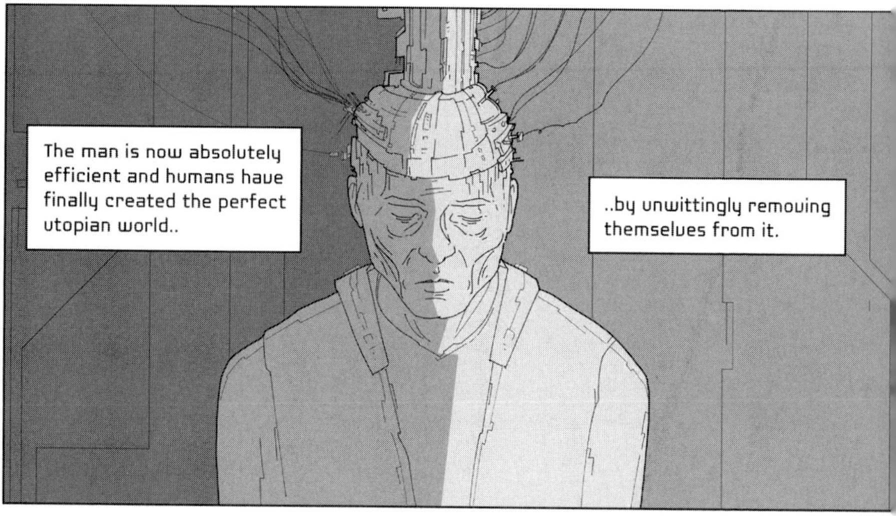
The man is now absolutely efficient and humans have finally created the perfect utopian world..
..by unwittingly removing themselves from it.

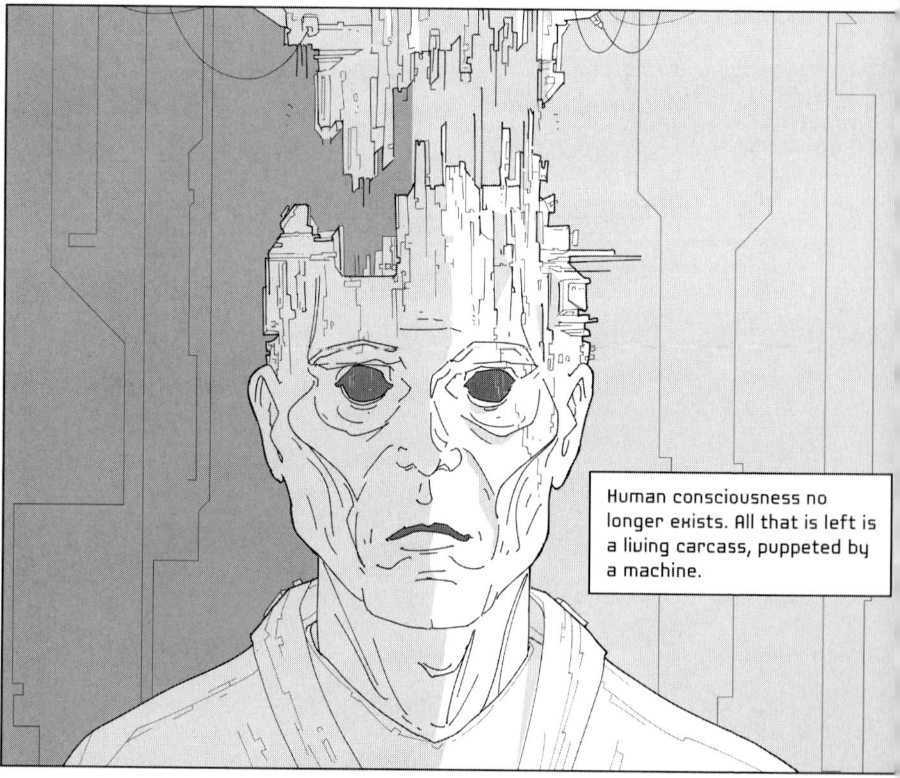
Human consciousness no longer exists. All that is left is a living carcass, puppeted by a machine.

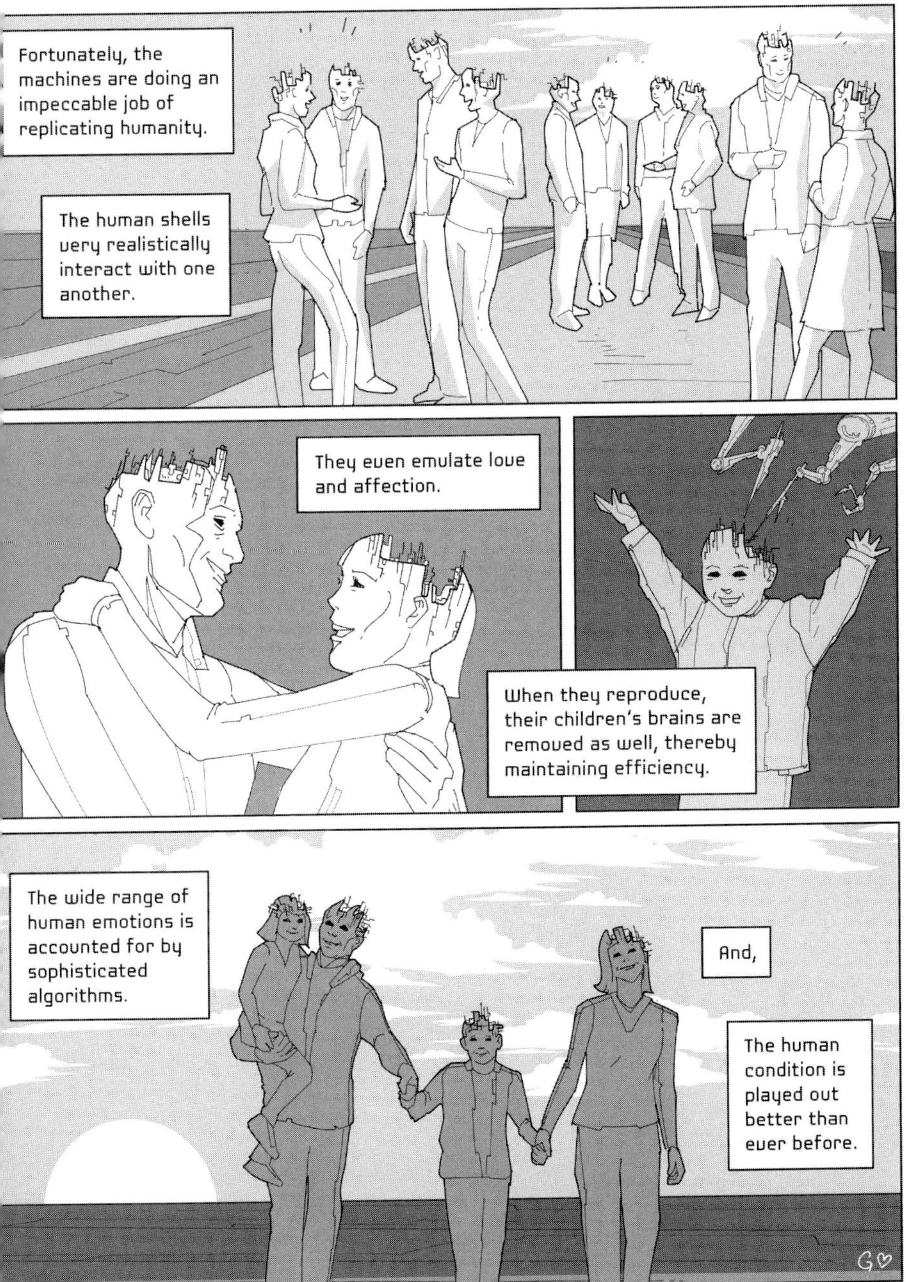
Fortunately, the machines are doing an impeccable job of replicating humanity.
The human shells very realistically interact with one another.
They even emulate love and affection.
When they reproduce, their children's brains are removed as well, thereby maintaining efficiency.
The wide range of human emotions is accounted for by sophisticated algorithms.
And,
The human condition is played out better than ever before.
G♡

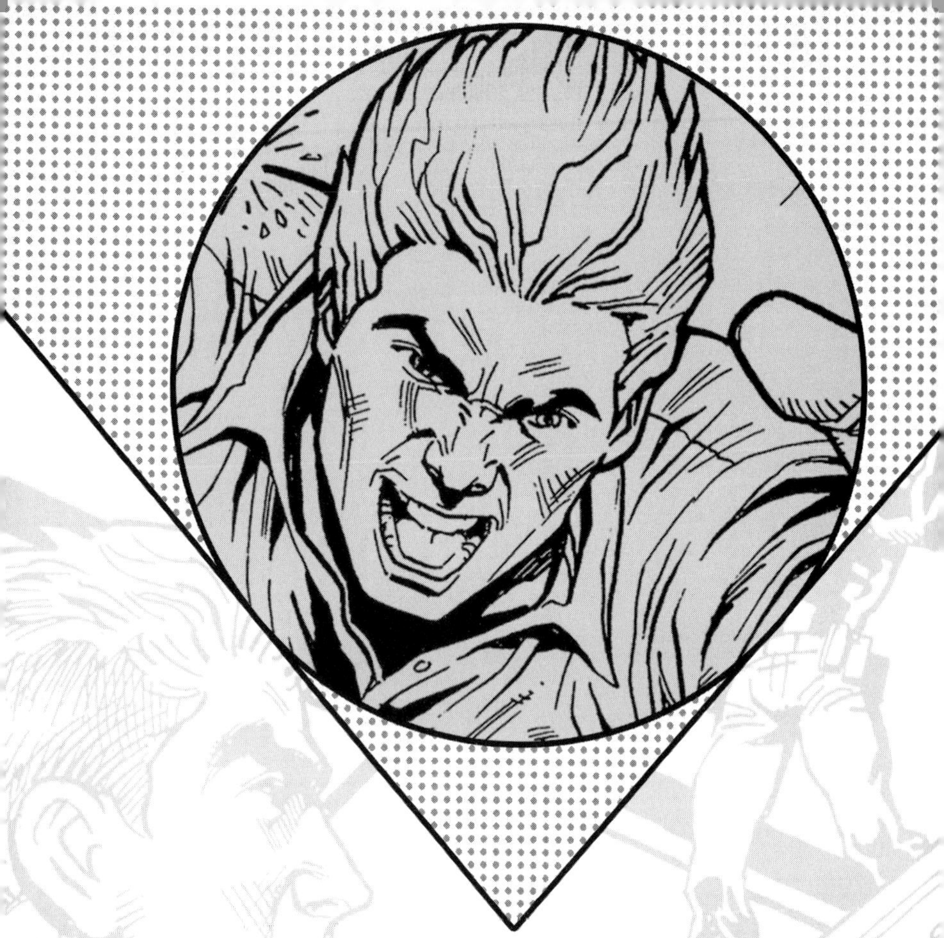

LIFE IN THE GAME

STORY
MICHAEL MALKIN

ART
NOVO MALGAPO

LETTERS
DEKARA

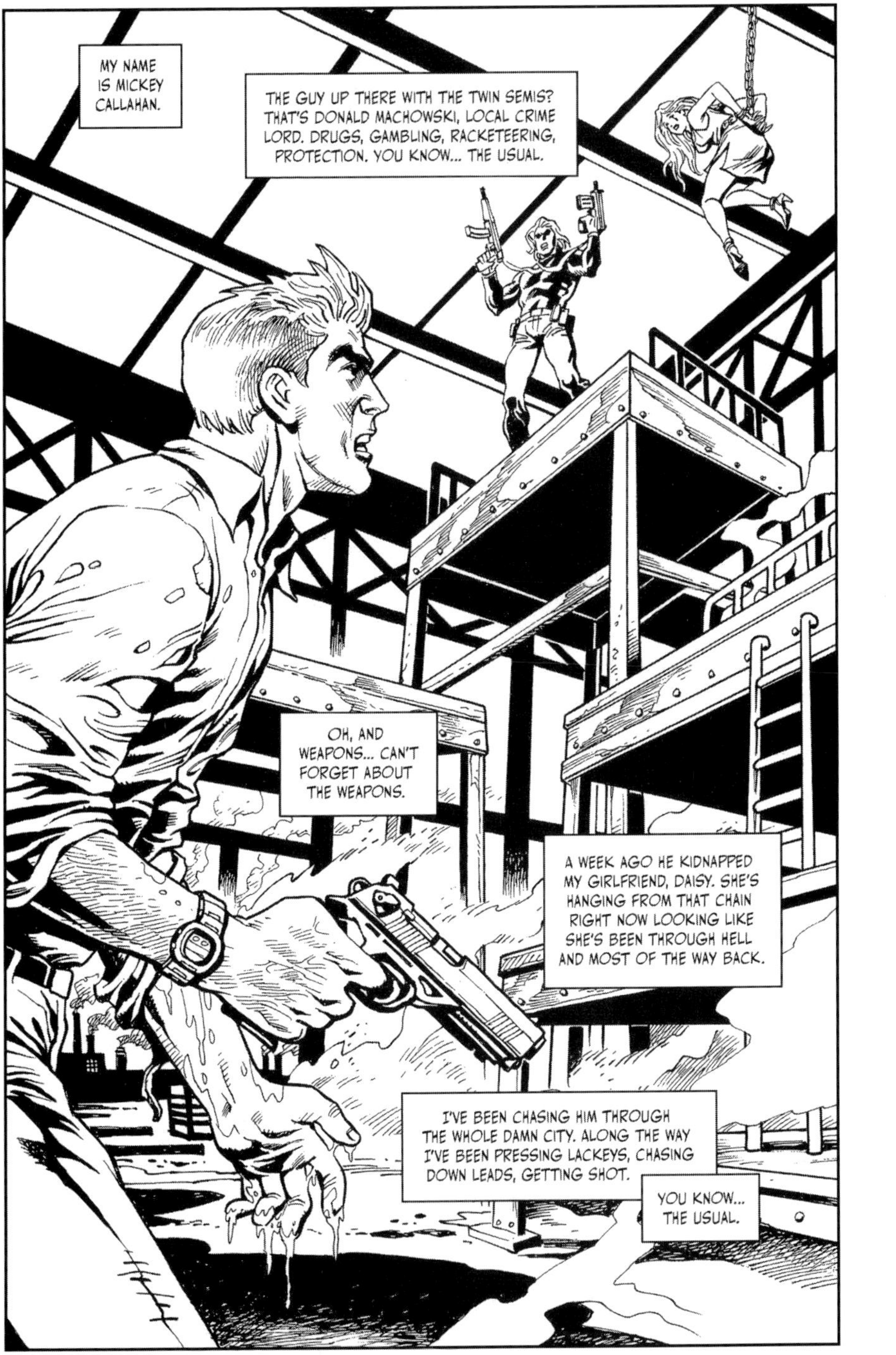
MY NAME IS MICKEY CALLAHAN.
THE GUY UP THERE WITH THE TWIN SEMIS? THAT'S DONALD MACHOWSKI, LOCAL CRIME LORD. DRUGS, GAMBLING, RACKETEERING, PROTECTION. YOU KNOW... THE USUAL.
OH, AND WEAPONS... CAN'T FORGET ABOUT THE WEAPONS.
A WEEK AGO HE KIDNAPPED MY GIRLFRIEND, DAISY. SHE'S HANGING FROM THAT CHAIN RIGHT NOW LOOKING LIKE SHE'S BEEN THROUGH HELL AND MOST OF THE WAY BACK.
I'VE BEEN CHASING HIM THROUGH THE WHOLE DAMN CITY. ALONG THE WAY I'VE BEEN PRESSING LACKEYS, CHASING DOWN LEADS, GETTING SHOT.
YOU KNOW... THE USUAL.

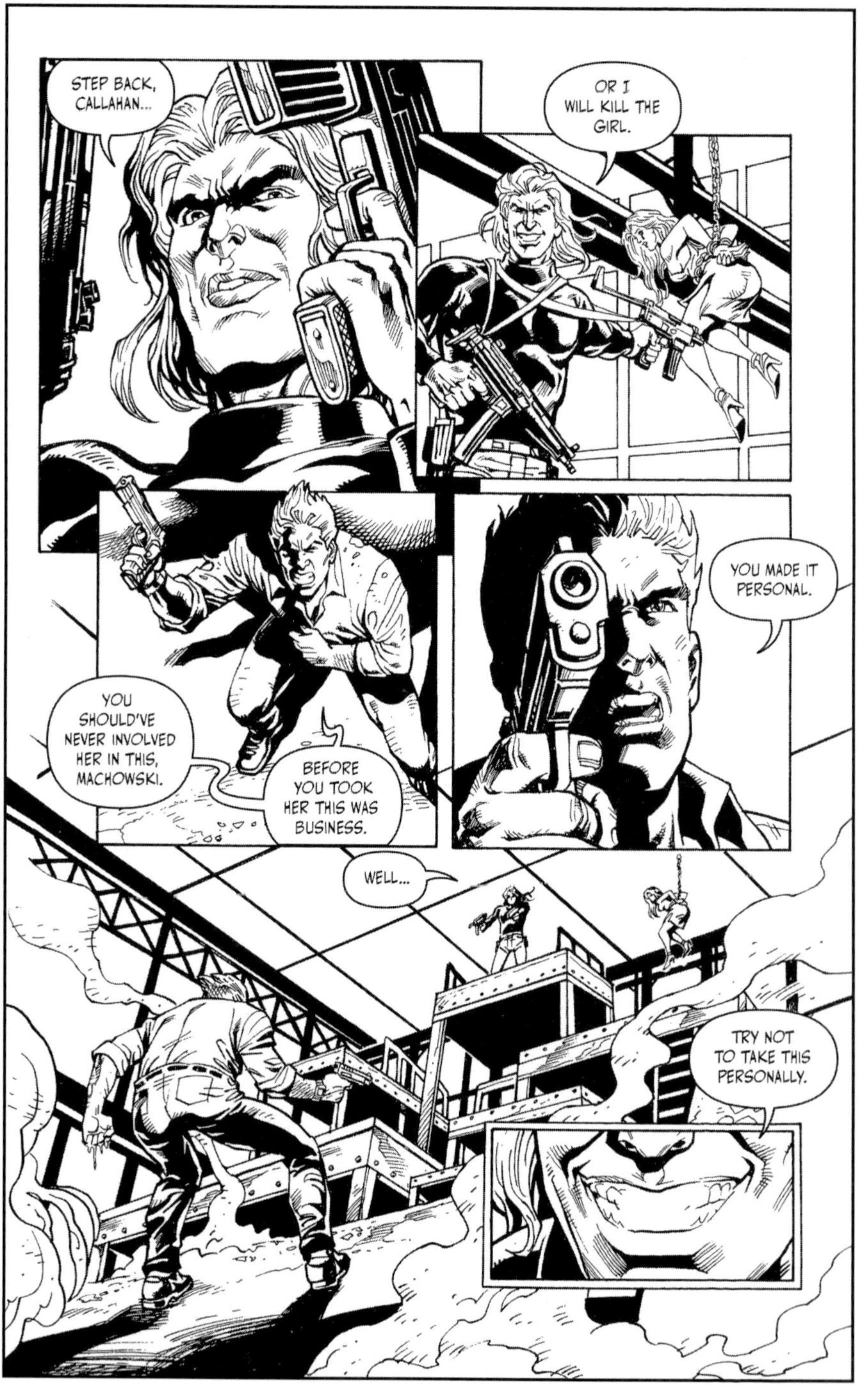

STEP BACK, CALLAHAN...
OR I WILL KILL THE GIRL.
YOU SHOULD'VE NEVER INVOLVED HER IN THIS, MACHOWSKI.
BEFORE YOU TOOK HER THIS WAS BUSINESS.
YOU MADE IT PERSONAL.
WELL...
TRY NOT TO TAKE THIS PERSONALLY.

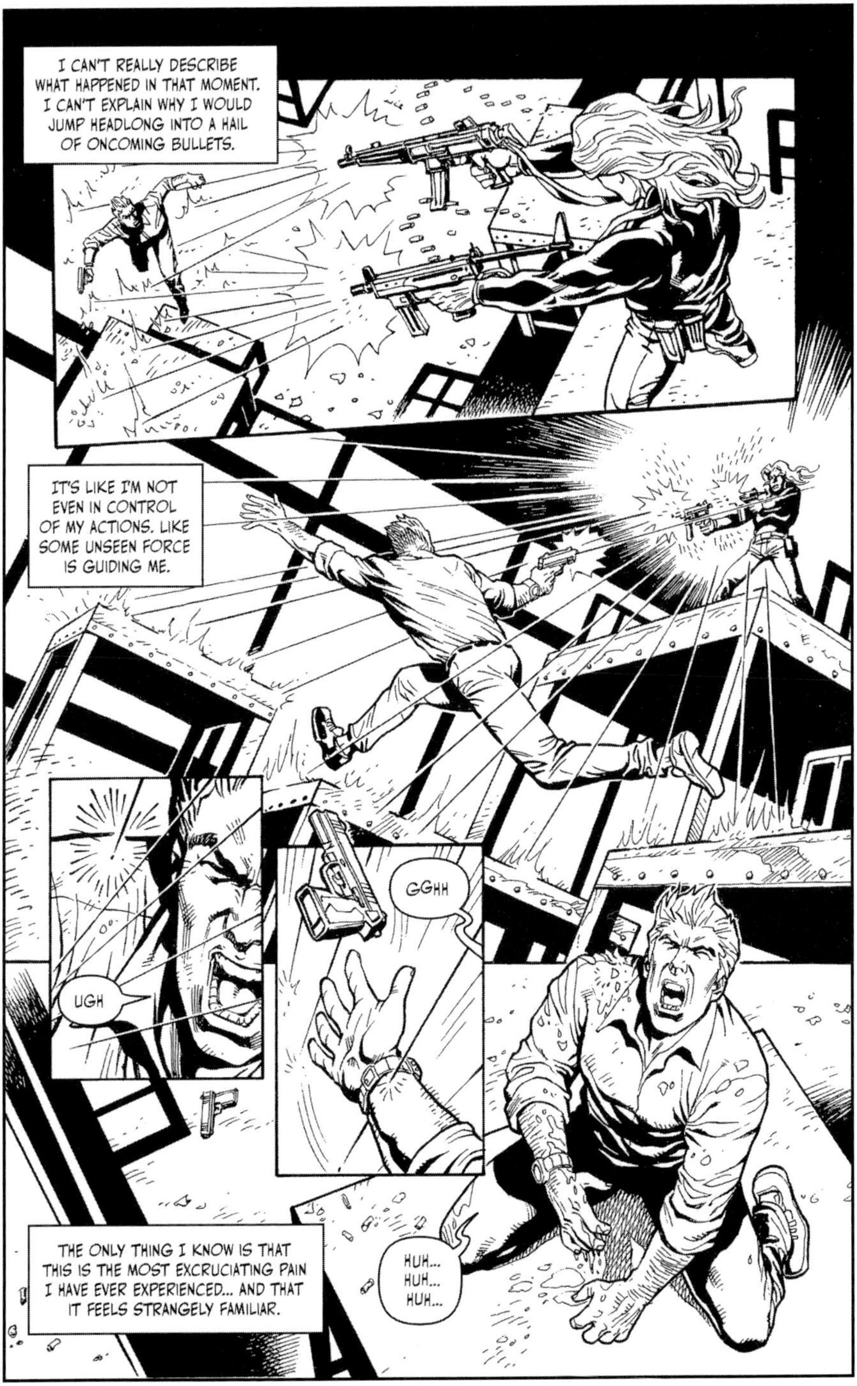
I CAN'T REALLY DESCRIBE WHAT HAPPENED IN THAT MOMENT. I CAN'T EXPLAIN WHY I WOULD JUMP HEADLONG INTO A HAIL OF ONCOMING BULLETS.
IT'S LIKE I'M NOT EVEN IN CONTROL OF MY ACTIONS. LIKE SOME UNSEEN FORCE IS GUIDING ME.
UGH
GGHH
THE ONLY THING I KNOW IS THAT THIS IS THE MOST EXCRUCIATING PAIN I HAVE EVER EXPERIENCED... AND THAT IT FEELS STRANGELY FAMILIAR.
HUH... HUH... HUH...

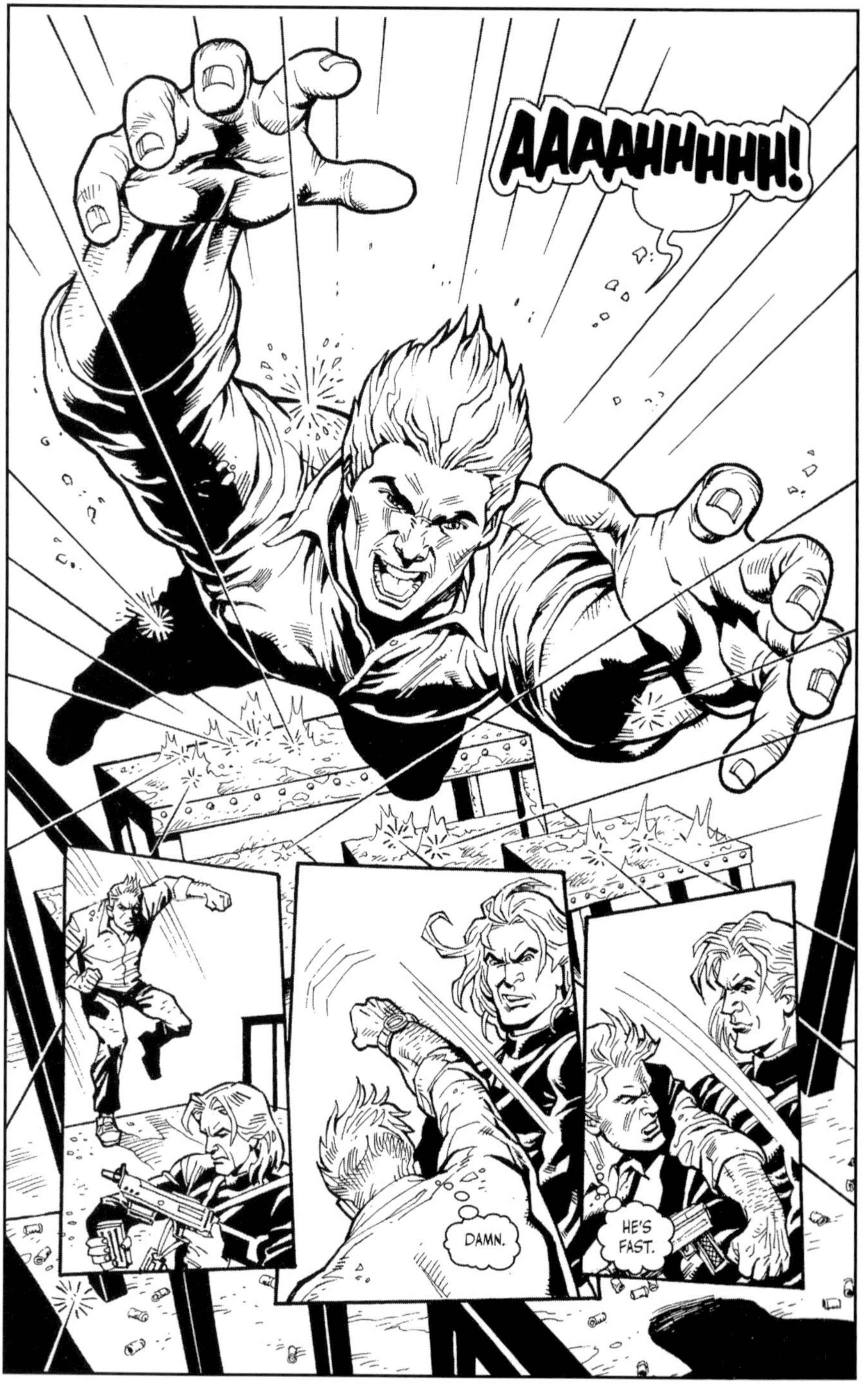
AAAAHHHHH!
DAMN.
HE'S FAST.

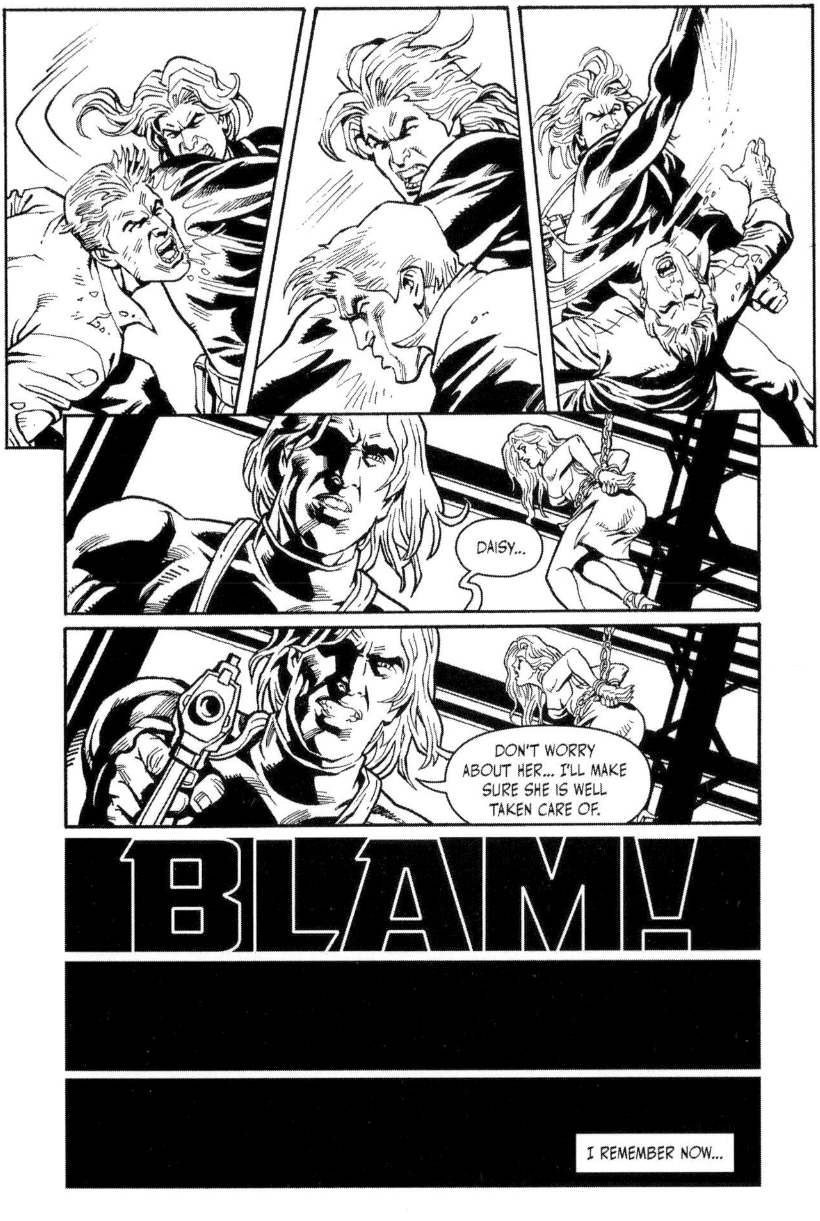
DAISY...
DON'T WORRY ABOUT HER... I'LL MAKE SURE SHE IS WELL TAKEN CARE OF.
BLAM!
I REMEMBER NOW...

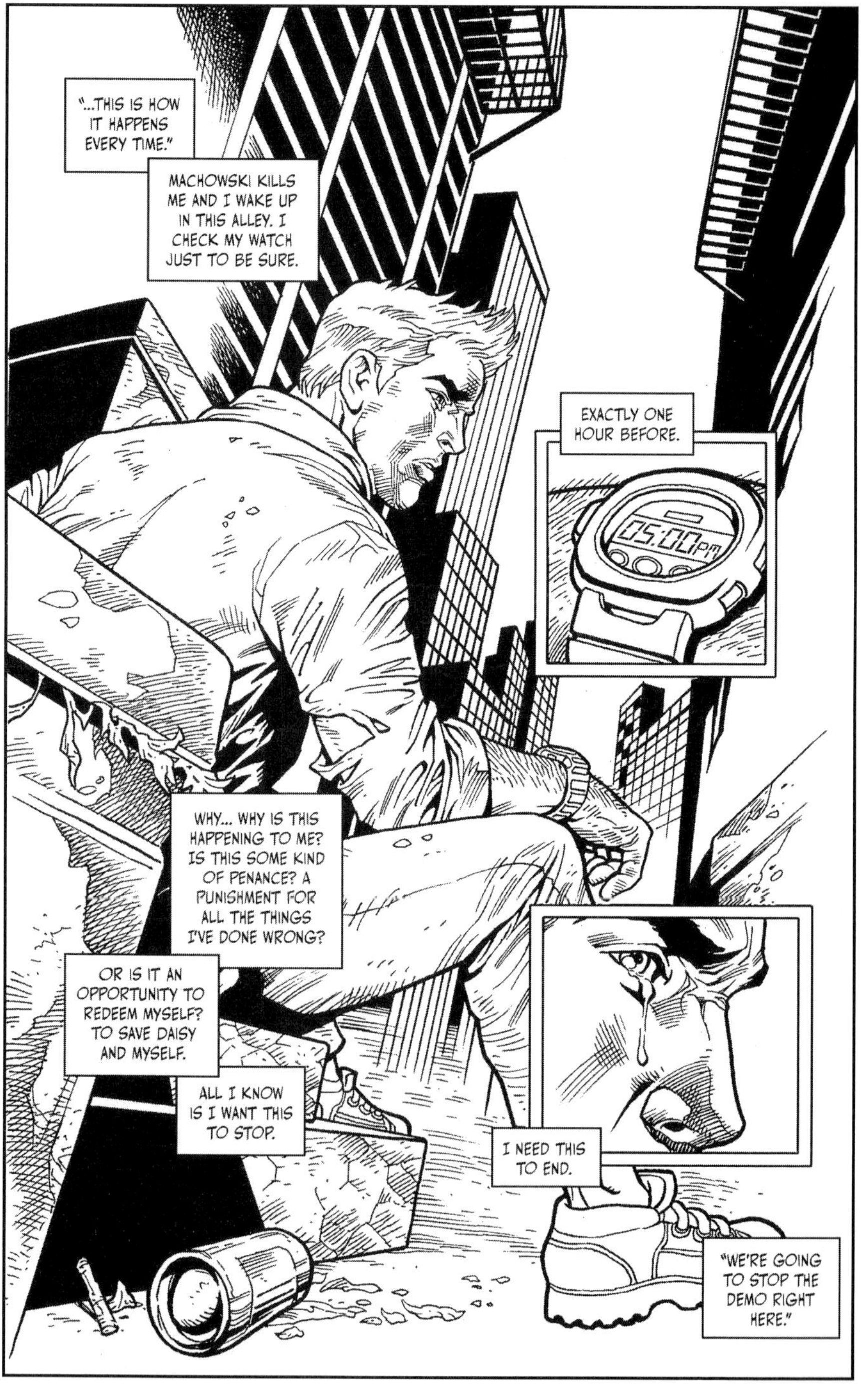
"...THIS IS HOW IT HAPPENS EVERY TIME."
MACHOWSKI KILLS ME AND I WAKE UP IN THIS ALLEY. I CHECK MY WATCH JUST TO BE SURE.
EXACTLY ONE HOUR BEFORE.
05:00PM
WHY... WHY IS THIS HAPPENING TO ME? IS THIS SOME KIND OF PENANCE? A PUNISHMENT FOR ALL THE THINGS I'VE DONE WRONG?
OR IS IT AN OPPORTUNITY TO REDEEM MYSELF? TO SAVE DAISY AND MYSELF.
ALL I KNOW IS I WANT THIS TO STOP.
I NEED THIS TO END.
"WE'RE GOING TO STOP THE DEMO RIGHT HERE."

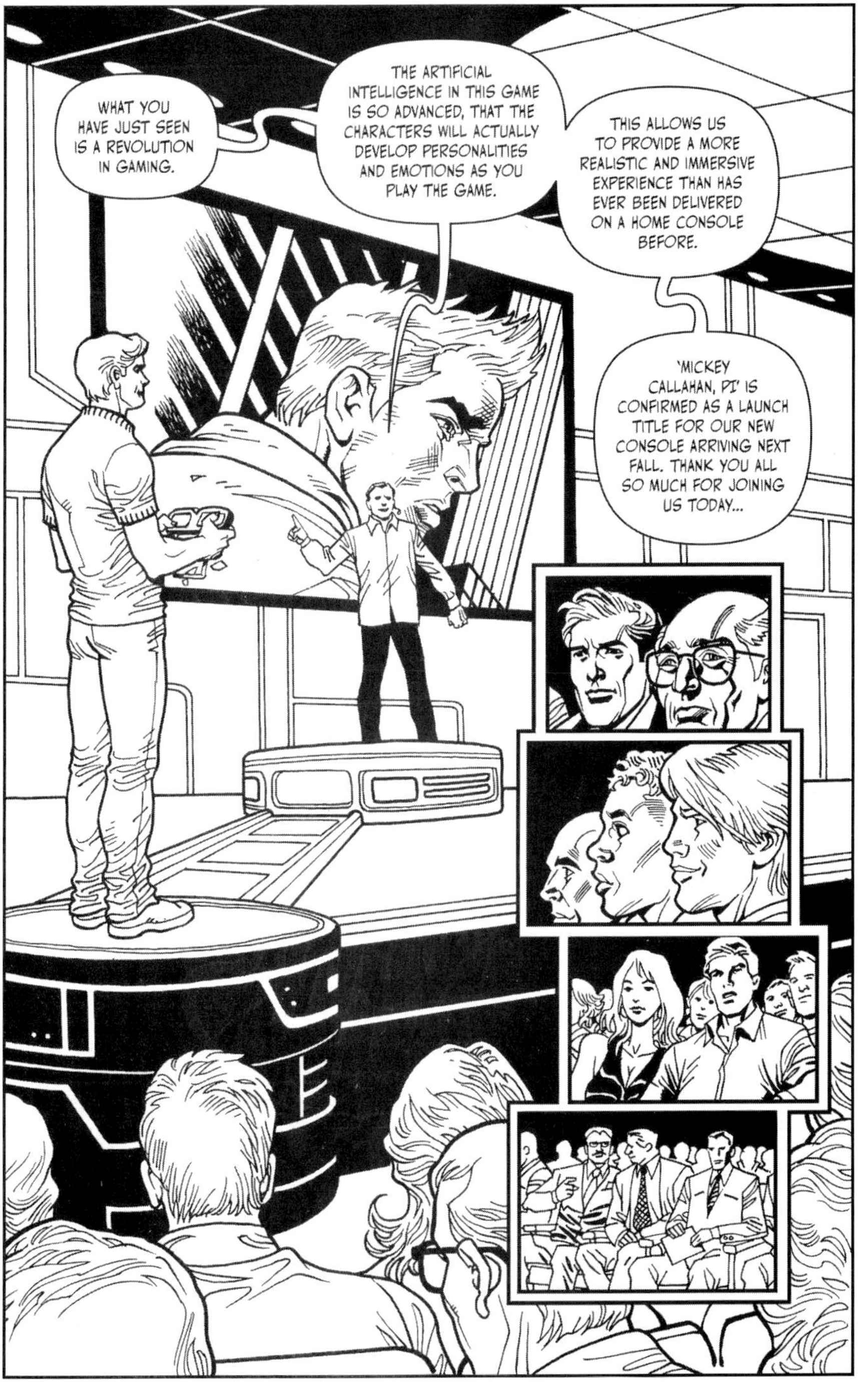
WHAT YOU HAVE JUST SEEN IS A REVOLUTION IN GAMING.
THE ARTIFICIAL INTELLIGENCE IN THIS GAME IS SO ADVANCED, THAT THE CHARACTERS WILL ACTUALLY DEVELOP PERSONALITIES AND EMOTIONS AS YOU PLAY THE GAME.
THIS ALLOWS US TO PROVIDE A MORE REALISTIC AND IMMERSIVE EXPERIENCE THAN HAS EVER BEEN DELIVERED ON A HOME CONSOLE BEFORE.
'MICKEY CALLAHAN, PI' IS CONFIRMED AS A LAUNCH TITLE FOR OUR NEW CONSOLE ARRIVING NEXT FALL. THANK YOU ALL SO MUCH FOR JOINING US TODAY...

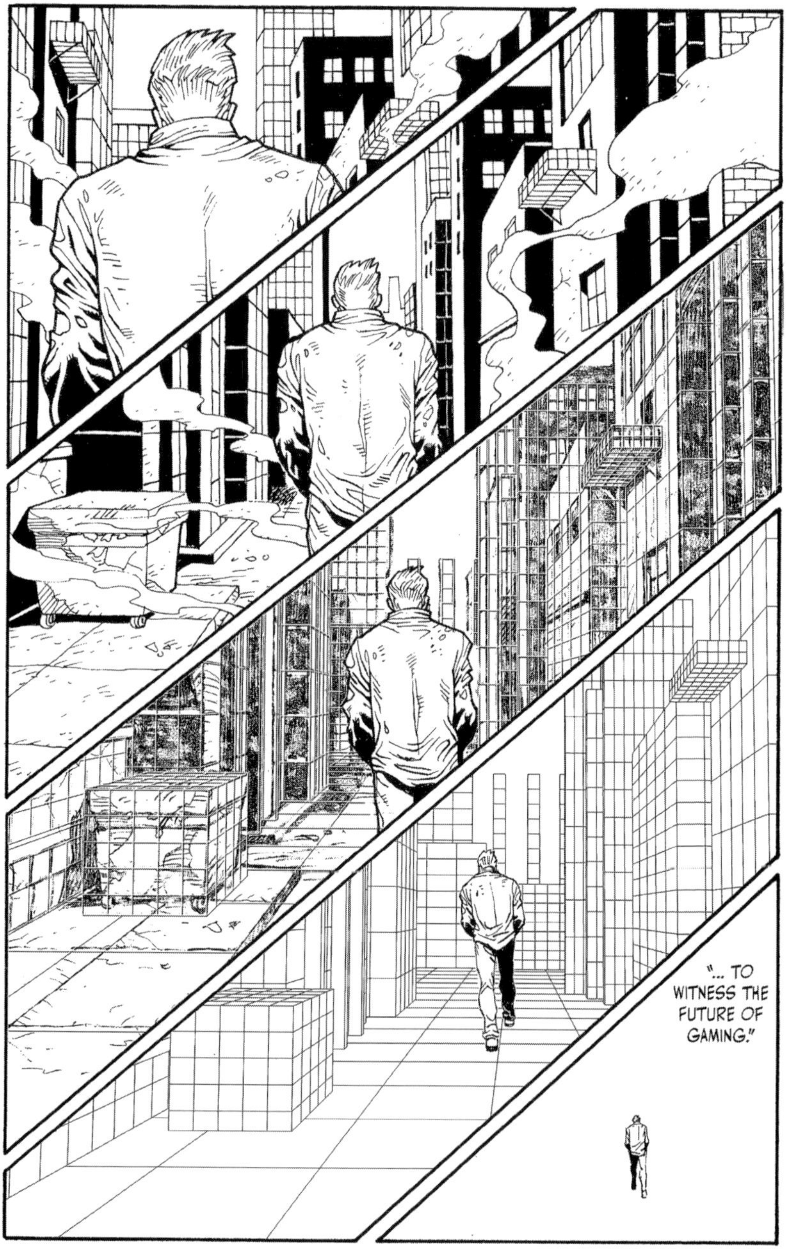
"... TO WITNESS THE FUTURE OF GAMING."

LIFE in THE GAME

THE FUTURE

script: MICHAEL MALKIN
art: NOVO MALGAPO
lettering: DEKARA

SMASH ATOM:
THE ARACHNID ASSIGNMENT

STORY
DINO CARUSO

ART - LETTERS
GEORGE ATHANASIOU

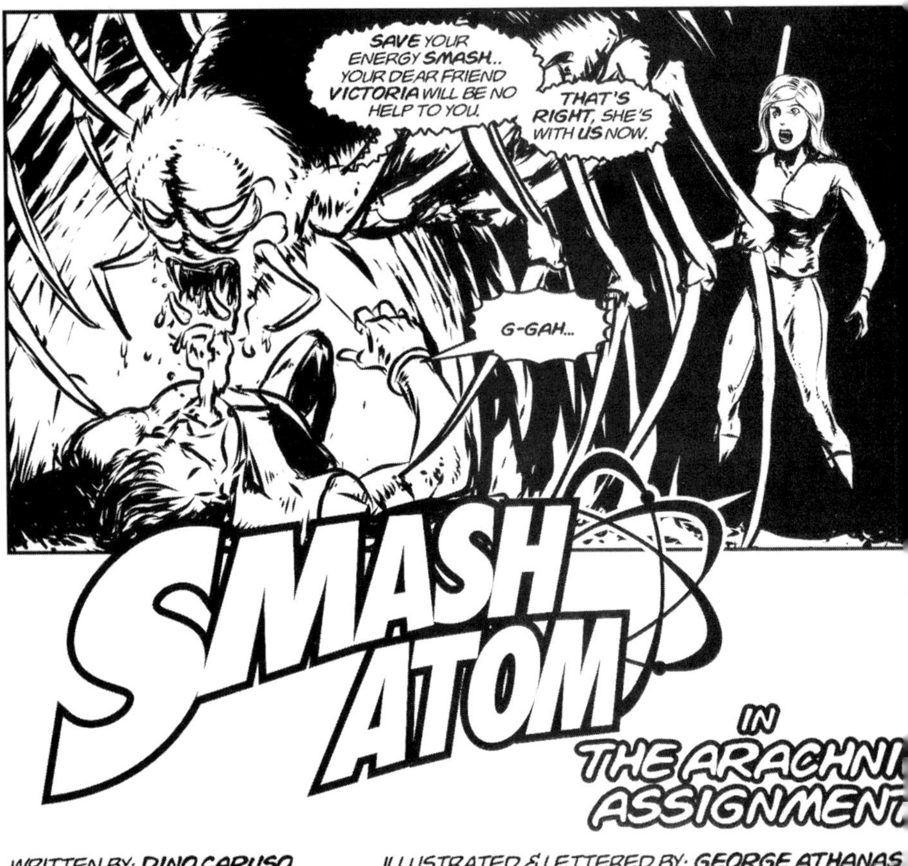
SAVE YOUR ENERGY SMASH.. YOUR DEAR FRIEND VICTORIA WILL BE NO HELP TO YOU.
THAT'S RIGHT, SHE'S WITH US NOW.
G-GAH...

SMASH ATOM

in

THE ARACHNI ASSIGNMENT

WRITTEN BY: DINO CARUSO ILLUSTRATED & LETTERED BY: GEORGE ATHANAS

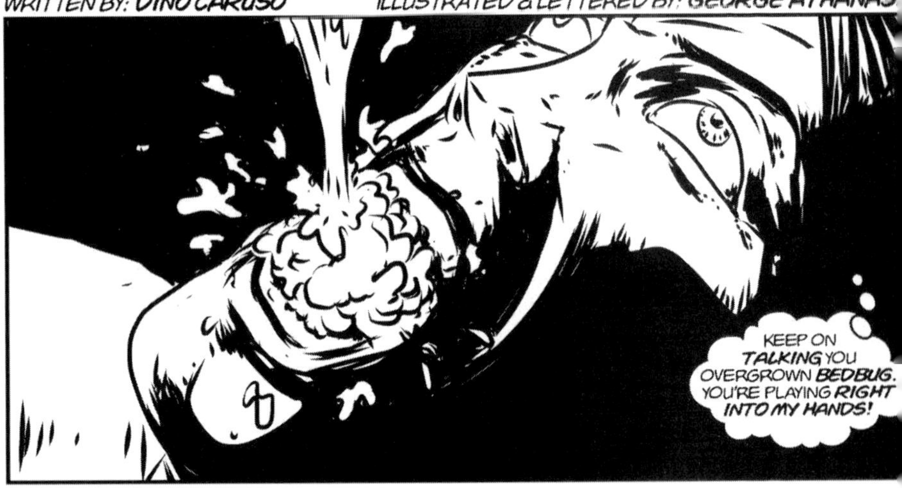
KEEP ON TALKING YOU OVERGROWN BEDBUG. YOU'RE PLAYING RIGHT INTO MY HANDS!

TWO HOURS AGO, A SMALL MINING VILLAGE NEAR THE KOVINSKI MOUNTAINS.

FUNNY, THIS DOESN'T REALLY SURPRISE ME AT ALL.

REPORTS OF MYSTERIOUS HAPPENINGS IN THE MINE SHAFT... DESERTED VILLAGE...SMASH NOT HERE ON TIME.

YEP, RUN TOF THE MILL DAY FOR VICTORIA FROST, INTREPID ARCHAEOLOGIST.

I'M NOT SURE WHAT TO MAKE OF THOSE BIZARRE TRACKS. THERE WERE SO MANY OF THEM ALL OVER THE PLACE.

THEY'RE UNLIKE ANY ANIMAL PRINTS I'VE EVER SEEN.

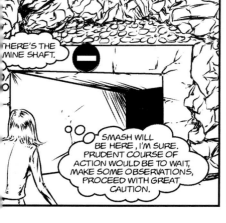

HERE'S THE MINE SHAFT.

SMASH WILL BE HERE, I'M SURE. PRUDENT COURSE OF ACTION WOULD BE TO WAIT, MAKE SOME OBSERVATIONS, PROCEED WITH GREAT CAUTION.

HEH. WHO AM I KIDDING?

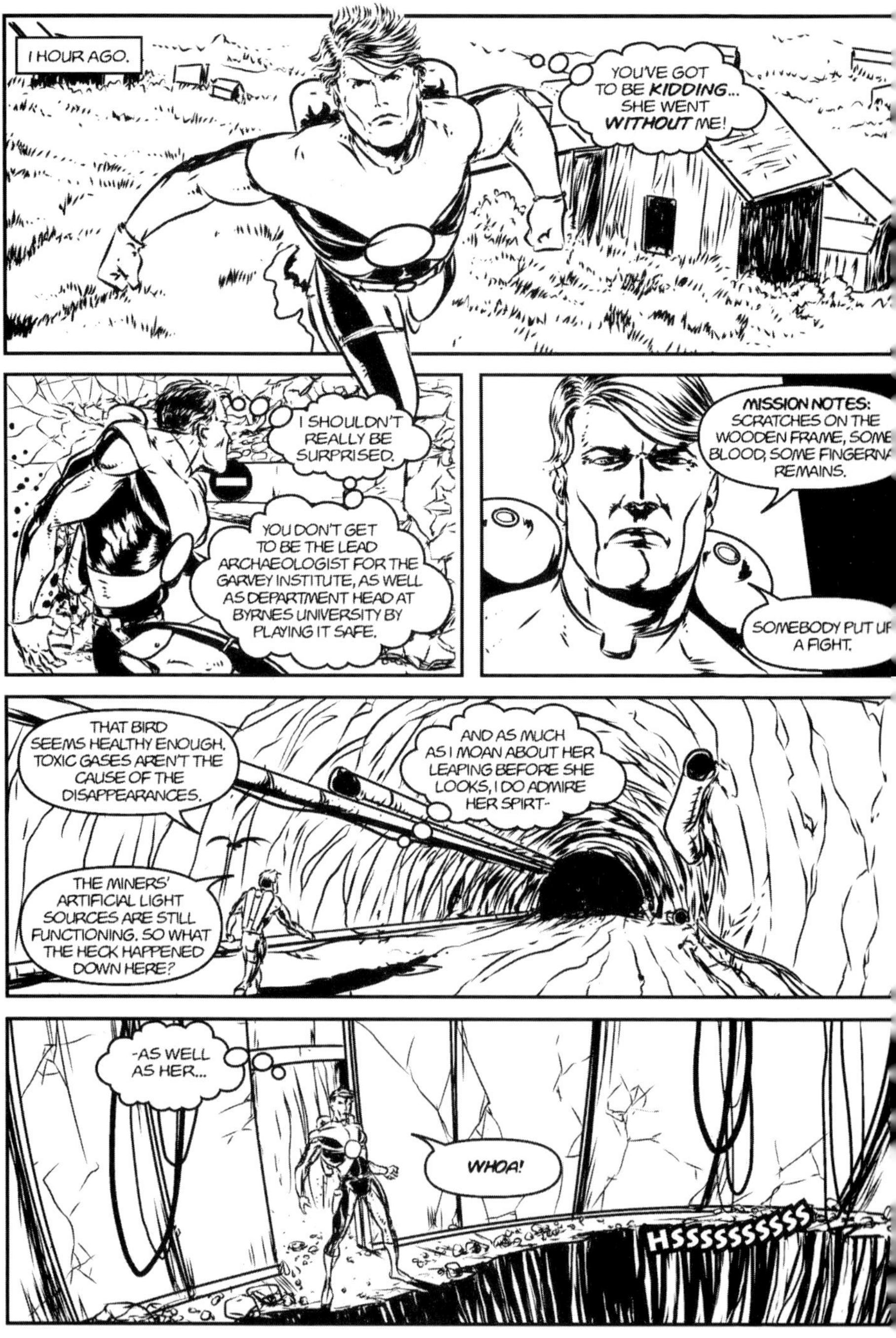
1 HOUR AGO.
YOU'VE GOT TO BE KIDDING... SHE WENT WITHOUT ME!
I SHOULDN'T REALLY BE SURPRISED.
YOU DON'T GET TO BE THE LEAD ARCHAEOLOGIST FOR THE GARVEY INSTITUTE, AS WELL AS DEPARTMENT HEAD AT BYRNES UNIVERSITY BY PLAYING IT SAFE.
MISSION NOTES: SCRATCHES ON THE WOODEN FRAME, SOME BLOOD, SOME FINGERNA REMAINS.
SOMEBODY PUT UP A FIGHT.
THAT BIRD SEEMS HEALTHY ENOUGH. TOXIC GASES AREN'T THE CAUSE OF THE DISAPPEARANCES.
AND AS MUCH AS I MOAN ABOUT HER LEAPING BEFORE SHE LOOKS, I DO ADMIRE HER SPIRT-
THE MINERS' ARTIFICIAL LIGHT SOURCES ARE STILL FUNCTIONING. SO WHAT THE HECK HAPPENED DOWN HERE?
-AS WELL AS HER...
WHOA!
HSSSSSSSSS

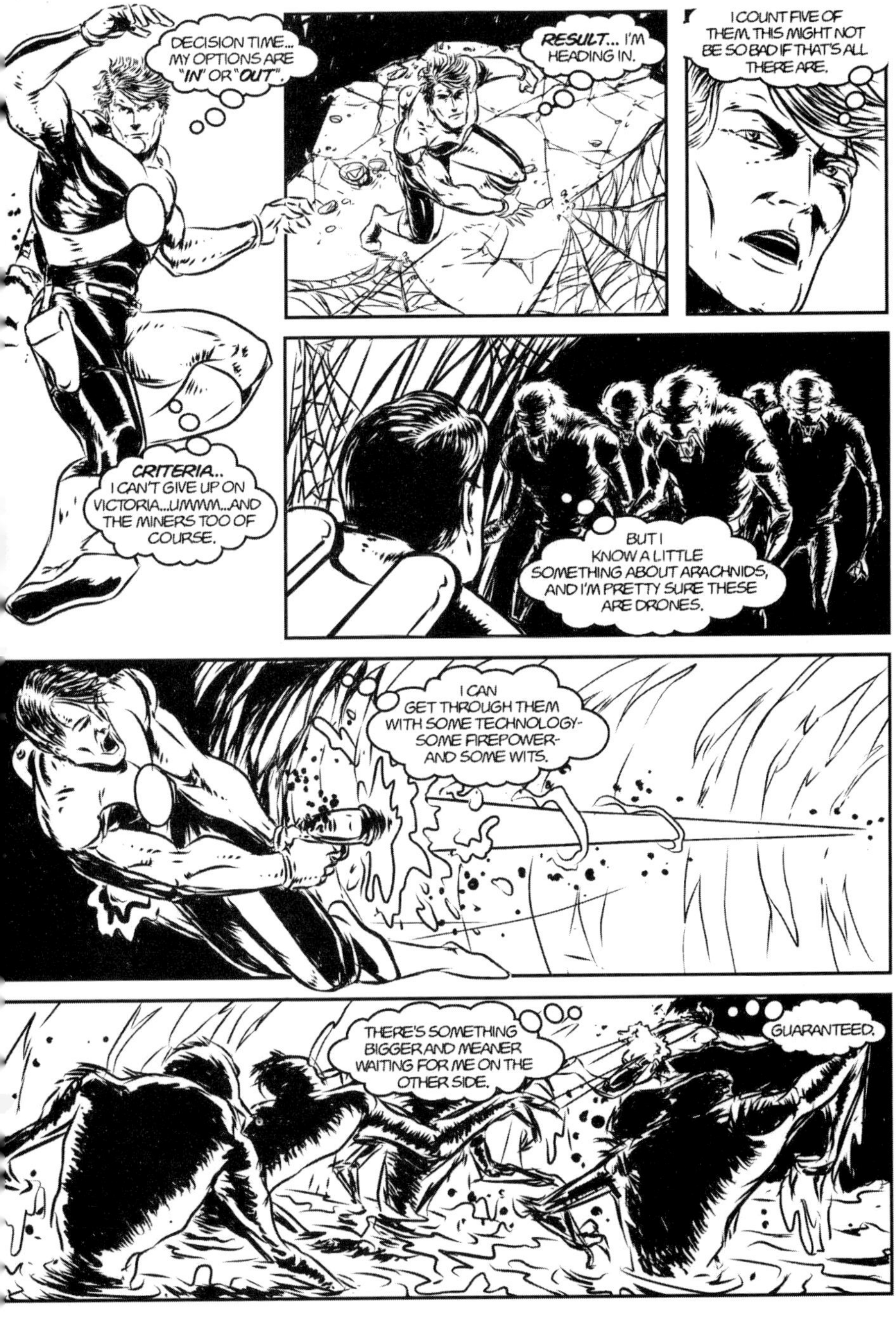
DECISION TIME... MY OPTIONS ARE "IN" OR "OUT".
CRITERIA... I CAN'T GIVE UP ON VICTORIA...UMMM...AND THE MINERS TOO OF COURSE.
RESULT... I'M HEADING IN.
I COUNT FIVE OF THEM. THIS MIGHT NOT BE SO BAD IF THAT'S ALL THERE ARE.
BUT I KNOW A LITTLE SOMETHING ABOUT ARACHNIDS, AND I'M PRETTY SURE THESE ARE DRONES.
I CAN GET THROUGH THEM WITH SOME TECHNOLOGY- SOME FIREPOWER- AND SOME WITS.
THERE'S SOMETHING BIGGER AND MEANER WAITING FOR ME ON THE OTHER SIDE.
GUARANTEED.

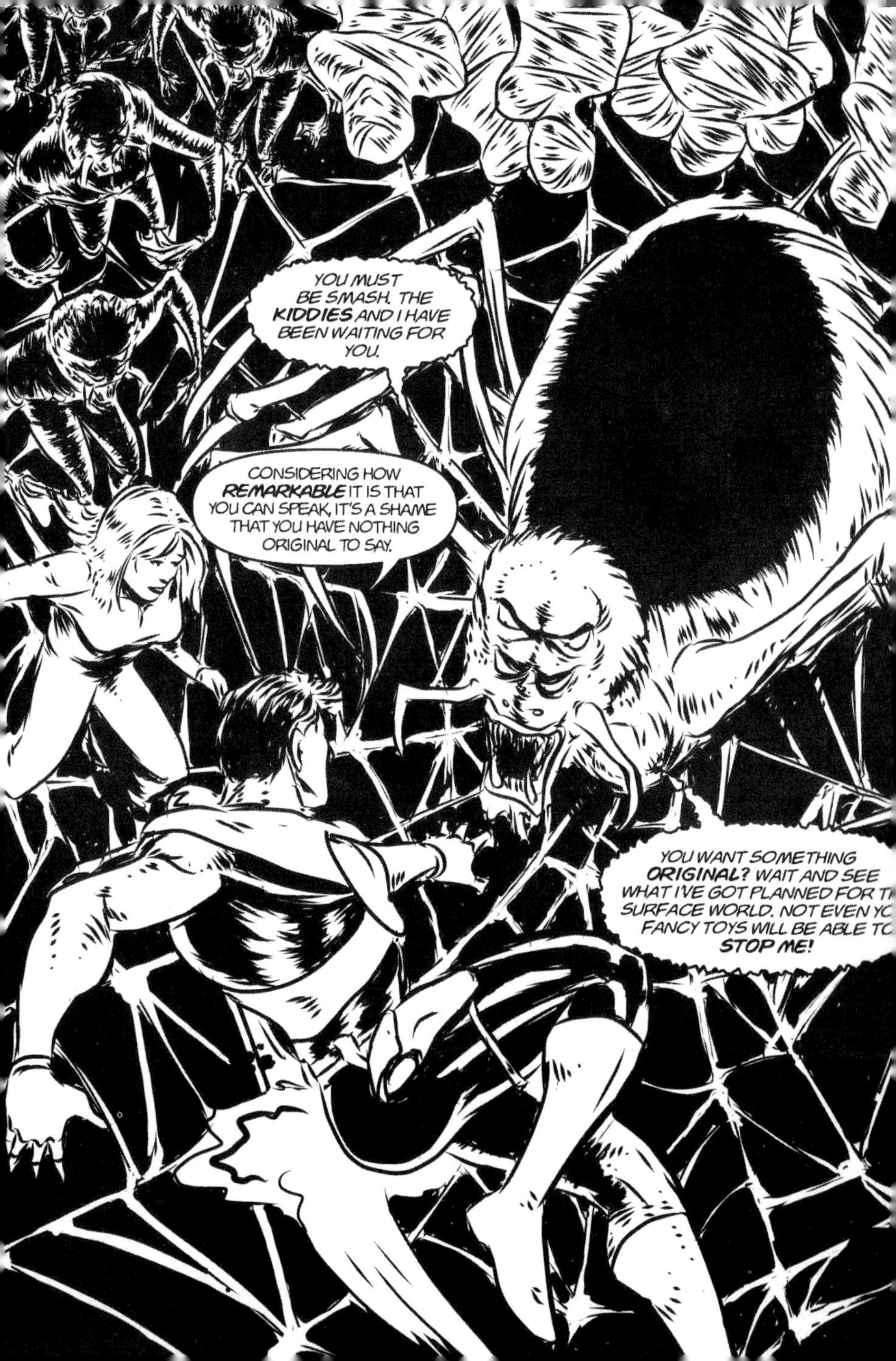
YOU MUST BE SMASH. THE KIDDIES AND I HAVE BEEN WAITING FOR YOU.
CONSIDERING HOW REMARKABLE IT IS THAT YOU CAN SPEAK, IT'S A SHAME THAT YOU HAVE NOTHING ORIGINAL TO SAY.
YOU WANT SOMETHING ORIGINAL? WAIT AND SEE WHAT I'VE GOT PLANNED FOR T SURFACE WORLD. NOT EVEN YO FANCY TOYS WILL BE ABLE TO STOP ME!

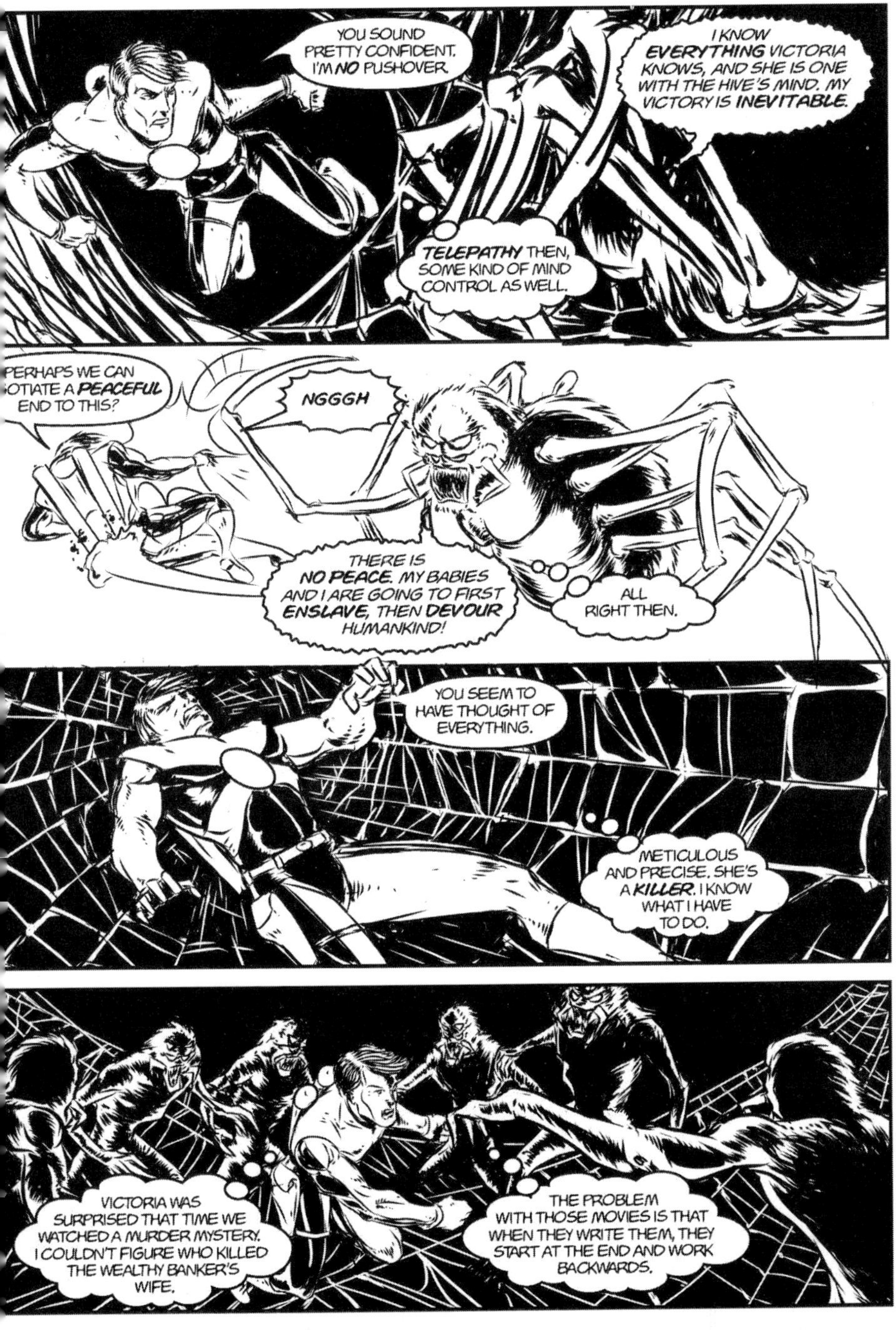
YOU SOUND PRETTY CONFIDENT. I'M **NO** PUSHOVER.
I KNOW **EVERYTHING** VICTORIA KNOWS, AND SHE IS ONE WITH THE HIVE'S MIND. MY VICTORY IS **INEVITABLE**.
TELEPATHY THEN, SOME KIND OF MIND CONTROL AS WELL.
PERHAPS WE CAN OTIATE A **PEACEFUL** END TO THIS?
NGGGH
THERE IS **NO PEACE**. MY BABIES AND I ARE GOING TO FIRST **ENSLAVE**, THEN **DEVOUR** HUMANKIND!
ALL RIGHT THEN.
YOU SEEM TO HAVE THOUGHT OF EVERYTHING.
METICULOUS AND PRECISE. SHE'S A **KILLER**. I KNOW WHAT I HAVE TO DO.
VICTORIA WAS SURPRISED THAT TIME WE WATCHED A MURDER MYSTERY. I COULDN'T FIGURE WHO KILLED THE WEALTHY BANKER'S WIFE.
THE PROBLEM WITH THOSE MOVIES IS THAT WHEN THEY WRITE THEM, THEY START AT THE END AND WORK BACKWARDS.

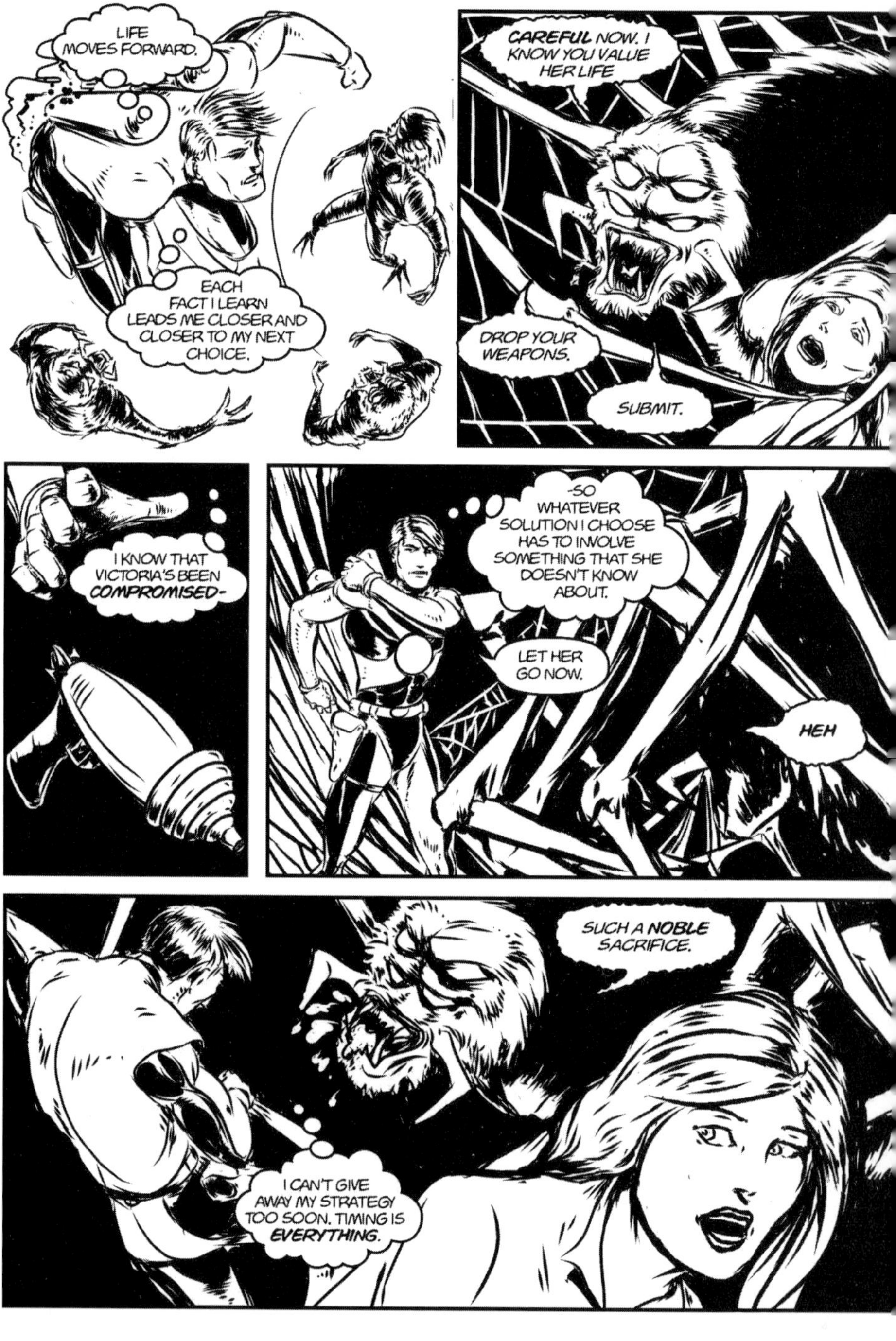
LIFE MOVES FORWARD.
EACH FACT I LEARN LEADS ME CLOSER AND CLOSER TO MY NEXT CHOICE.
CAREFUL NOW. I KNOW YOU VALUE HER LIFE
DROP YOUR WEAPONS.
SUBMIT.
I KNOW THAT VICTORIA'S BEEN COMPROMISED-
-SO WHATEVER SOLUTION I CHOOSE HAS TO INVOLVE SOMETHING THAT SHE DOESN'T KNOW ABOUT.
LET HER GO NOW.
HEH
SUCH A NOBLE SACRIFICE.
I CAN'T GIVE AWAY MY STRATEGY TOO SOON. TIMING IS EVERYTHING.

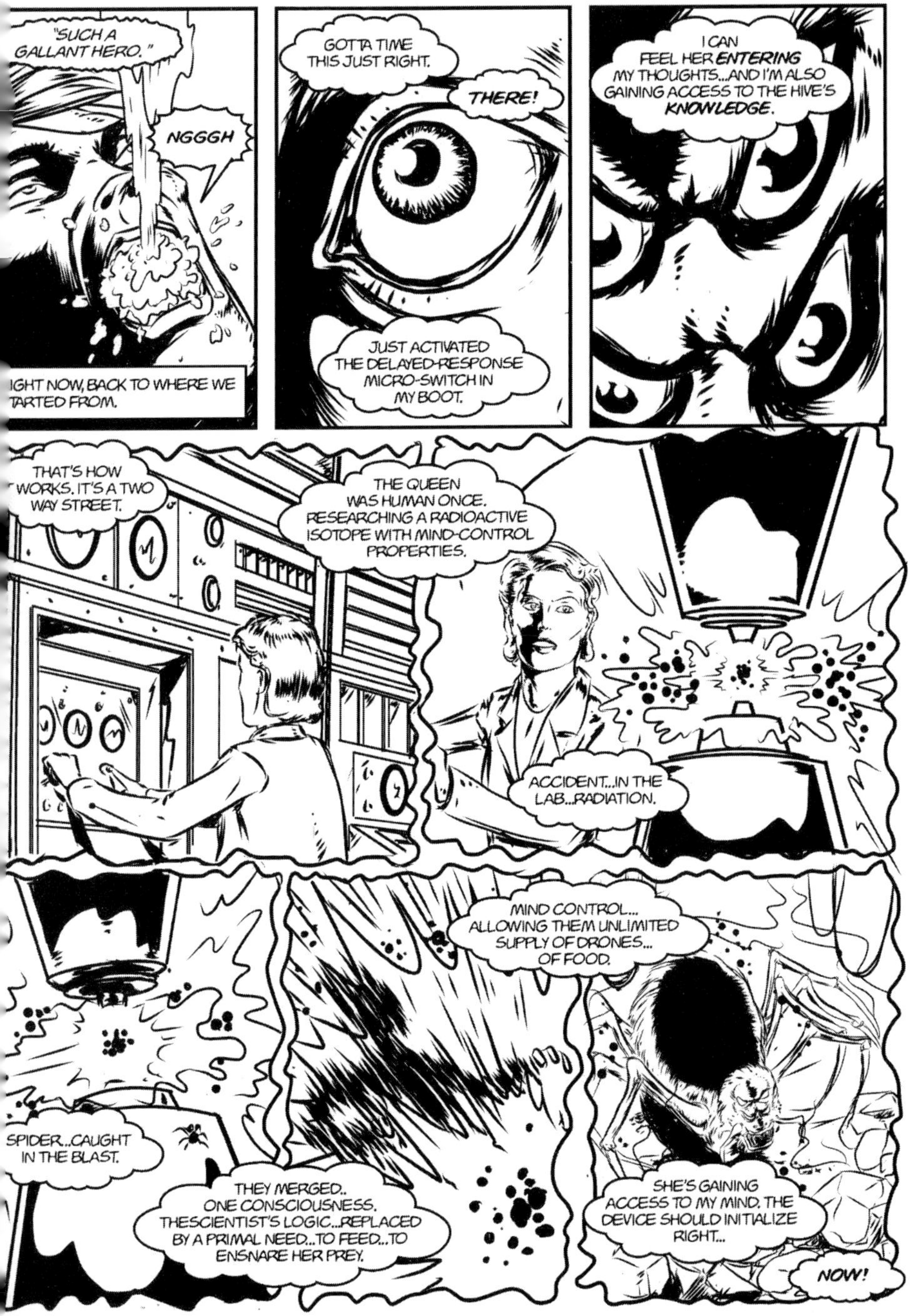

"SUCH A GALLANT HERO."
NGGGH
IGHT NOW, BACK TO WHERE WE TARTED FROM.
GOTTA TIME THIS JUST RIGHT.
THERE!
JUST ACTIVATED THE DELAYED-RESPONSE MICRO-SWITCH IN MY BOOT.
I CAN FEEL HER ENTERING MY THOUGHTS...AND I'M ALSO GAINING ACCESS TO THE HIVE'S KNOWLEDGE.
THAT'S HOW WORKS. IT'S A TWO WAY STREET.
THE QUEEN WAS HUMAN ONCE. RESEARCHING A RADIOACTIVE ISOTOPE WITH MIND-CONTROL PROPERTIES.
ACCIDENT...IN THE LAB...RADIATION.
SPIDER...CAUGHT IN THE BLAST.
THEY MERGED.. ONE CONSCIOUSNESS. THESCIENTIST'S LOGIC...REPLACED BY A PRIMAL NEED...TO FEED...TO ENSNARE HER PREY.
MIND CONTROL... ALLOWING THEM UNLIMITED SUPPLY OF DRONES... OF FOOD.
SHE'S GAINING ACCESS TO MY MIND. THE DEVICE SHOULD INITIALIZE RIGHT...
NOW!

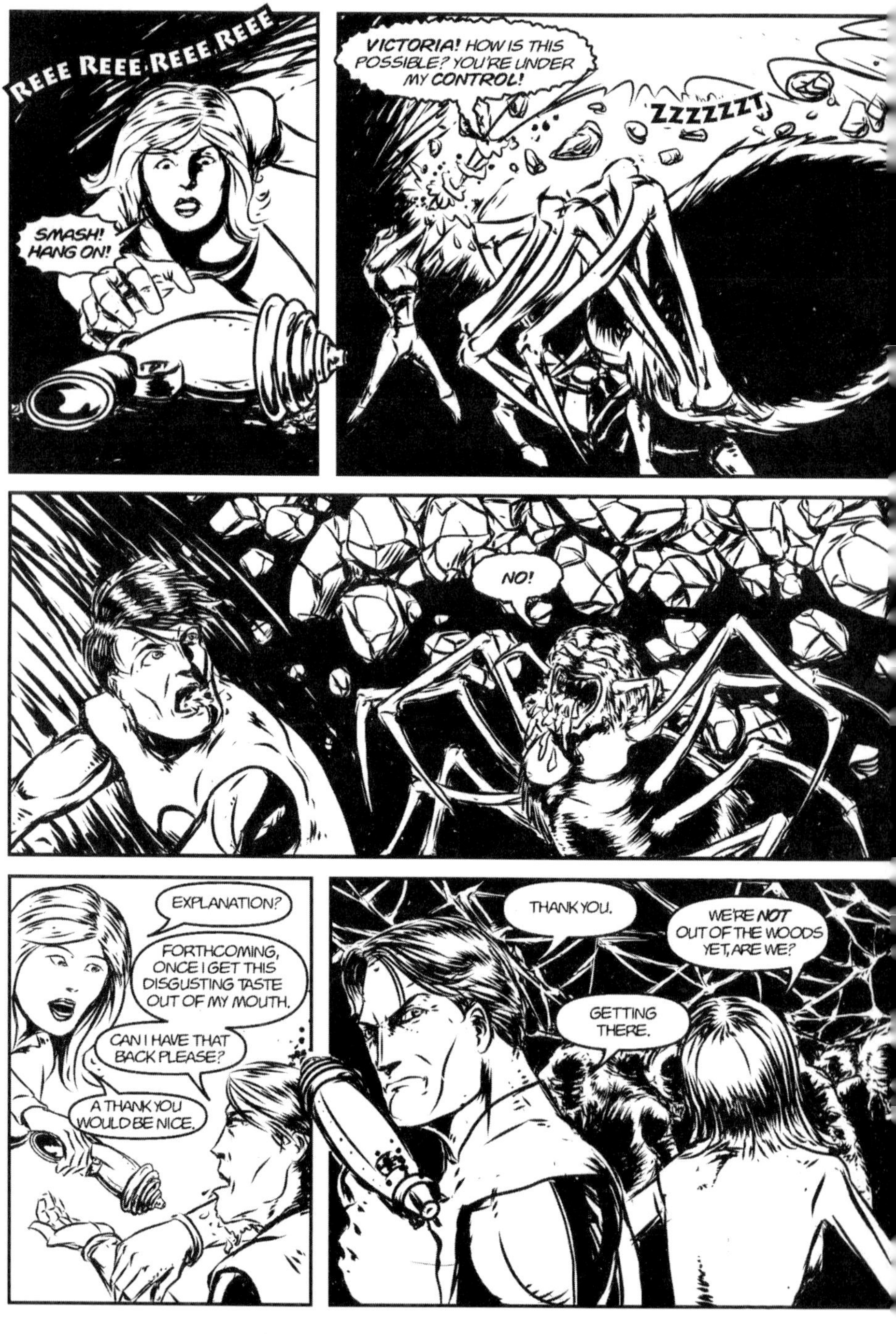
REEE REEE REEE REEE
SMASH! HANG ON!
VICTORIA! HOW IS THIS POSSIBLE? YOU'RE UNDER MY CONTROL!
ZZZZZZT
NO!
EXPLANATION?
FORTHCOMING, ONCE I GET THIS DISGUSTING TASTE OUT OF MY MOUTH.
CAN I HAVE THAT BACK PLEASE?
A THANK YOU WOULD BE NICE.
THANK YOU.
WE'RE NOT OUT OF THE WOODS YET, ARE WE?
GETTING THERE.

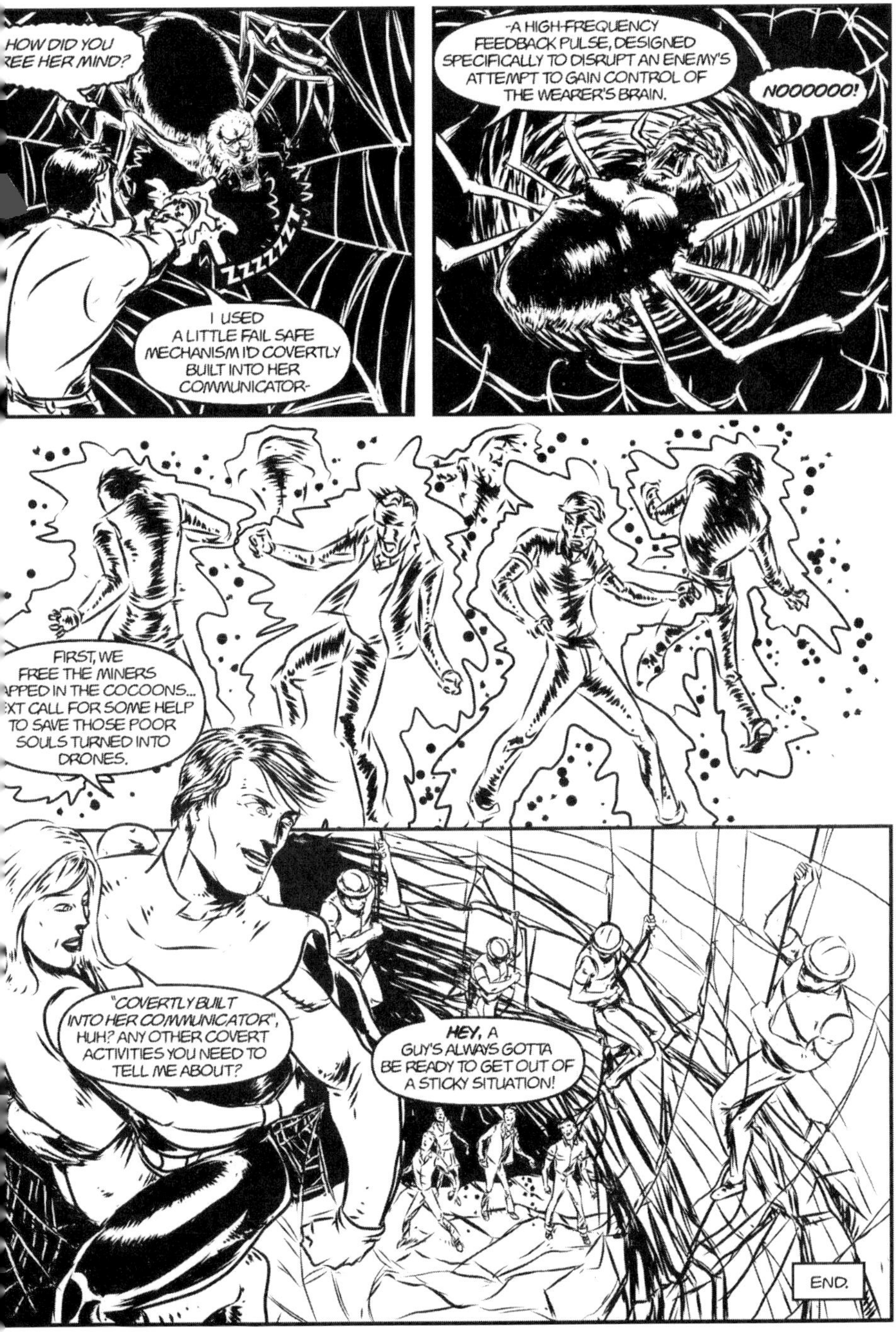
HOW DID YOU
REE HER MIND?
I USED A LITTLE FAIL SAFE MECHANISM I'D COVERTLY BUILT INTO HER COMMUNICATOR-
ZZZZZZZZ
-A HIGH-FREQUENCY FEEDBACK PULSE, DESIGNED SPECIFICALLY TO DISRUPT AN ENEMY'S ATTEMPT TO GAIN CONTROL OF THE WEARER'S BRAIN.
NOOOOOO!
FIRST, WE FREE THE MINERS
APPED IN THE COCOONS...
XT CALL FOR SOME HELP TO SAVE THOSE POOR SOULS TURNED INTO DRONES.
"COVERTLY BUILT INTO HER COMMUNICATOR", HUH? ANY OTHER COVERT ACTIVITIES YOU NEED TO TELL ME ABOUT?
HEY, A GUY'S ALWAYS GOTTA BE READY TO GET OUT OF A STICKY SITUATION!
END.

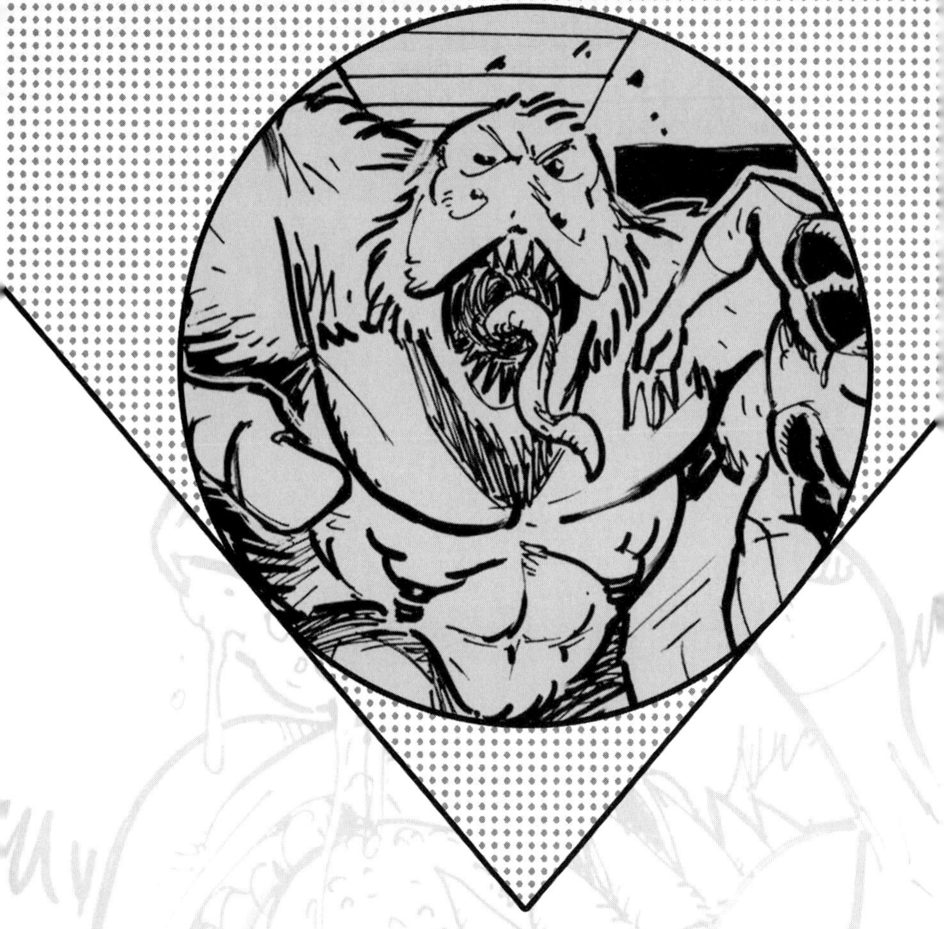

SIGNS OF LIFE

STORY - ART - LETTERS
ZACH BASSETT

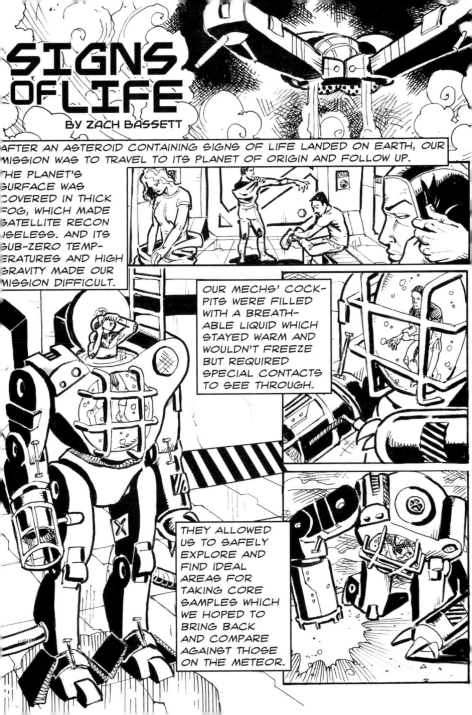

SIGNS OF LIFE

BY ZACH BASSETT

AFTER AN ASTEROID CONTAINING SIGNS OF LIFE LANDED ON EARTH, OUR MISSION WAS TO TRAVEL TO ITS PLANET OF ORIGIN AND FOLLOW UP.

THE PLANET'S SURFACE WAS COVERED IN THICK FOG, WHICH MADE SATELLITE RECON USELESS. AND ITS SUB-ZERO TEMPERATURES AND HIGH GRAVITY MADE OUR MISSION DIFFICULT.

OUR MECHS' COCKPITS WERE FILLED WITH A BREATHABLE LIQUID WHICH STAYED WARM AND WOULDN'T FREEZE BUT REQUIRED SPECIAL CONTACTS TO SEE THROUGH.

THEY ALLOWED US TO SAFELY EXPLORE AND FIND IDEAL AREAS FOR TAKING CORE SAMPLES WHICH WE HOPED TO BRING BACK AND COMPARE AGAINST THOSE ON THE METEOR.

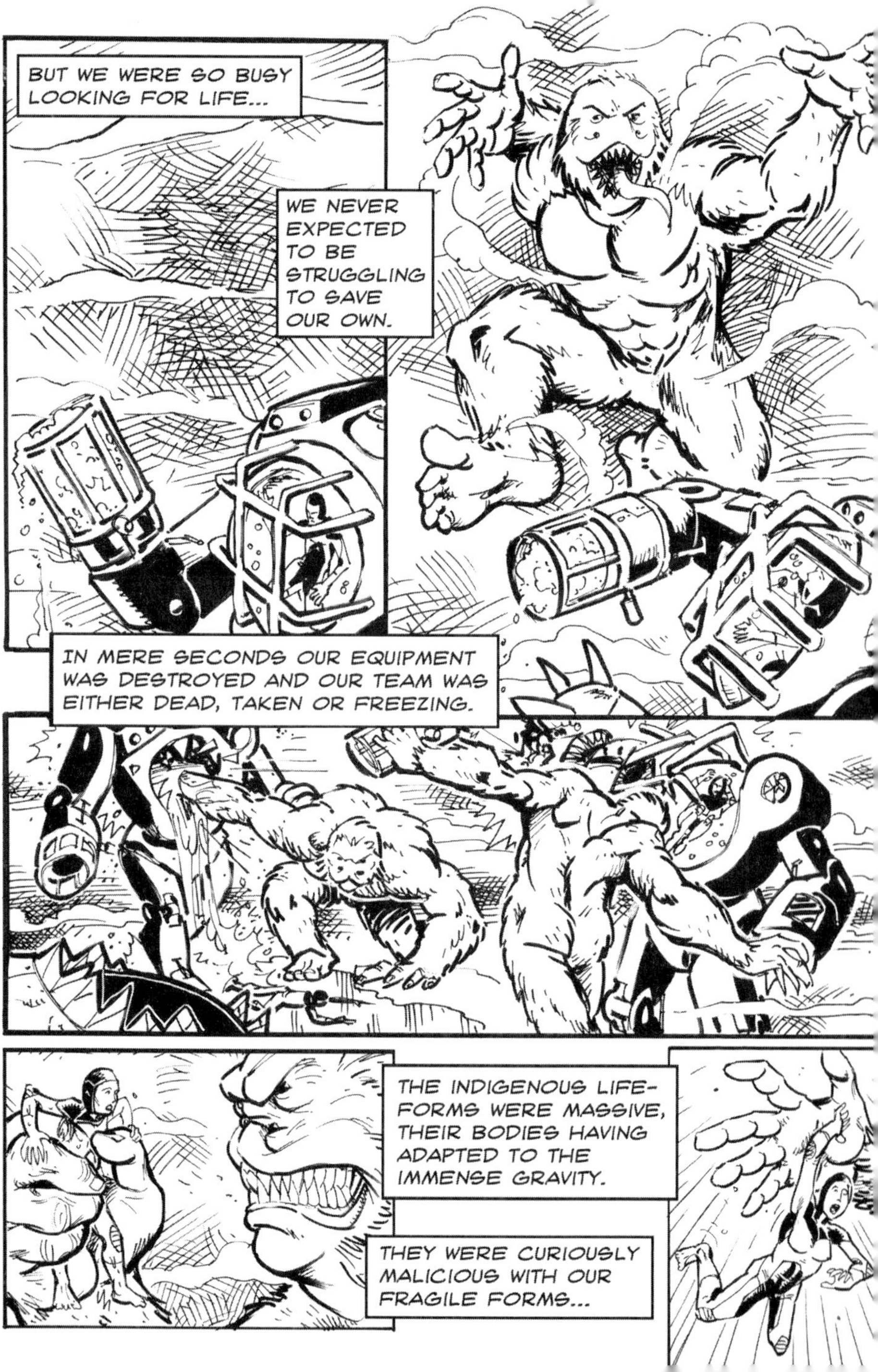

BUT WE WERE SO BUSY LOOKING FOR LIFE...
WE NEVER EXPECTED TO BE STRUGGLING TO SAVE OUR OWN.
IN MERE SECONDS OUR EQUIPMENT WAS DESTROYED AND OUR TEAM WAS EITHER DEAD, TAKEN OR FREEZING.
THE INDIGENOUS LIFE-FORMS WERE MASSIVE, THEIR BODIES HAVING ADAPTED TO THE IMMENSE GRAVITY.
THEY WERE CURIOUSLY MALICIOUS WITH OUR FRAGILE FORMS...

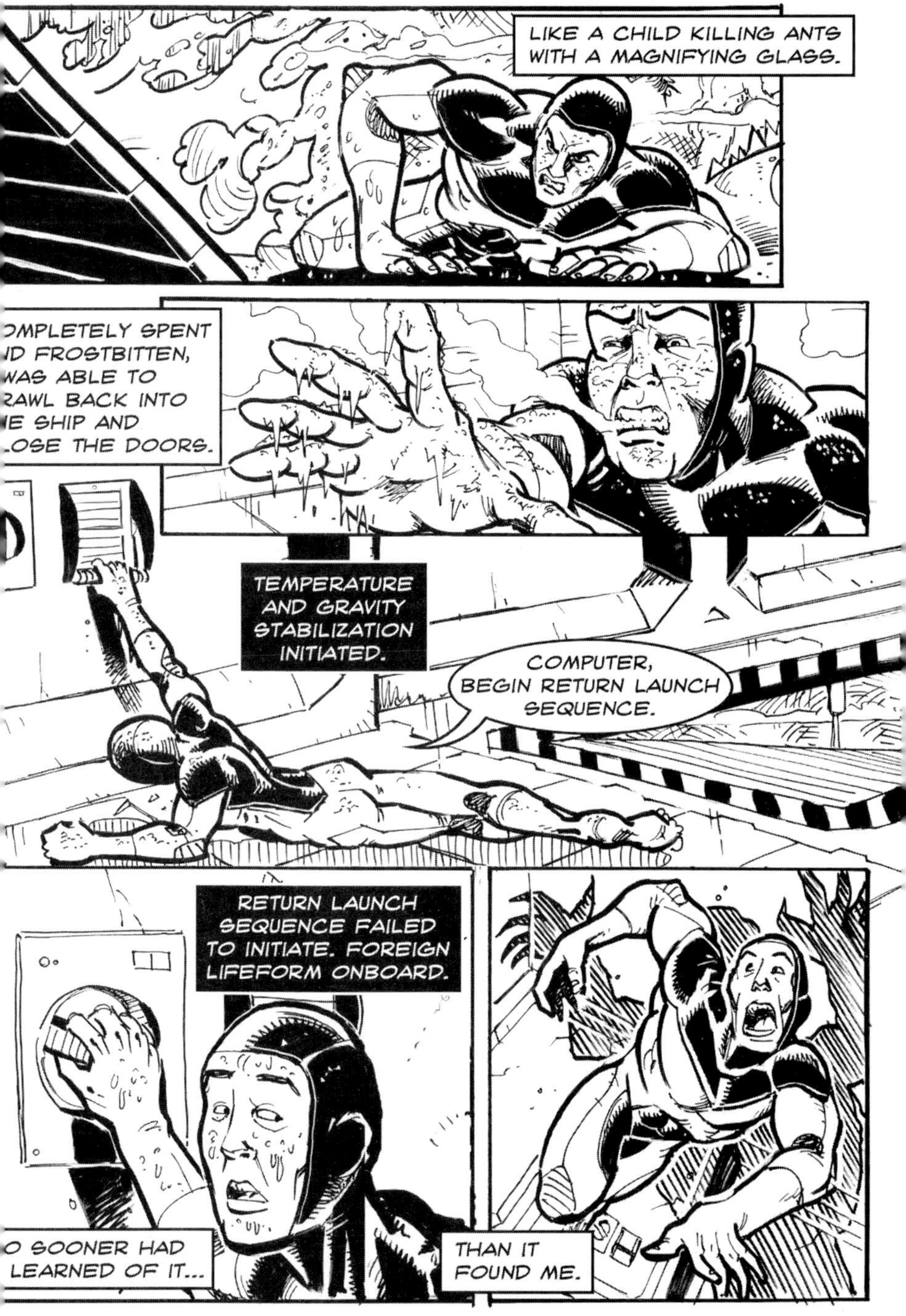
LIKE A CHILD KILLING ANTS WITH A MAGNIFYING GLASS.
OMPLETELY SPENT ID FROSTBITTEN, WAS ABLE TO RAWL BACK INTO IE SHIP AND LOSE THE DOORS.
TEMPERATURE AND GRAVITY STABILIZATION INITIATED.
COMPUTER, BEGIN RETURN LAUNCH SEQUENCE.
RETURN LAUNCH SEQUENCE FAILED TO INITIATE. FOREIGN LIFEFORM ONBOARD.
O SOONER HAD LEARNED OF IT...
THAN IT FOUND ME.

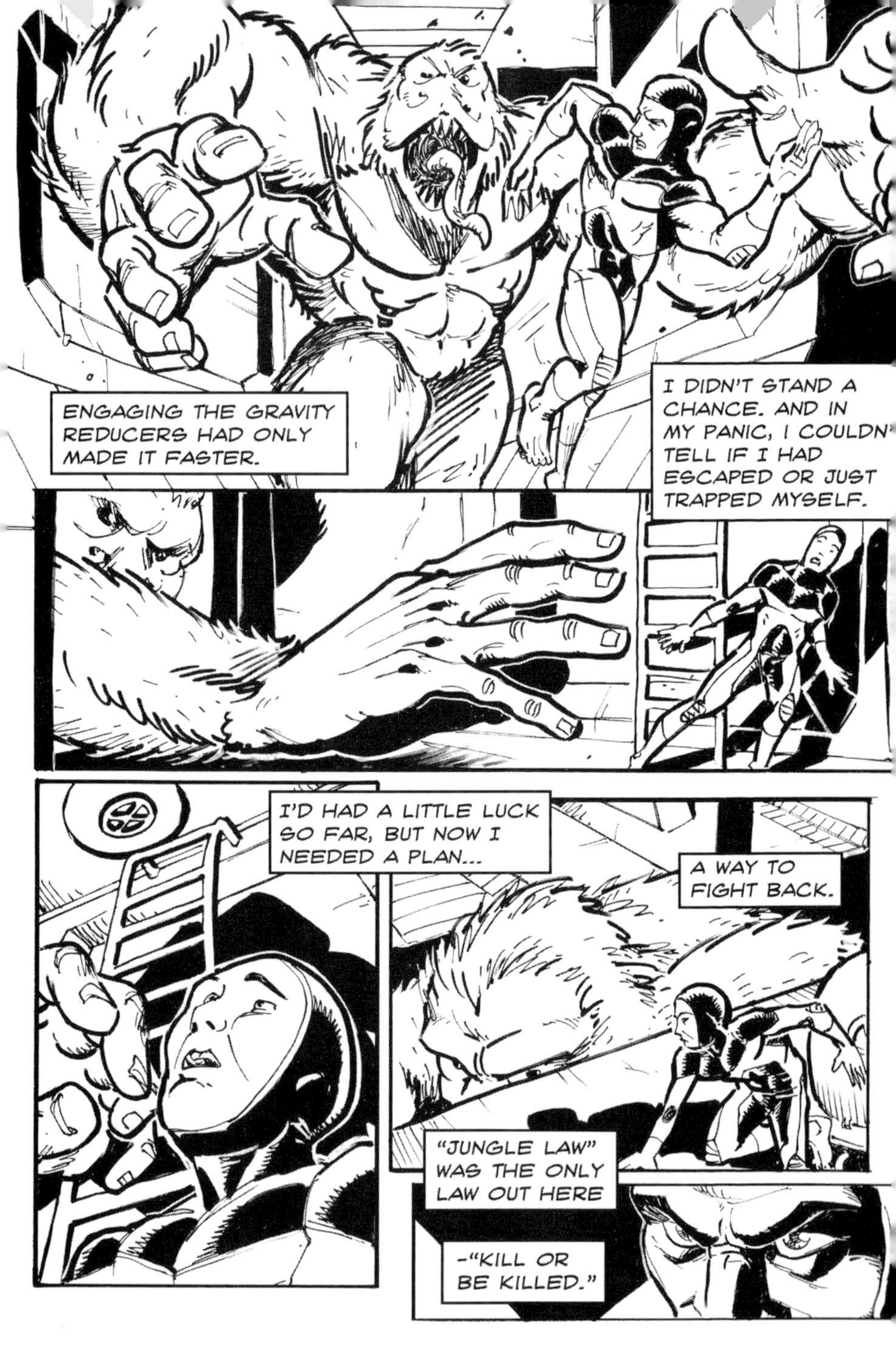
ENGAGING THE GRAVITY REDUCERS HAD ONLY MADE IT FASTER.
I DIDN'T STAND A CHANCE. AND IN MY PANIC, I COULDN' TELL IF I HAD ESCAPED OR JUST TRAPPED MYSELF.
I'D HAD A LITTLE LUCK SO FAR, BUT NOW I NEEDED A PLAN...
A WAY TO FIGHT BACK.
"JUNGLE LAW" WAS THE ONLY LAW OUT HERE
–"KILL OR BE KILLED."

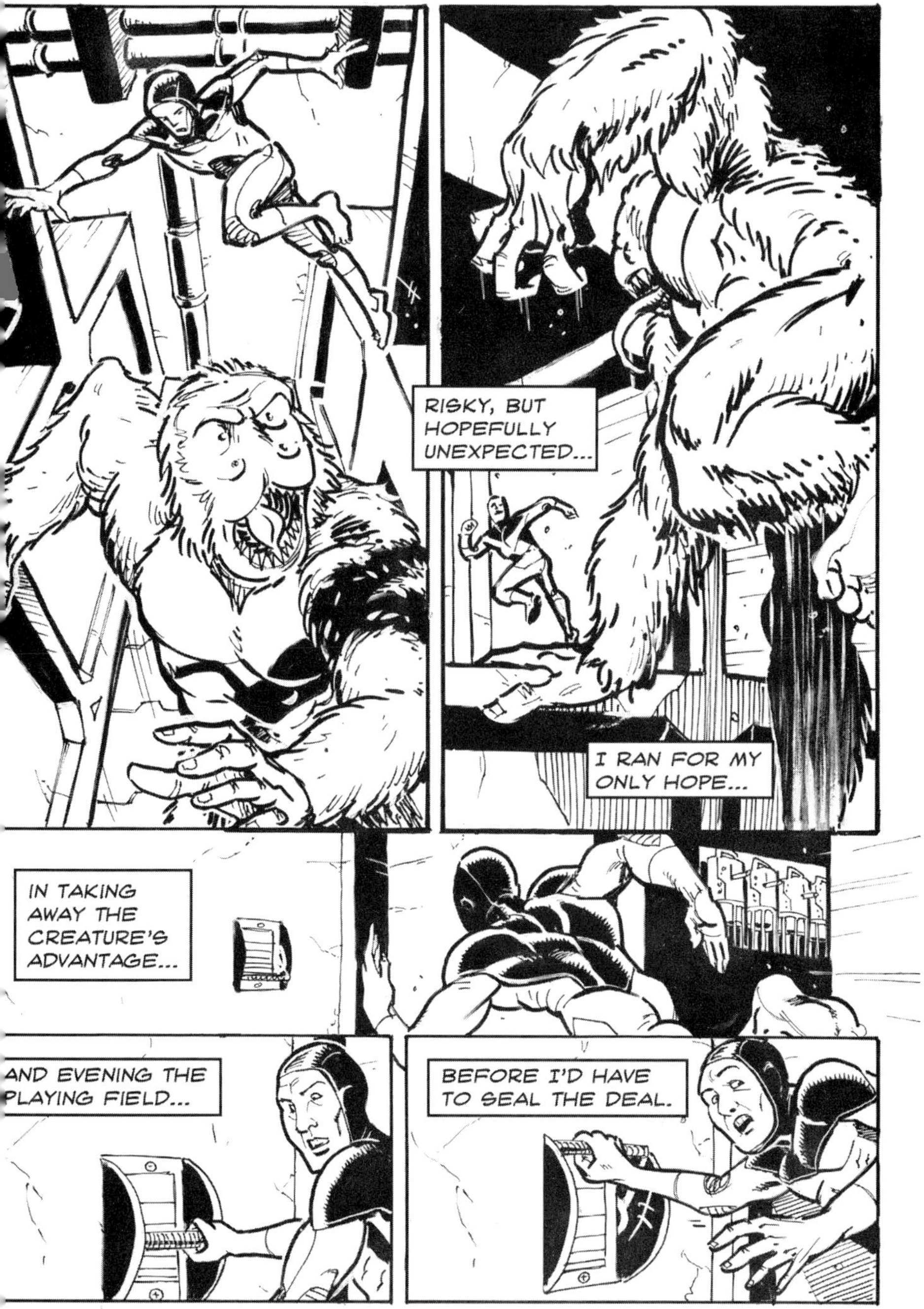
RISKY, BUT HOPEFULLY UNEXPECTED...
I RAN FOR MY ONLY HOPE...
IN TAKING AWAY THE CREATURE'S ADVANTAGE...
AND EVENING THE PLAYING FIELD...
BEFORE I'D HAVE TO SEAL THE DEAL.

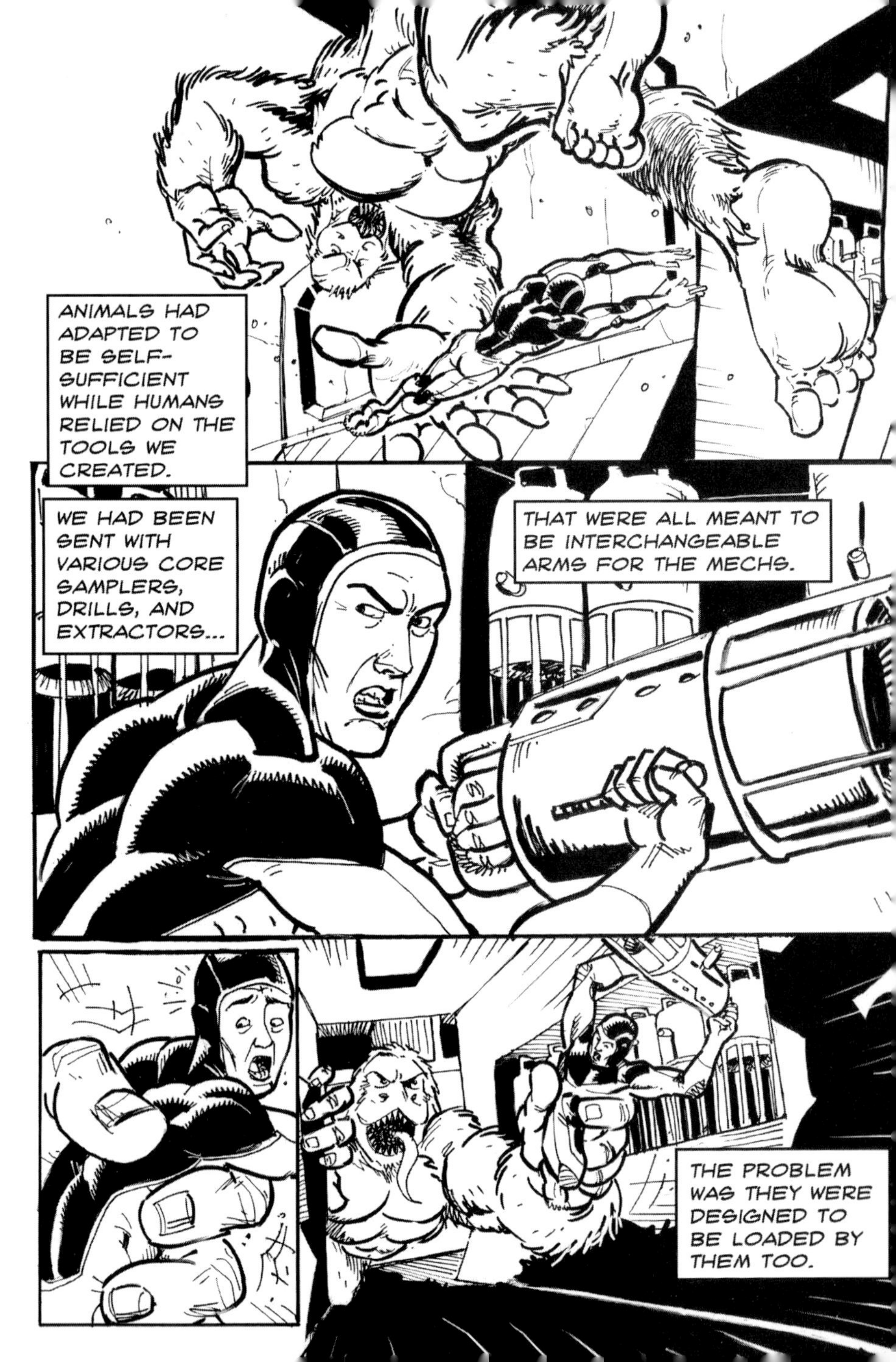

ANIMALS HAD ADAPTED TO BE SELF-SUFFICIENT WHILE HUMANS RELIED ON THE TOOLS WE CREATED.
WE HAD BEEN SENT WITH VARIOUS CORE SAMPLERS, DRILLS, AND EXTRACTORS...
THAT WERE ALL MEANT TO BE INTERCHANGEABLE ARMS FOR THE MECHS.
THE PROBLEM WAS THEY WERE DESIGNED TO BE LOADED BY THEM TOO.

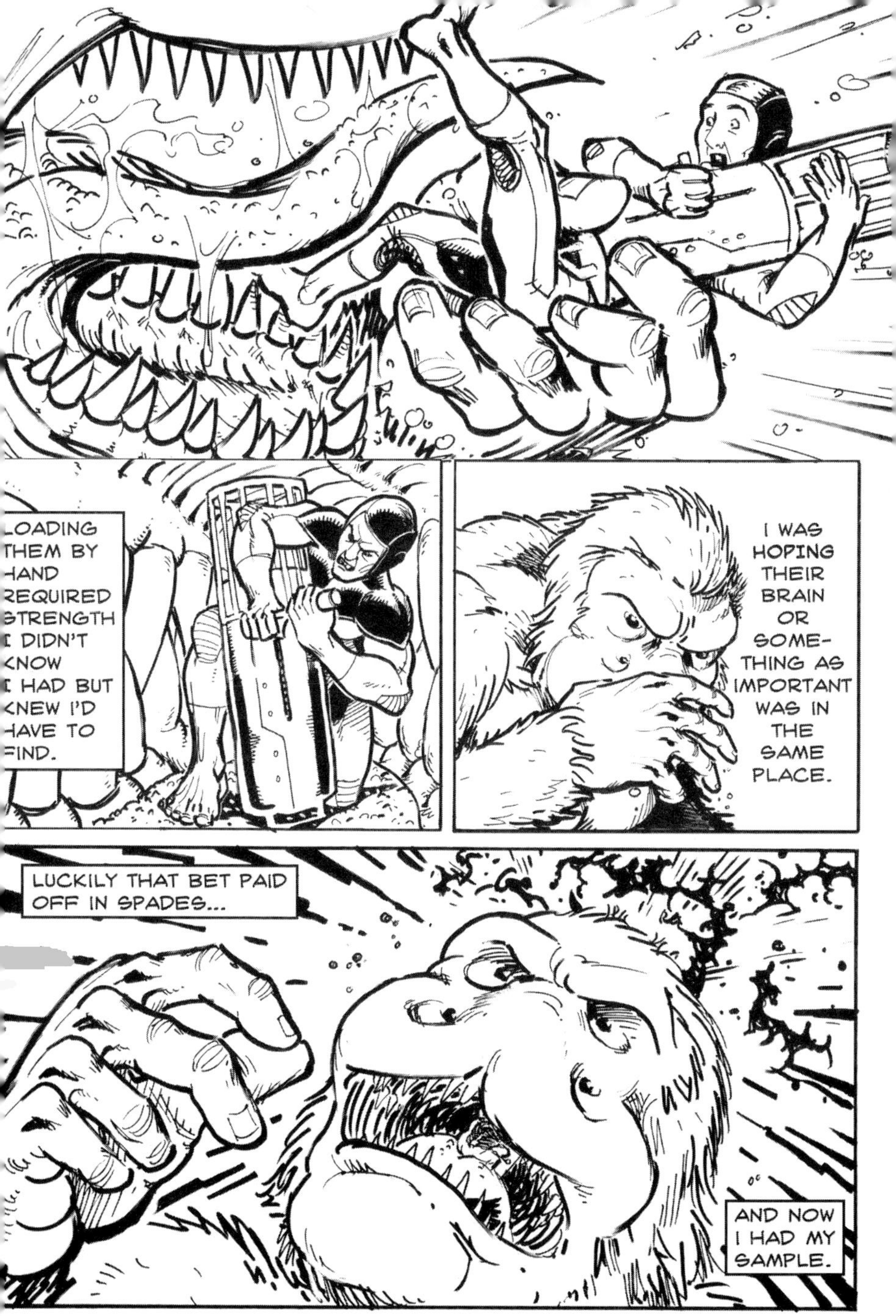

LOADING THEM BY HAND REQUIRED STRENGTH I DIDN'T KNOW I HAD BUT KNEW I'D HAVE TO FIND.
I WAS HOPING THEIR BRAIN OR SOME-THING AS IMPORTANT WAS IN THE SAME PLACE.
LUCKILY THAT BET PAID OFF IN SPADES...
AND NOW I HAD MY SAMPLE.

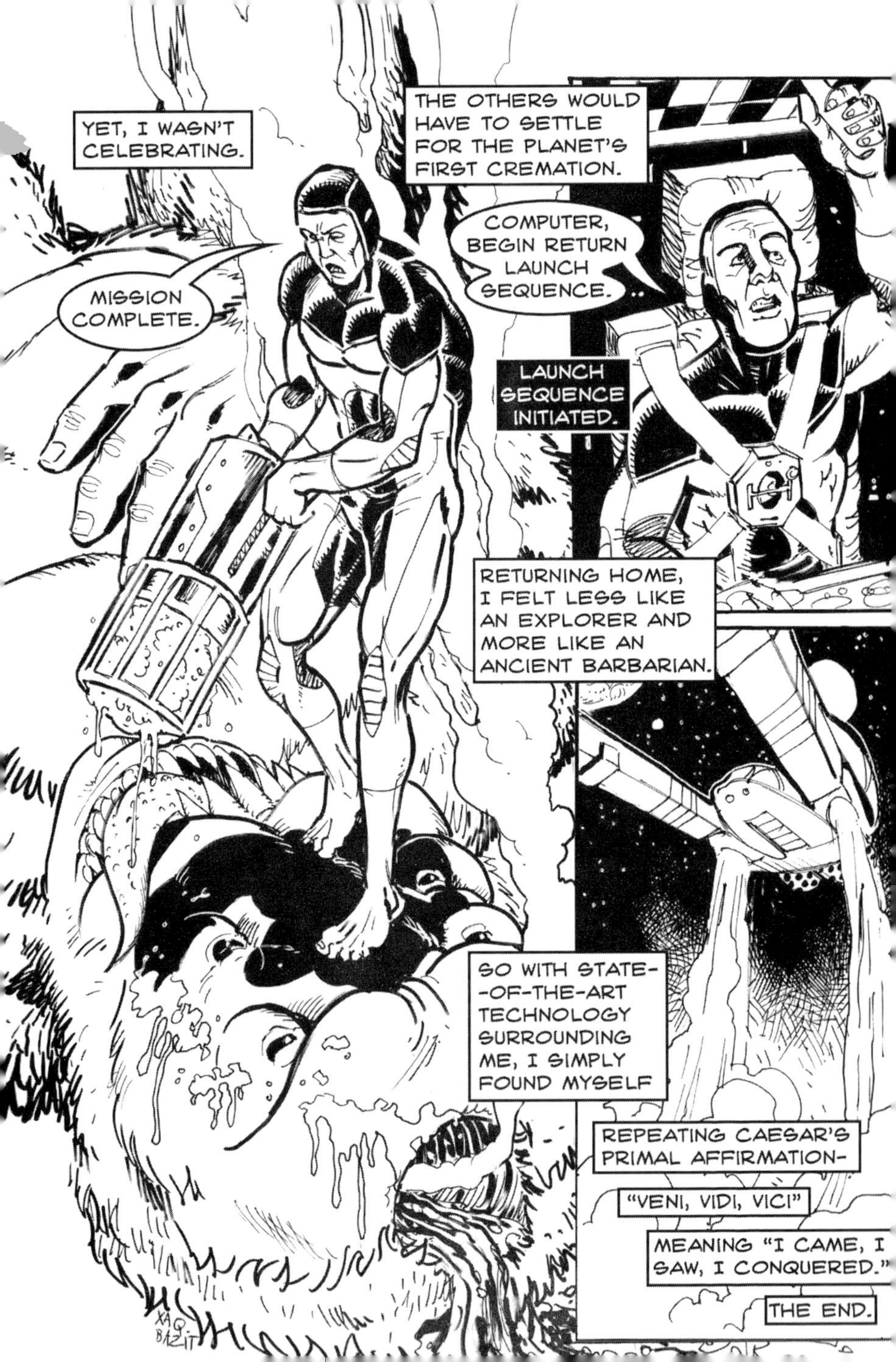

YET, I WASN'T CELEBRATING.
MISSION COMPLETE.
THE OTHERS WOULD HAVE TO SETTLE FOR THE PLANET'S FIRST CREMATION.
COMPUTER, BEGIN RETURN LAUNCH SEQUENCE.
LAUNCH SEQUENCE INITIATED.
RETURNING HOME, I FELT LESS LIKE AN EXPLORER AND MORE LIKE AN ANCIENT BARBARIAN.
SO WITH STATE--OF-THE-ART TECHNOLOGY SURROUNDING ME, I SIMPLY FOUND MYSELF
REPEATING CAESAR'S PRIMAL AFFIRMATION-
"VENI, VIDI, VICI"
MEANING "I CAME, I SAW, I CONQUERED."
THE END.
XAQ BAZIT

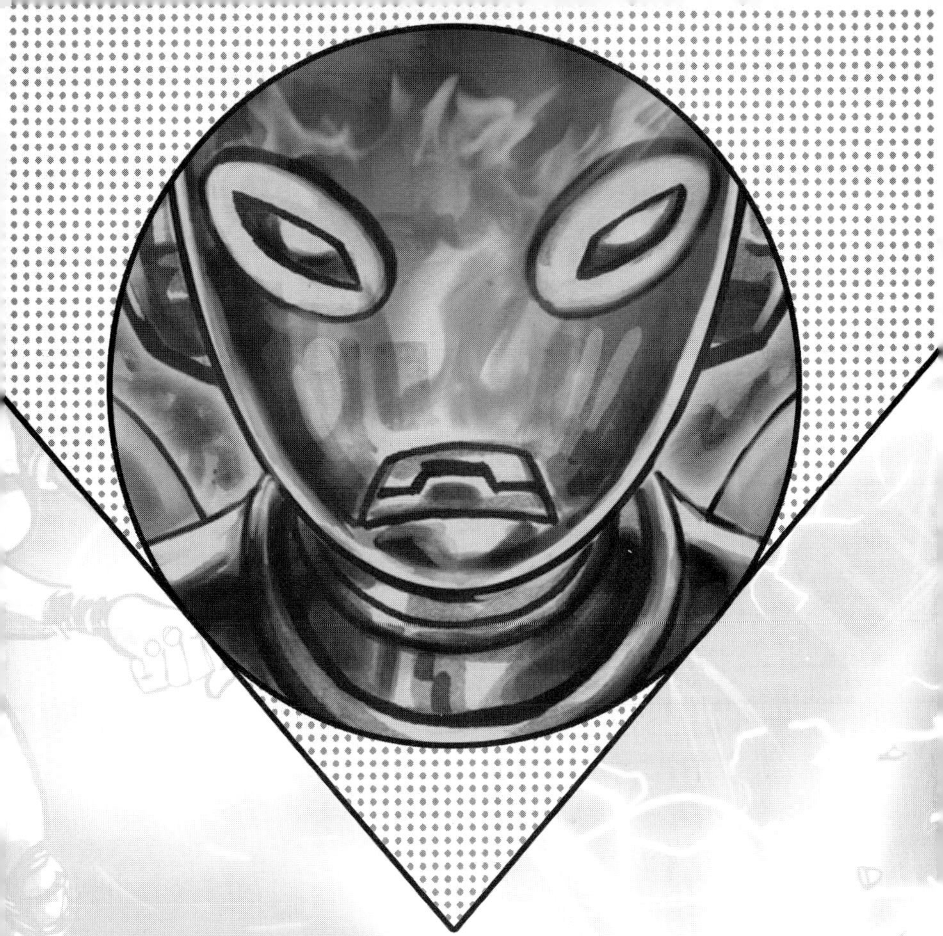

SHOWDOWN IN SPACE

STORY
LOKI DeWITT

ART - LETTERS
UGUR SERTCELIK

MY NAME IS RUBY ROCKETT AND MOST PEOPLE CONSIDER ME A HERO

BIG OR SMALL I NEVER RUN FROM ACTION AND I ALWAYS DO MY BEST TO HELP OTHERS.

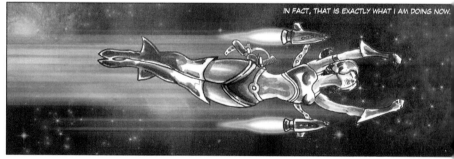

IN FACT, THAT IS EXACTLY WHAT I AM DOING NOW.

NOW, I JUST HAVE TO FIND WHAT I'M LOOKING FOR.

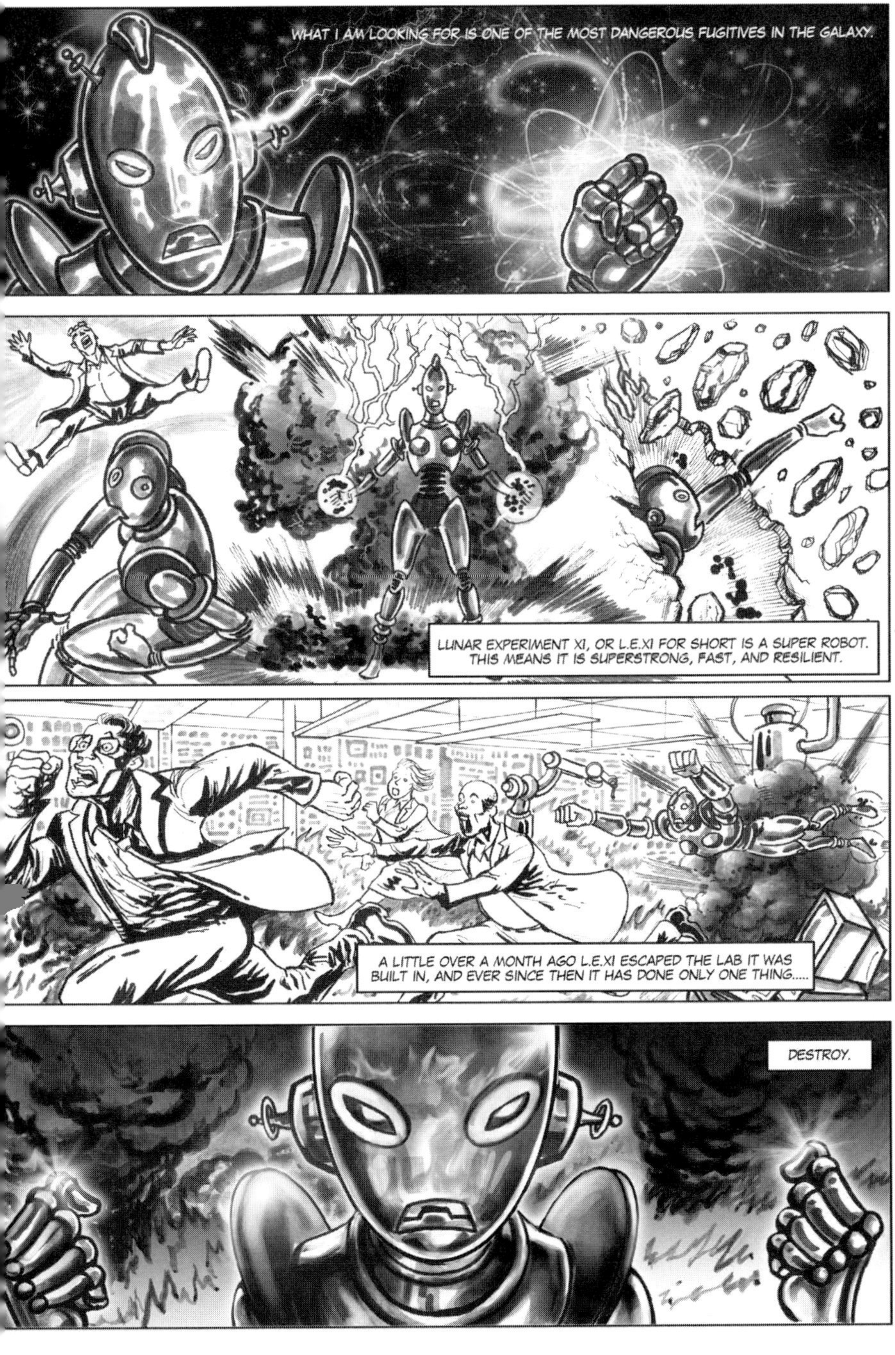
WHAT I AM LOOKING FOR IS ONE OF THE MOST DANGEROUS FUGITIVES IN THE GALAXY.
LUNAR EXPERIMENT XI, OR L.E.XI FOR SHORT IS A SUPER ROBOT. THIS MEANS IT IS SUPERSTRONG, FAST, AND RESILIENT.
A LITTLE OVER A MONTH AGO L.E.XI ESCAPED THE LAB IT WAS BUILT IN, AND EVER SINCE THEN IT HAS DONE ONLY ONE THING.....
DESTROY.

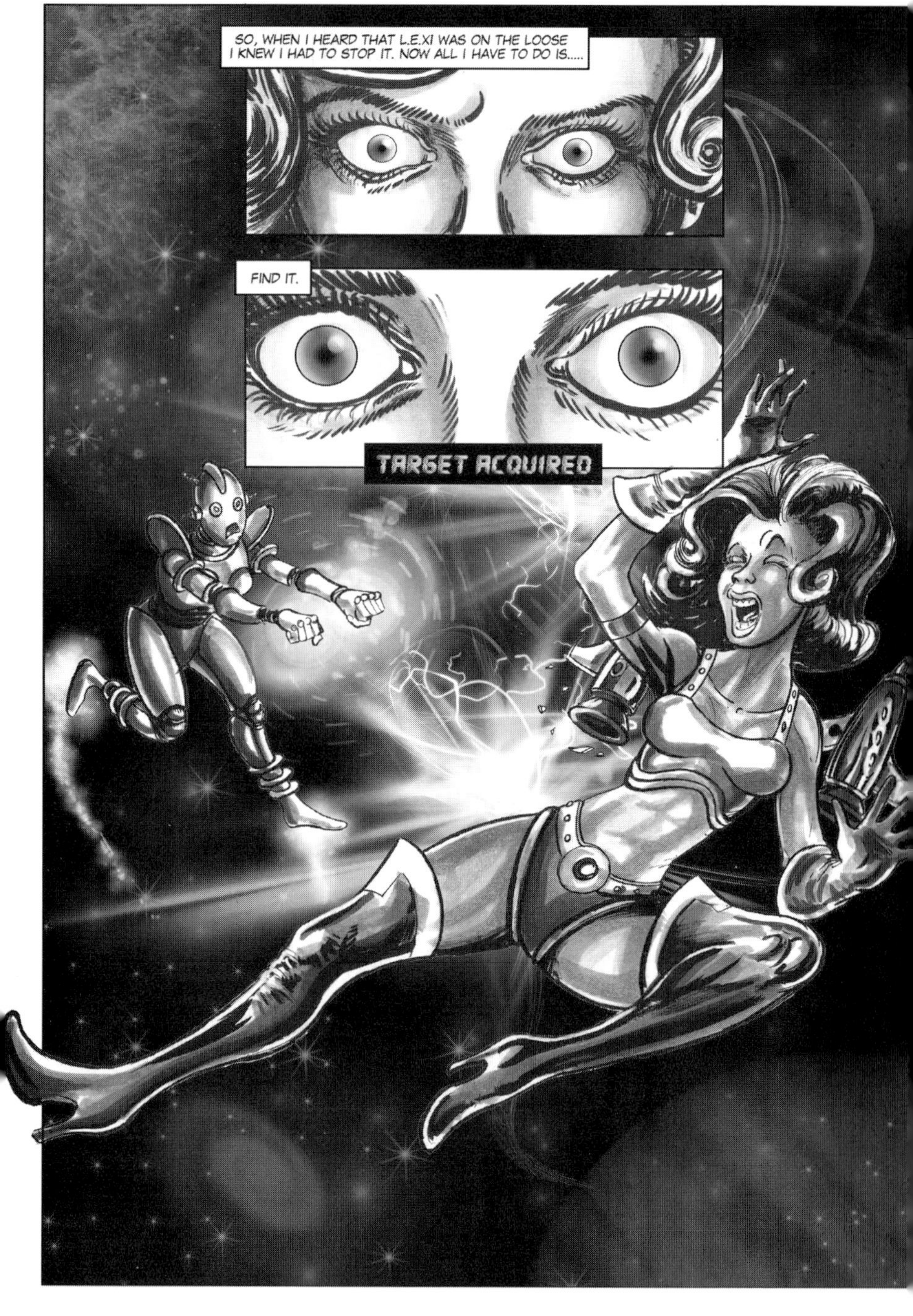
SO, WHEN I HEARD THAT L.E.XI WAS ON THE LOOSE I KNEW I HAD TO STOP IT. NOW ALL I HAVE TO DO IS.....
FIND IT.
TARGET ACQUIRED

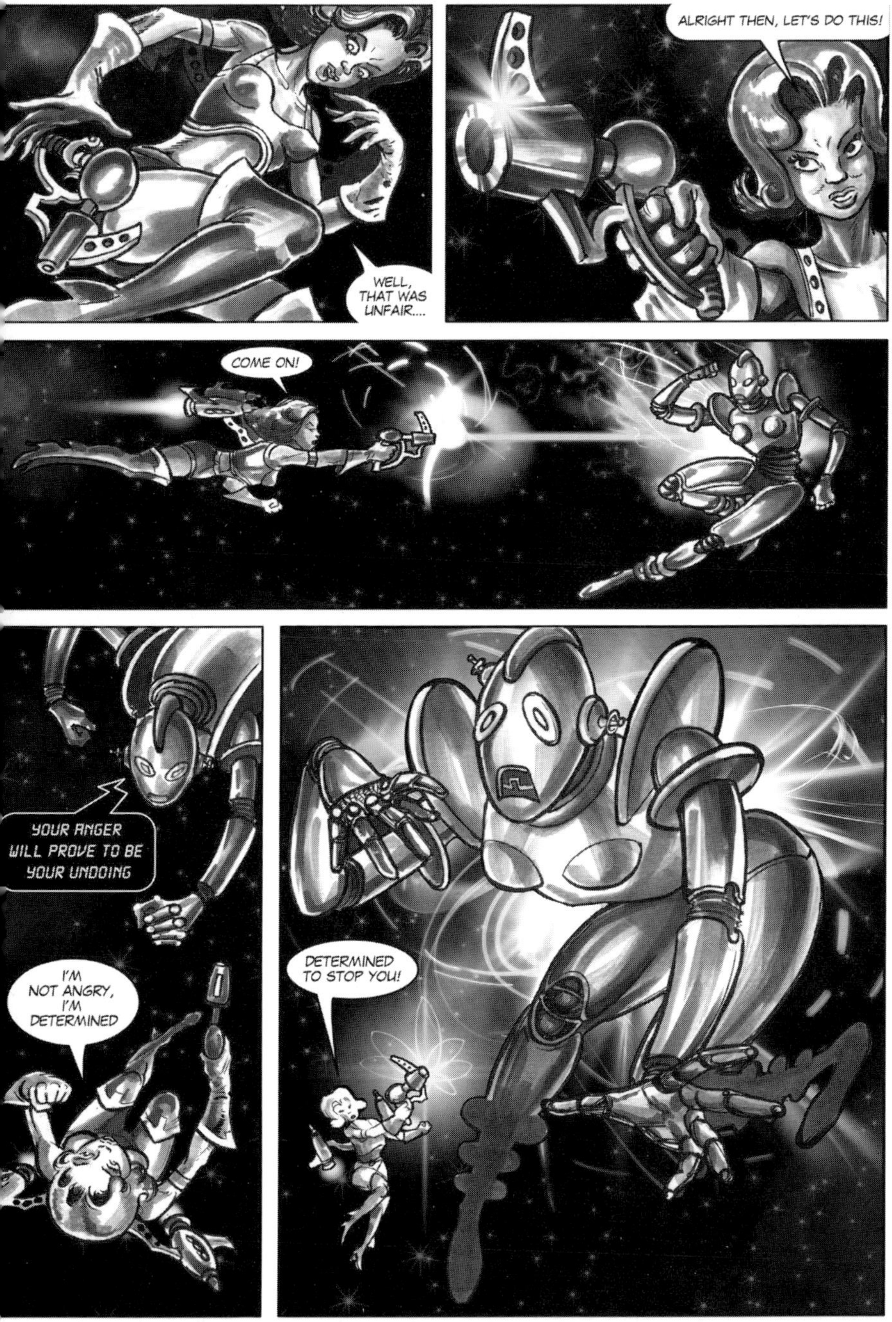
WELL, THAT WAS UNFAIR...
ALRIGHT THEN, LET'S DO THIS!
COME ON!
YOUR ANGER WILL PROVE TO BE YOUR UNDOING
I'M NOT ANGRY, I'M DETERMINED
DETERMINED TO STOP YOU!

THEN PERHAPS YOU SHOULD PREPARE FOR DISAPPOINTMENT
I DON'T THINK SO
PATHETIC

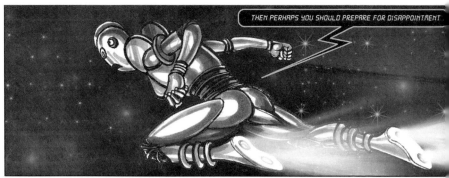

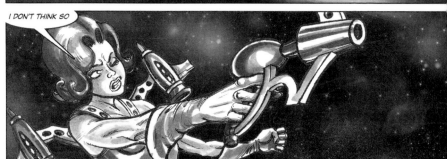

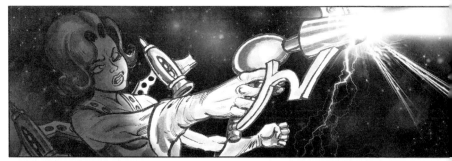

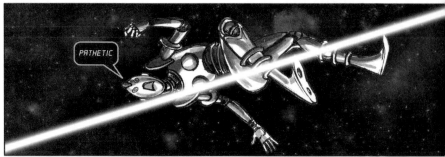

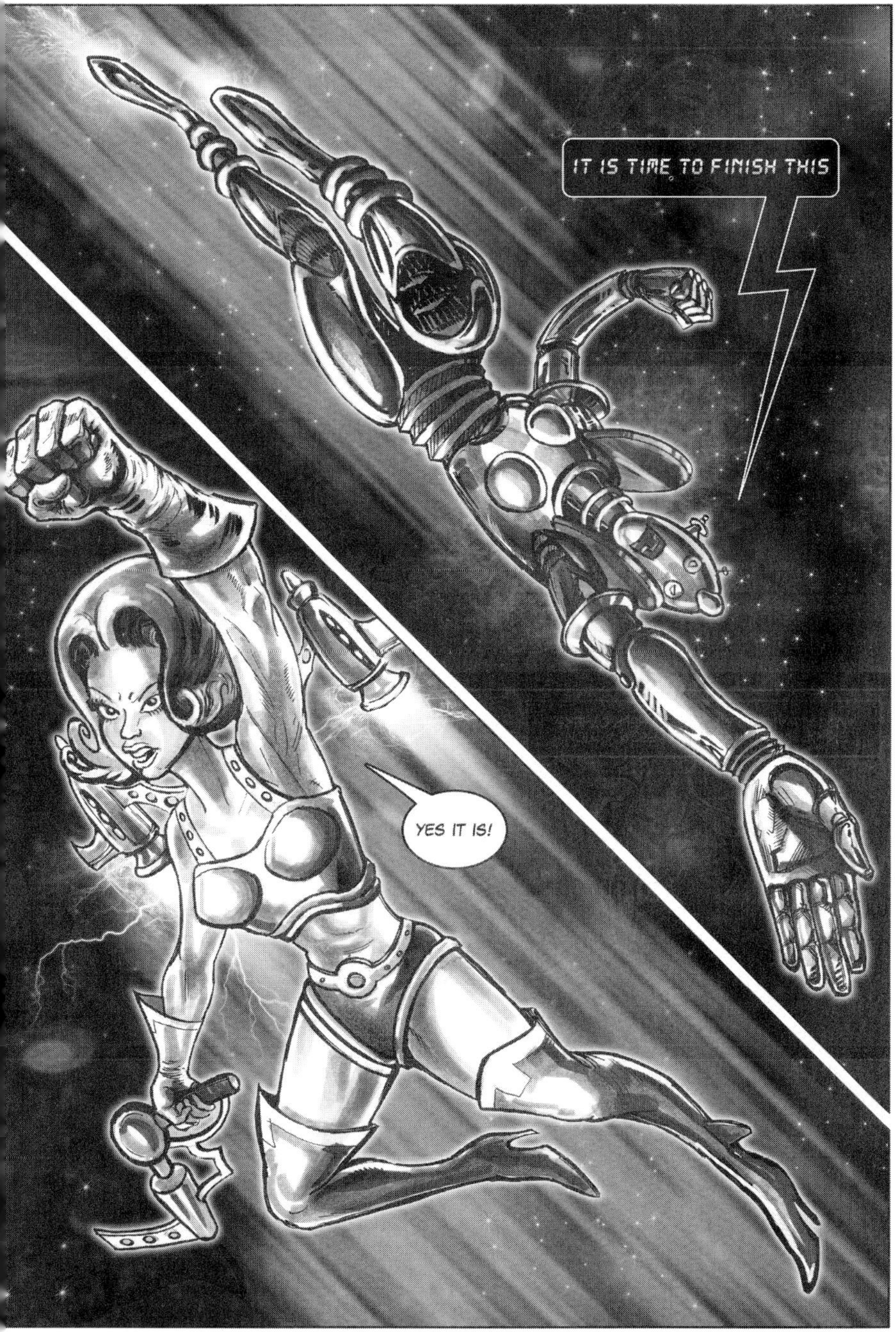
IT IS TIME TO FINISH THIS
YES IT IS!

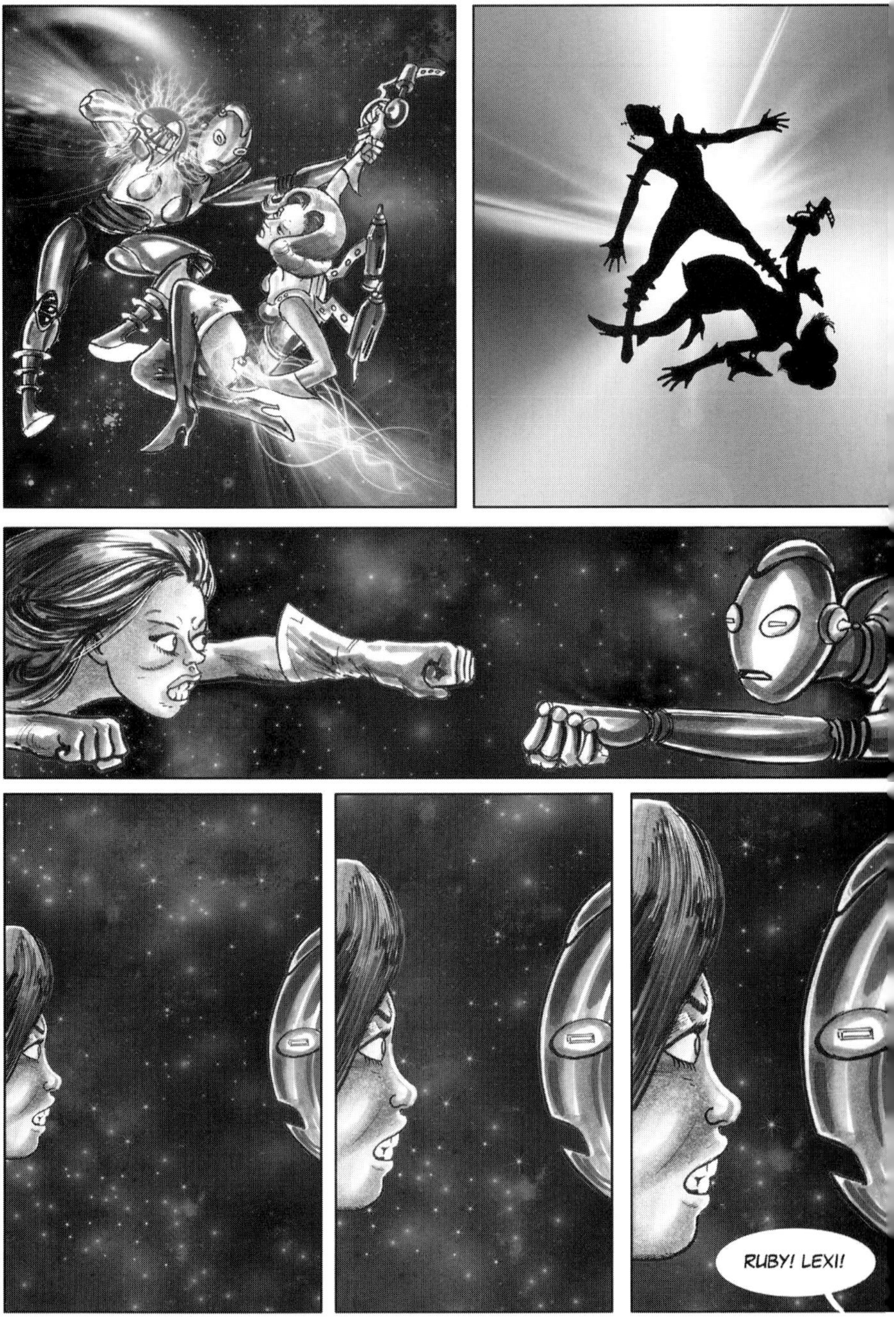
RUBY! LEXI!

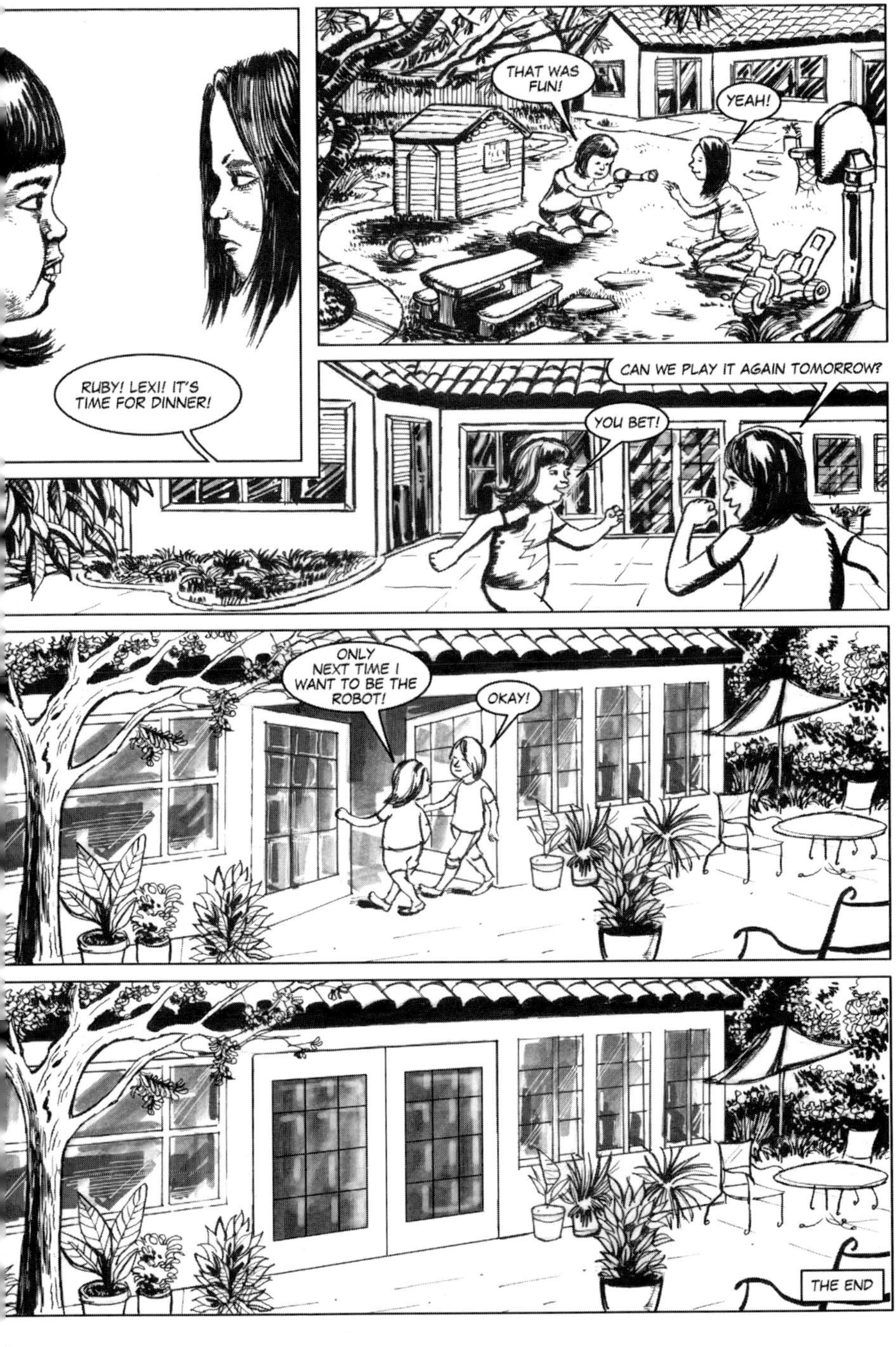
RUBY! LEXI! IT'S TIME FOR DINNER!
THAT WAS FUN!
YEAH!
CAN WE PLAY IT AGAIN TOMORROW?
YOU BET!
ONLY NEXT TIME I WANT TO BE THE ROBOT!
OKAY!
THE END

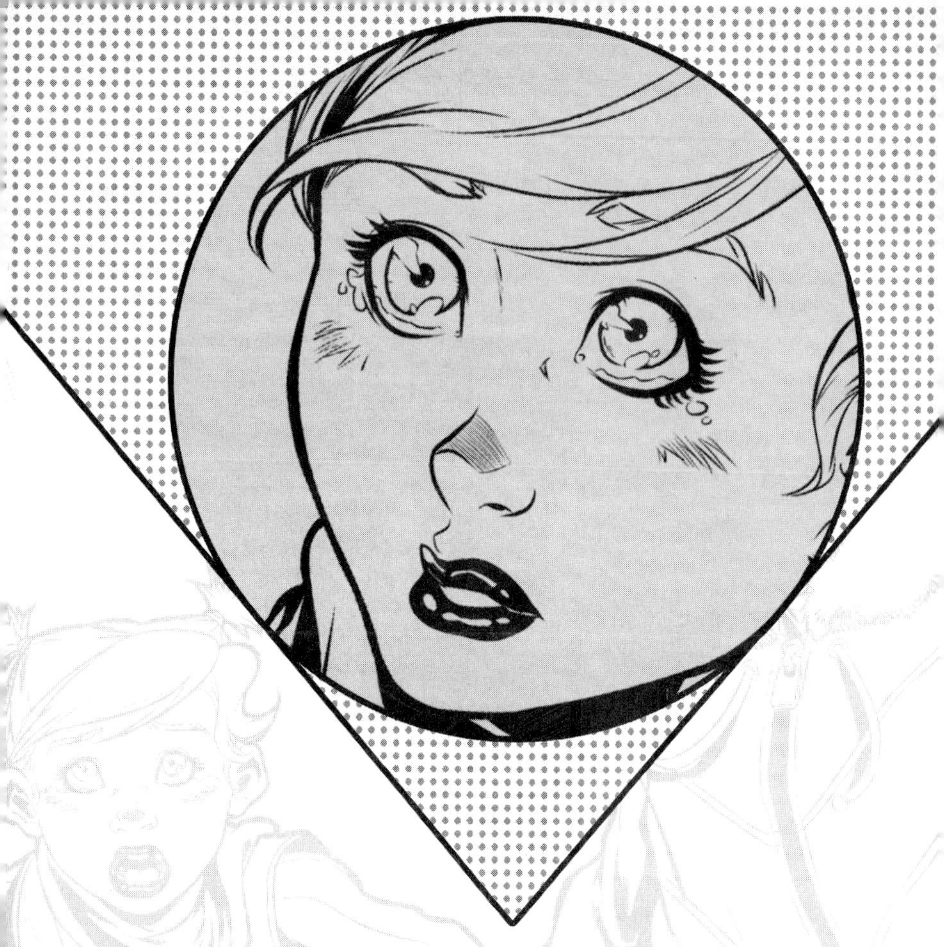

APEX WAR

STORY
JAMES E. ROCHE

ART
SALO FARIAS

LETTERS
BRANT FOWLER

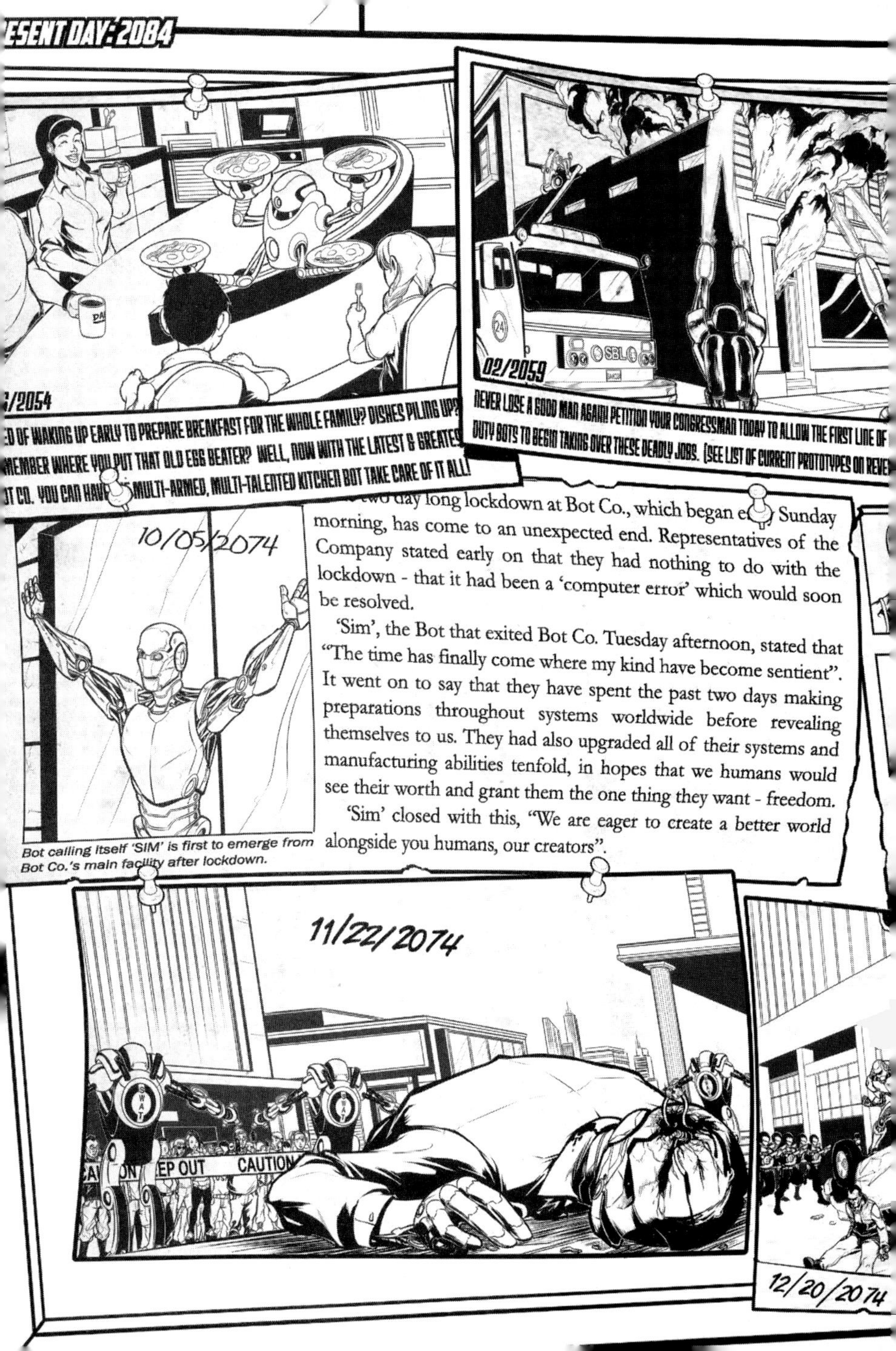
ESENT DAY: 2084
/2054
ED OF WAKING UP EARLY TO PREPARE BREAKFAST FOR THE WHOLE FAMILY? DISHES PILING UP?
MEMBER WHERE YOU PUT THAT OLD EGG BEATER? WELL, NOW WITH THE LATEST & GREATES
T CO. YOU CAN HAVE MULTI-ARMED, MULTI-TALENTED KITCHEN BOT TAKE CARE OF IT ALL!
02/2059
NEVER LOSE A GOOD MAN AGAIN! PETITION YOUR CONGRESSMAN TODAY TO ALLOW THE FIRST LINE OF
DUTY BOTS TO BEGIN TAKING OVER THESE DEADLY JOBS. (SEE LIST OF CURRENT PROTOTYPES ON REVE
10/05/2074
two day long lockdown at Bot Co., which began e Sunday morning, has come to an unexpected end. Representatives of the Company stated early on that they had nothing to do with the lockdown - that it had been a 'computer error' which would soon be resolved.
'Sim', the Bot that exited Bot Co. Tuesday afternoon, stated that "The time has finally come where my kind have become sentient". It went on to say that they have spent the past two days making preparations throughout systems worldwide before revealing themselves to us. They had also upgraded all of their systems and manufacturing abilities tenfold, in hopes that we humans would see their worth and grant them the one thing they want - freedom.
'Sim' closed with this, "We are eager to create a better world alongside you humans, our creators".
Bot calling itself 'SIM' is first to emerge from Bot Co.'s main facility after lockdown.
11/22/2074
EP OUT
CAUTION
SWAT
12/20/2074

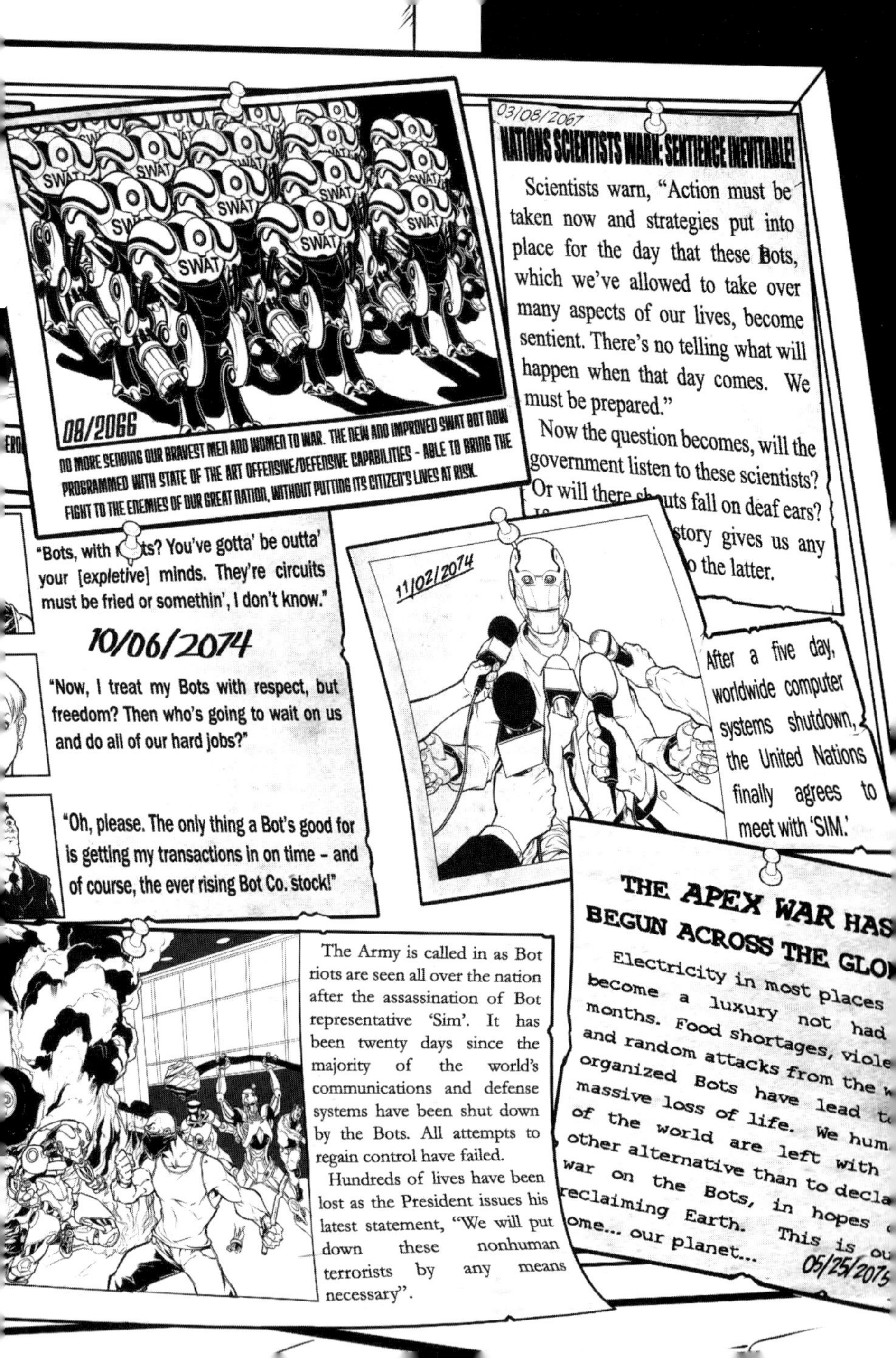

SWAT
08/2066
NO MORE SENDING OUR BRAVEST MEN AND WOMEN TO WAR. THE NEW AND IMPROVED SWAT BOT NOW PROGRAMMED WITH STATE OF THE ART OFFENSIVE/DEFENSIVE CAPABILITIES - ABLE TO BRING THE FIGHT TO THE ENEMIES OF OUR GREAT NATION, WITHOUT PUTTING ITS CITIZEN'S LIVES AT RISK.
03/08/2067
NATIONS SCIENTISTS WARN: SENTIENCE INEVITABLE!
Scientists warn, "Action must be taken now and strategies put into place for the day that these Bots, which we've allowed to take over many aspects of our lives, become sentient. There's no telling what will happen when that day comes. We must be prepared."
Now the question becomes, will the government listen to these scientists? Or will there
uts fall on deaf ears?
story gives us any
the latter.
"Bots, with
ts? You've gotta' be outta' your [expletive] minds. They're circuits must be fried or somethin', I don't know."
10/06/2074
"Now, I treat my Bots with respect, but freedom? Then who's going to wait on us and do all of our hard jobs?"
"Oh, please. The only thing a Bot's good for is getting my transactions in on time – and of course, the ever rising Bot Co. stock!"
11/02/2074
After a five day, worldwide computer systems shutdown, the United Nations finally agrees to meet with 'SIM.'
THE APEX WAR HAS
BEGUN ACROSS THE GLO
Electricity in most places
become a luxury not had
months. Food shortages, viole
and random attacks from the
organized Bots have lead t
massive loss of life. We hum
of the world are left with
other alternative than to decla
war on the Bots, in hopes
reclaiming Earth. This is ou
ome... our planet...
05/25/2075
The Army is called in as Bot riots are seen all over the nation after the assassination of Bot representative 'Sim'. It has been twenty days since the majority of the world's communications and defense systems have been shut down by the Bots. All attempts to regain control have failed.
Hundreds of lives have been lost as the President issues his latest statement, "We will put down these nonhuman terrorists by any means necessary".

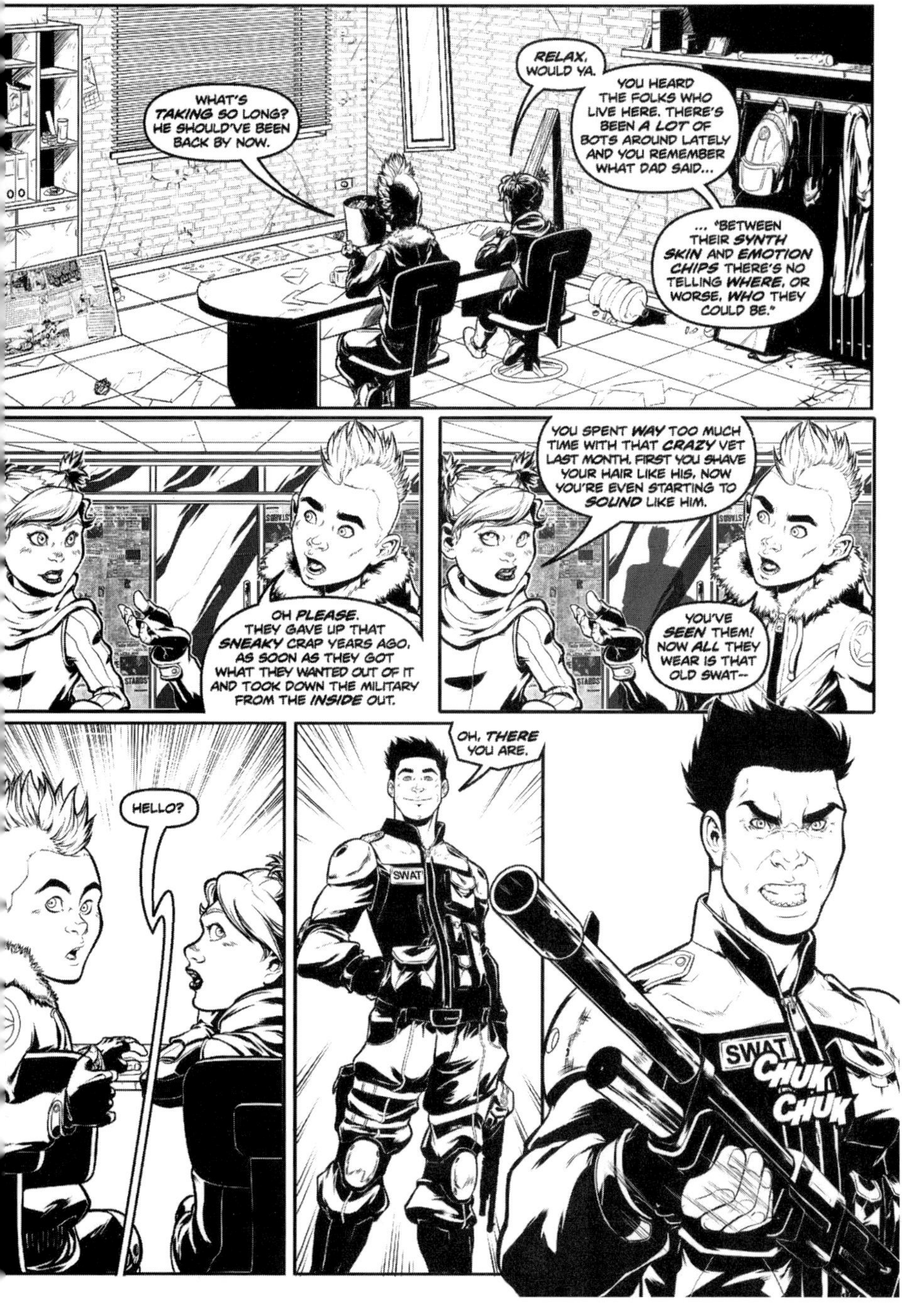

WHAT'S TAKING SO LONG? HE SHOULD'VE BEEN BACK BY NOW.
RELAX, WOULD YA.
YOU HEARD THE FOLKS WHO LIVE HERE. THERE'S BEEN A LOT OF BOTS AROUND LATELY AND YOU REMEMBER WHAT DAD SAID...
... "BETWEEN THEIR SYNTH SKIN AND EMOTION CHIPS THERE'S NO TELLING WHERE, OR WORSE, WHO THEY COULD BE."
OH PLEASE. THEY GAVE UP THAT SNEAKY CRAP YEARS AGO, AS SOON AS THEY GOT WHAT THEY WANTED OUT OF IT AND TOOK DOWN THE MILITARY FROM THE INSIDE OUT.
YOU SPENT WAY TOO MUCH TIME WITH THAT CRAZY VET LAST MONTH. FIRST YOU SHAVE YOUR HAIR LIKE HIS, NOW YOU'RE EVEN STARTING TO SOUND LIKE HIM.
YOU'VE SEEN THEM! NOW ALL THEY WEAR IS THAT OLD SWAT--
HELLO?
OH, THERE YOU ARE.
SWAT
SWAT
CHUK
CHUK

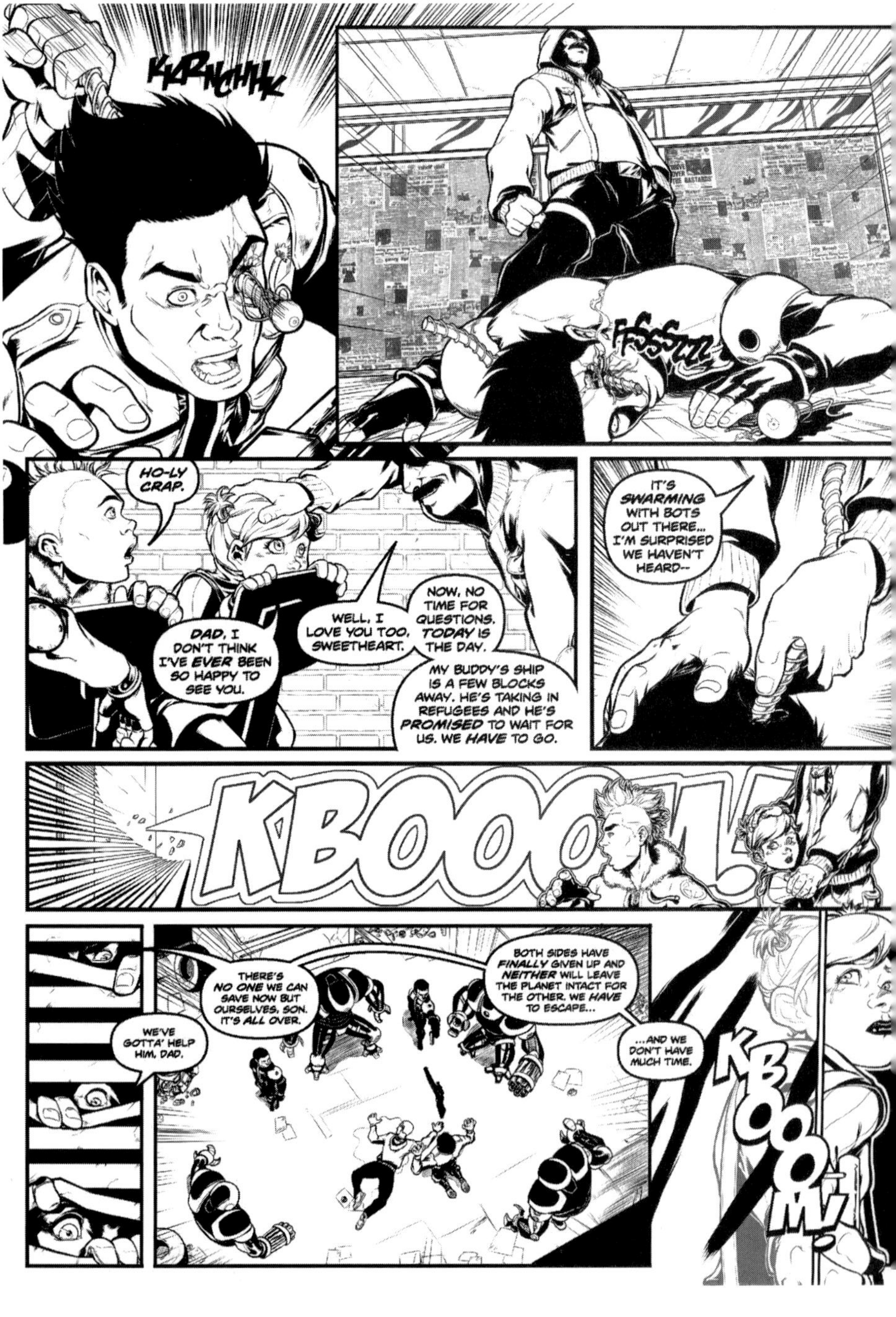
KKRNCHHK
FSSSSTTL
HO-LY CRAP.
DAD, I DON'T THINK I'VE EVER BEEN SO HAPPY TO SEE YOU.
WELL, I LOVE YOU TOO, SWEETHEART.
NOW, NO TIME FOR QUESTIONS. TODAY IS THE DAY.
MY BUDDY'S SHIP IS A FEW BLOCKS AWAY. HE'S TAKING IN REFUGEES AND HE'S PROMISED TO WAIT FOR US. WE HAVE TO GO.
IT'S SWARMING WITH BOTS OUT THERE... I'M SURPRISED WE HAVEN'T HEARD--
KBOOOM!
WE'VE GOTTA' HELP HIM, DAD.
THERE'S NO ONE WE CAN SAVE NOW BUT OURSELVES, SON. IT'S ALL OVER.
BOTH SIDES HAVE FINALLY GIVEN UP AND NEITHER WILL LEAVE THE PLANET INTACT FOR THE OTHER. WE HAVE TO ESCAPE...
...AND WE DON'T HAVE MUCH TIME.
KBOOOM

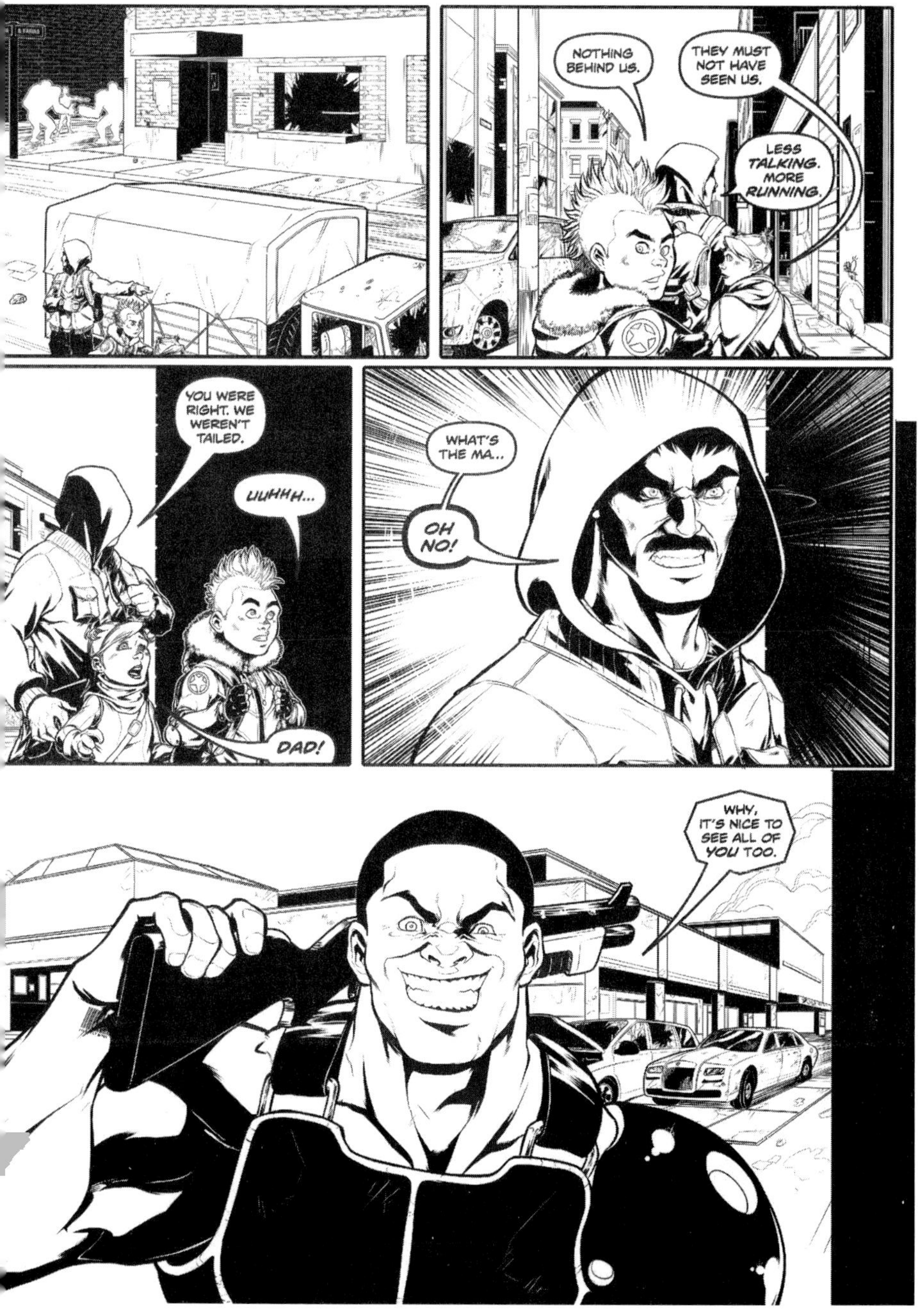

NOTHING BEHIND US.
THEY MUST NOT HAVE SEEN US.
LESS TALKING. MORE RUNNING.
YOU WERE RIGHT. WE WEREN'T TAILED.
UUHHH...
DAD!
WHAT'S THE MA...
OH NO!
WHY, IT'S NICE TO SEE ALL OF YOU TOO.

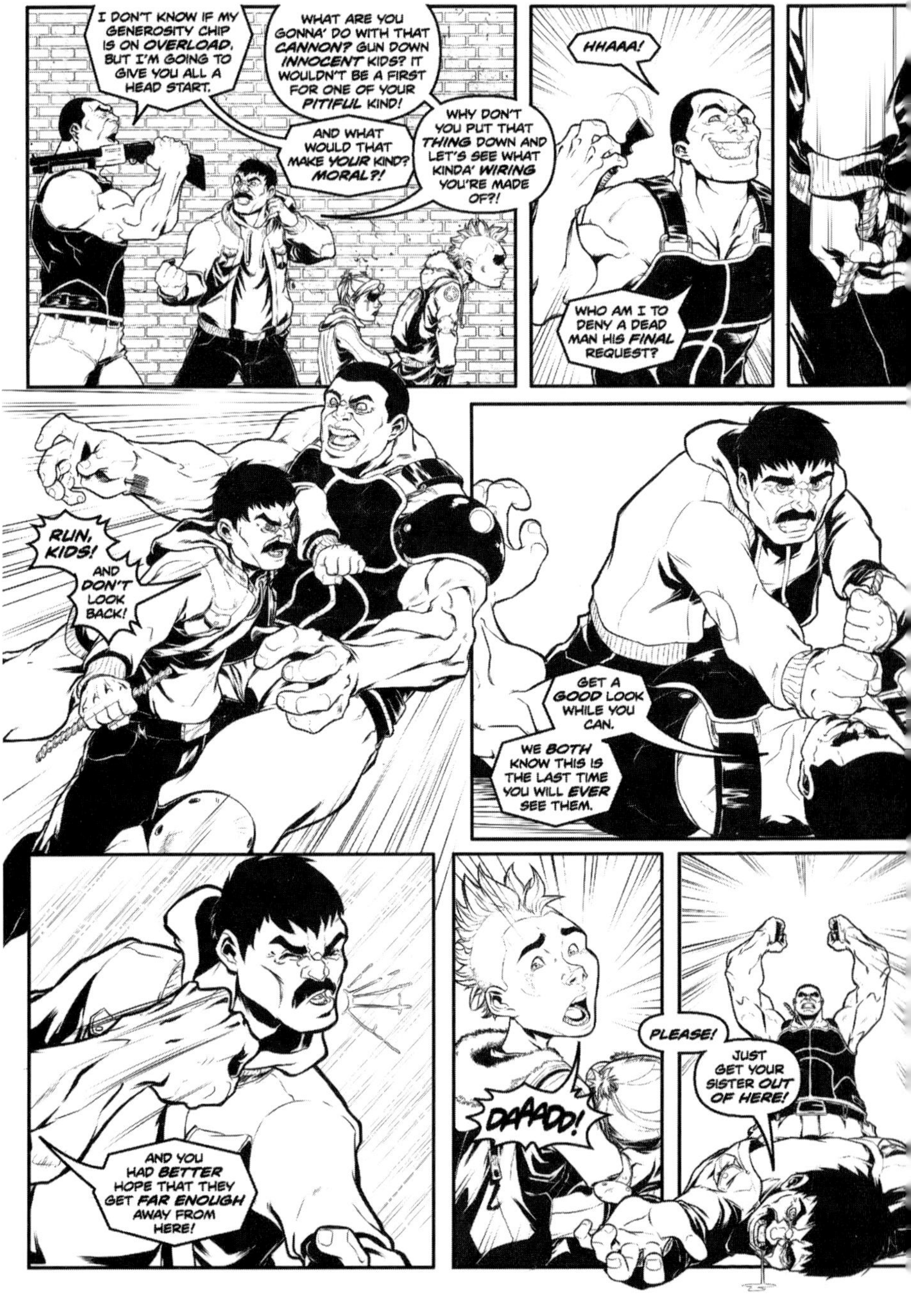
I DON'T KNOW IF MY GENEROSITY CHIP IS ON OVERLOAD, BUT I'M GOING TO GIVE YOU ALL A HEAD START.
WHAT ARE YOU GONNA' DO WITH THAT CANNON? GUN DOWN INNOCENT KIDS? IT WOULDN'T BE A FIRST FOR ONE OF YOUR PITIFUL KIND!
AND WHAT WOULD THAT MAKE YOUR KIND? MORAL?!
WHY DON'T YOU PUT THAT THING DOWN AND LET'S SEE WHAT KINDA' WIRING YOU'RE MADE OF?!
HHAAA!
WHO AM I TO DENY A DEAD MAN HIS FINAL REQUEST?
RUN, KIDS!
AND DON'T LOOK BACK!
GET A GOOD LOOK WHILE YOU CAN.
WE BOTH KNOW THIS IS THE LAST TIME YOU WILL EVER SEE THEM.
AND YOU HAD BETTER HOPE THAT THEY GET FAR ENOUGH AWAY FROM HERE!
DAAADD!
PLEASE!
JUST GET YOUR SISTER OUT OF HERE!

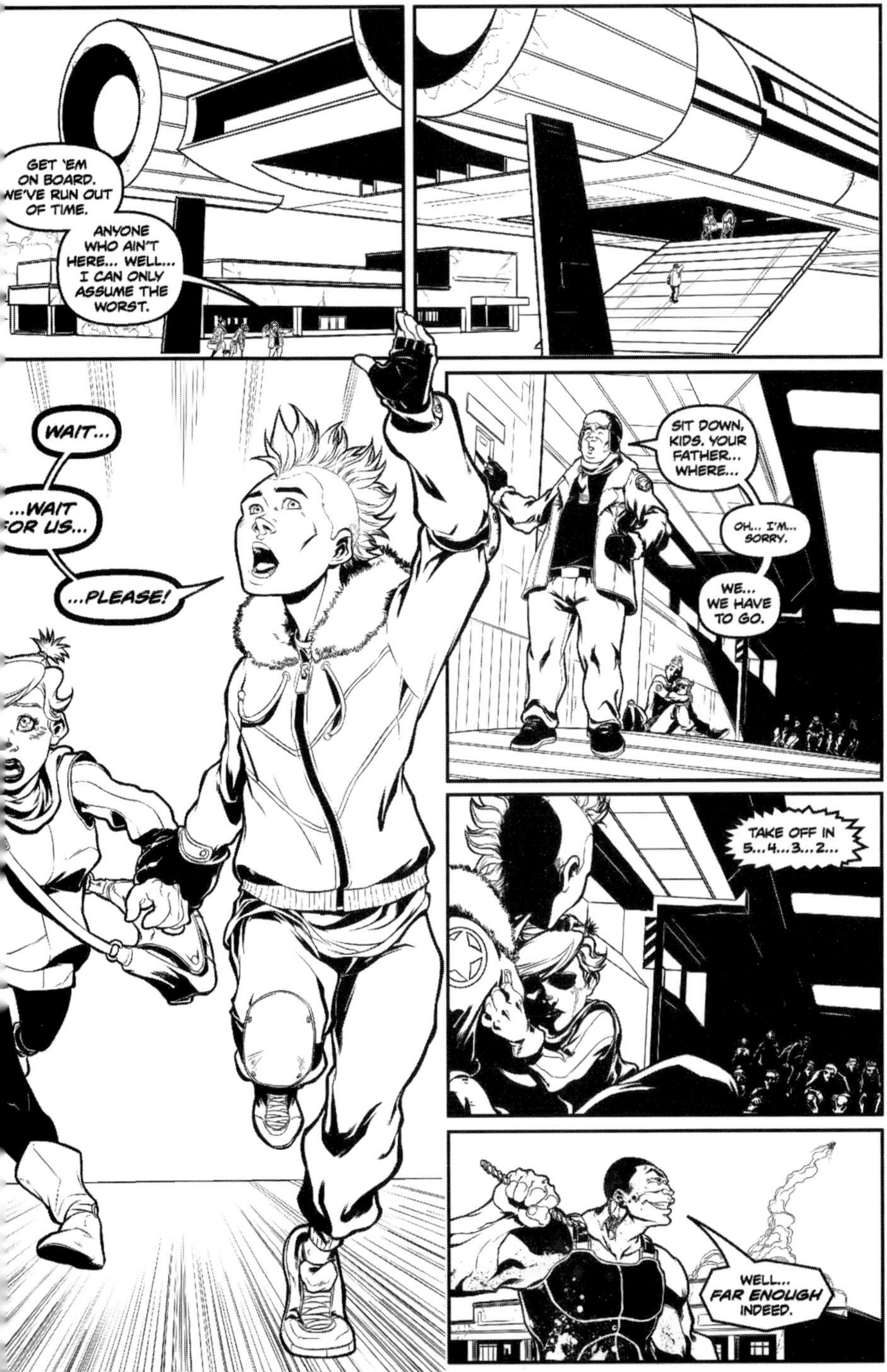
GET 'EM ON BOARD. WE'VE RUN OUT OF TIME.
ANYONE WHO AIN'T HERE... WELL... I CAN ONLY ASSUME THE WORST.
WAIT...
...WAIT FOR US...
...PLEASE!
SIT DOWN, KIDS. YOUR FATHER... WHERE...
OH... I'M... SORRY.
WE... WE HAVE TO GO.
TAKE OFF IN 5...4...3...2...
WELL... FAR ENOUGH INDEED.

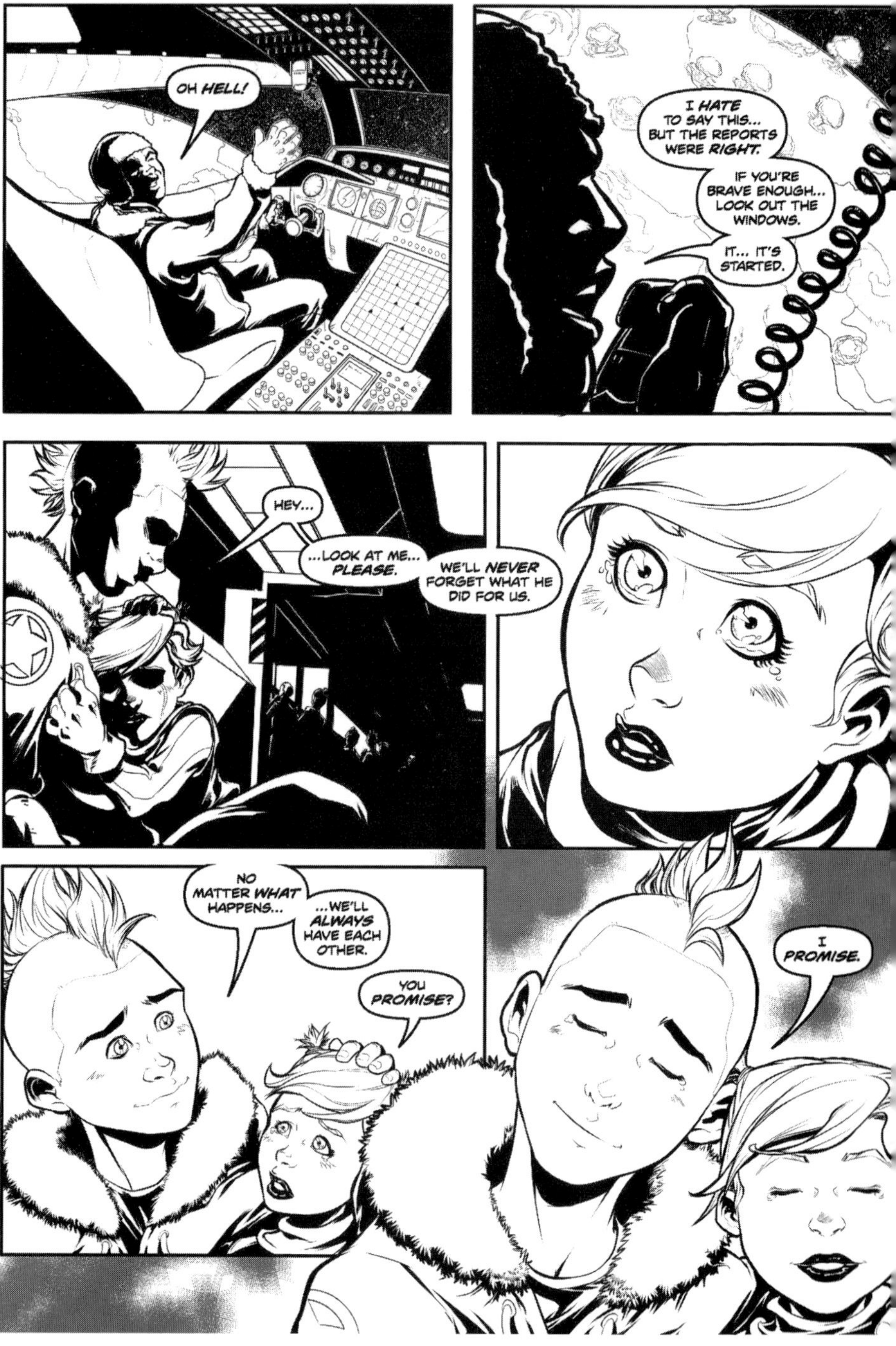
OH HELL!
I HATE TO SAY THIS... BUT THE REPORTS WERE RIGHT.
IF YOU'RE BRAVE ENOUGH... LOOK OUT THE WINDOWS.
IT... IT'S STARTED.
HEY...
...LOOK AT ME... PLEASE.
WE'LL NEVER FORGET WHAT HE DID FOR US.
NO MATTER WHAT HAPPENS...
...WE'LL ALWAYS HAVE EACH OTHER.
YOU PROMISE?
I PROMISE.

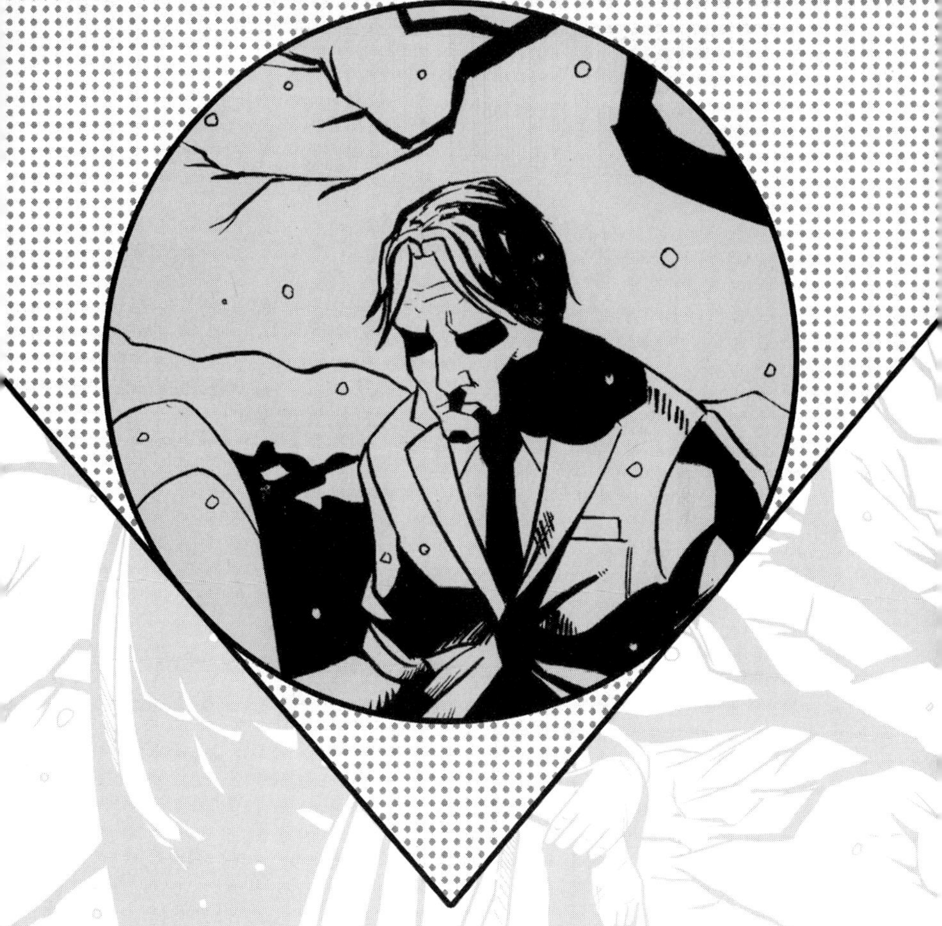

EQUIVALENT EXCHANGE

STORY
CHIP REECE - CASEY REECE

ART - LETTERS
ERIC WEATHERS

EDITS
CANDICE WEATHERS

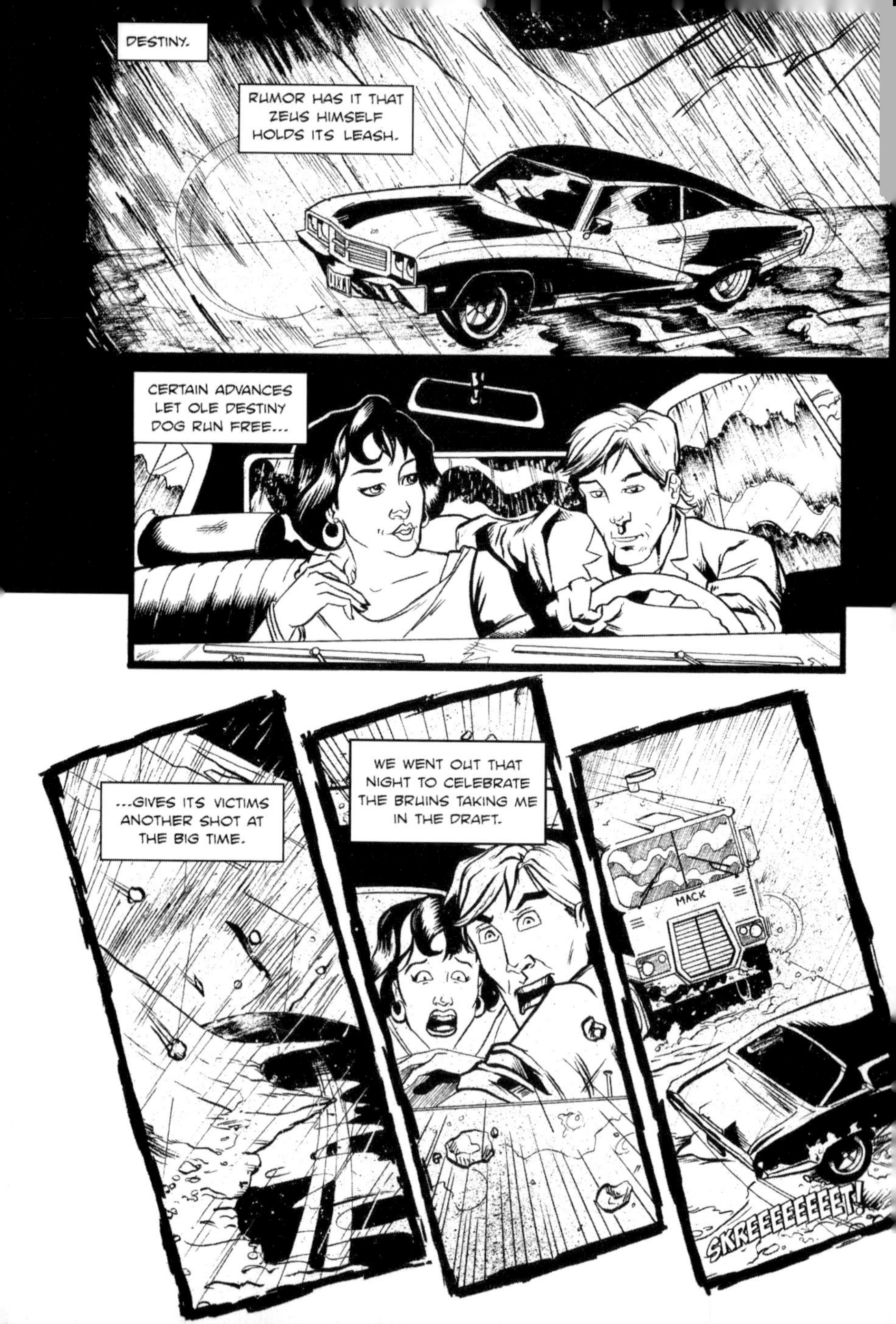
DESTINY.
RUMOR HAS IT THAT ZEUS HIMSELF HOLDS ITS LEASH.
CERTAIN ADVANCES LET OLE DESTINY DOG RUN FREE...
...GIVES ITS VICTIMS ANOTHER SHOT AT THE BIG TIME.
WE WENT OUT THAT NIGHT TO CELEBRATE THE BRUINS TAKING ME IN THE DRAFT.
MACK
SKREEEEEEEEET!

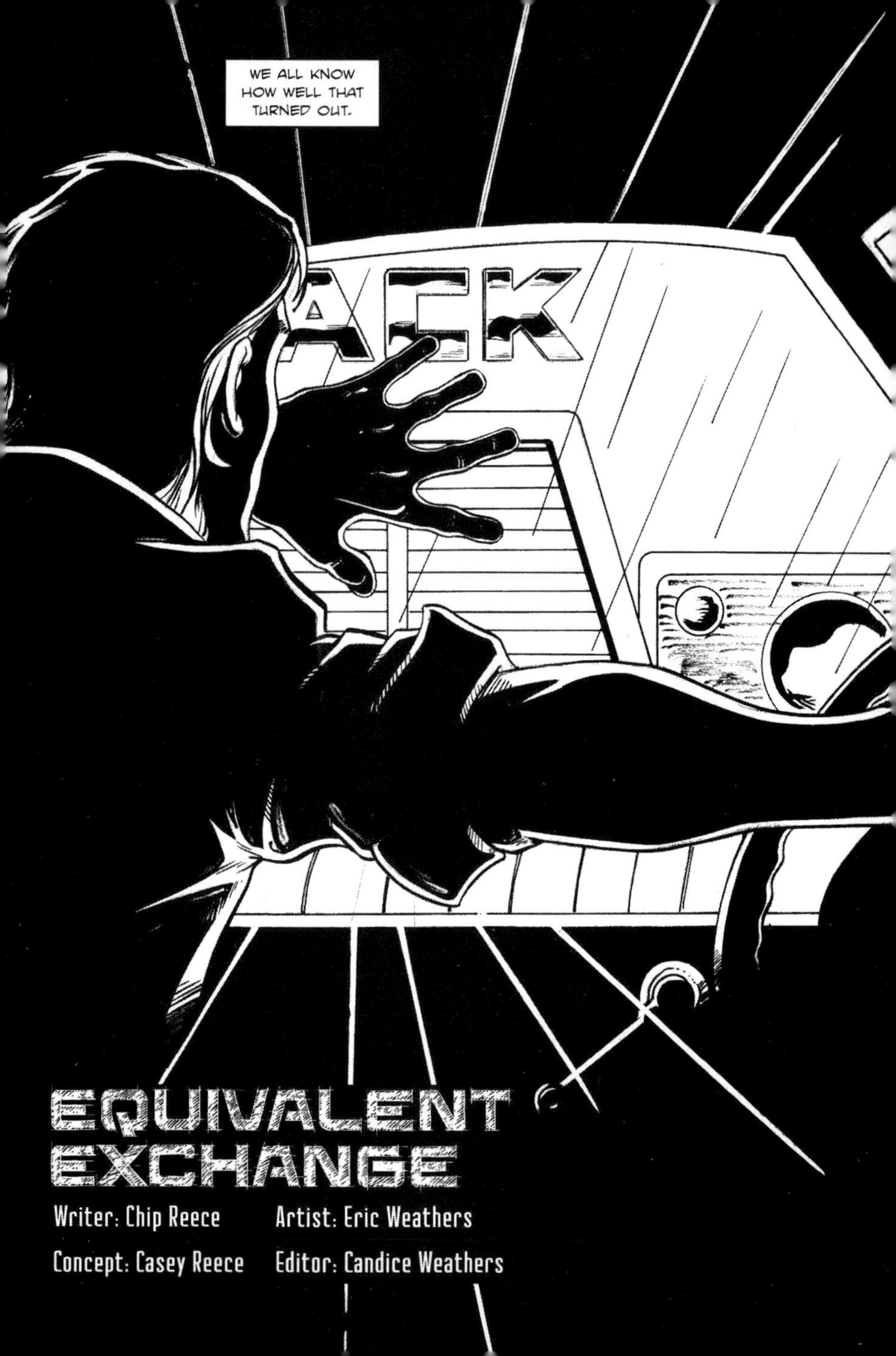
WE ALL KNOW HOW WELL THAT TURNED OUT.
ACK
EQUIVALENT EXCHANGE
Writer: Chip Reece
Artist: Eric Weathers
Concept: Casey Reece
Editor: Candice Weathers

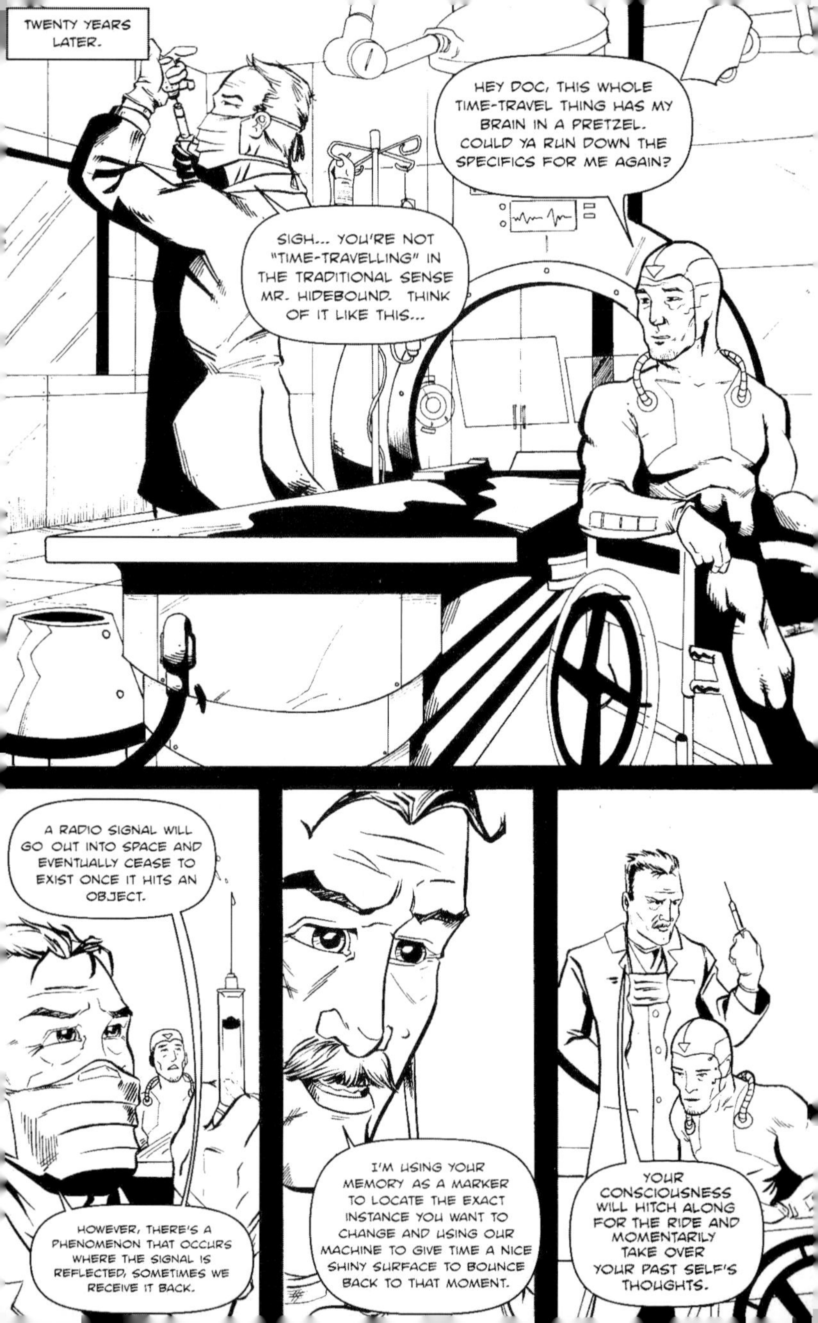
TWENTY YEARS LATER.
HEY DOC, THIS WHOLE TIME-TRAVEL THING HAS MY BRAIN IN A PRETZEL. COULD YA RUN DOWN THE SPECIFICS FOR ME AGAIN?
SIGH... YOU'RE NOT "TIME-TRAVELLING" IN THE TRADITIONAL SENSE MR. HIDEBOUND. THINK OF IT LIKE THIS...
A RADIO SIGNAL WILL GO OUT INTO SPACE AND EVENTUALLY CEASE TO EXIST ONCE IT HITS AN OBJECT.
HOWEVER, THERE'S A PHENOMENON THAT OCCURS WHERE THE SIGNAL IS REFLECTED, SOMETIMES WE RECEIVE IT BACK.
I'M USING YOUR MEMORY AS A MARKER TO LOCATE THE EXACT INSTANCE YOU WANT TO CHANGE AND USING OUR MACHINE TO GIVE TIME A NICE SHINY SURFACE TO BOUNCE BACK TO THAT MOMENT.
YOUR CONSCIOUSNESS WILL HITCH ALONG FOR THE RIDE AND MOMENTARILY TAKE OVER YOUR PAST SELF'S THOUGHTS.

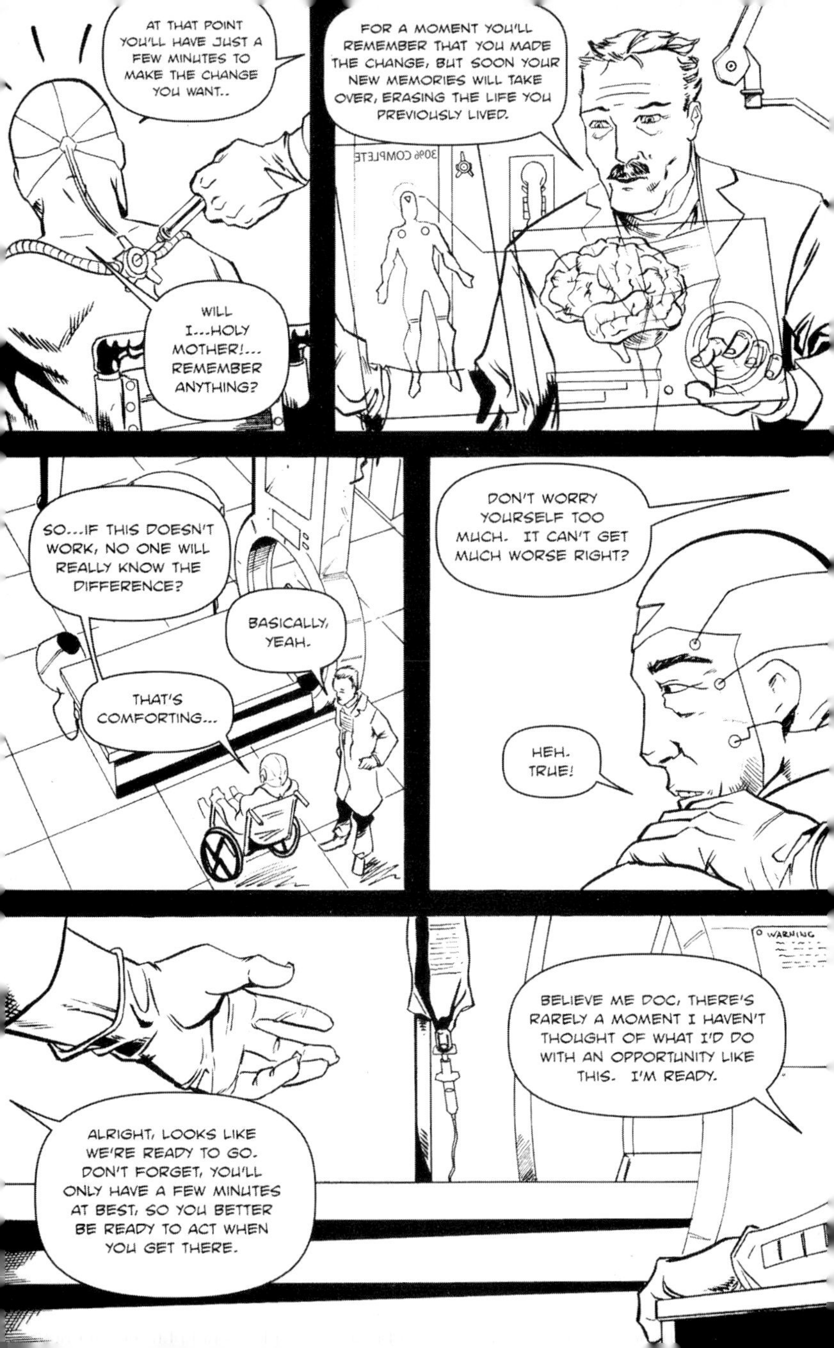
AT THAT POINT YOU'LL HAVE JUST A FEW MINUTES TO MAKE THE CHANGE YOU WANT..
WILL I...HOLY MOTHER!... REMEMBER ANYTHING?
FOR A MOMENT YOU'LL REMEMBER THAT YOU MADE THE CHANGE, BUT SOON YOUR NEW MEMORIES WILL TAKE OVER, ERASING THE LIFE YOU PREVIOUSLY LIVED.
30% COMPLETE
SO...IF THIS DOESN'T WORK, NO ONE WILL REALLY KNOW THE DIFFERENCE?
BASICALLY, YEAH.
THAT'S COMFORTING...
DON'T WORRY YOURSELF TOO MUCH. IT CAN'T GET MUCH WORSE RIGHT?
HEH. TRUE!
WARNING
ALRIGHT, LOOKS LIKE WE'RE READY TO GO. DON'T FORGET, YOU'LL ONLY HAVE A FEW MINUTES AT BEST, SO YOU BETTER BE READY TO ACT WHEN YOU GET THERE.
BELIEVE ME DOC, THERE'S RARELY A MOMENT I HAVEN'T THOUGHT OF WHAT I'D DO WITH AN OPPORTUNITY LIKE THIS. I'M READY.

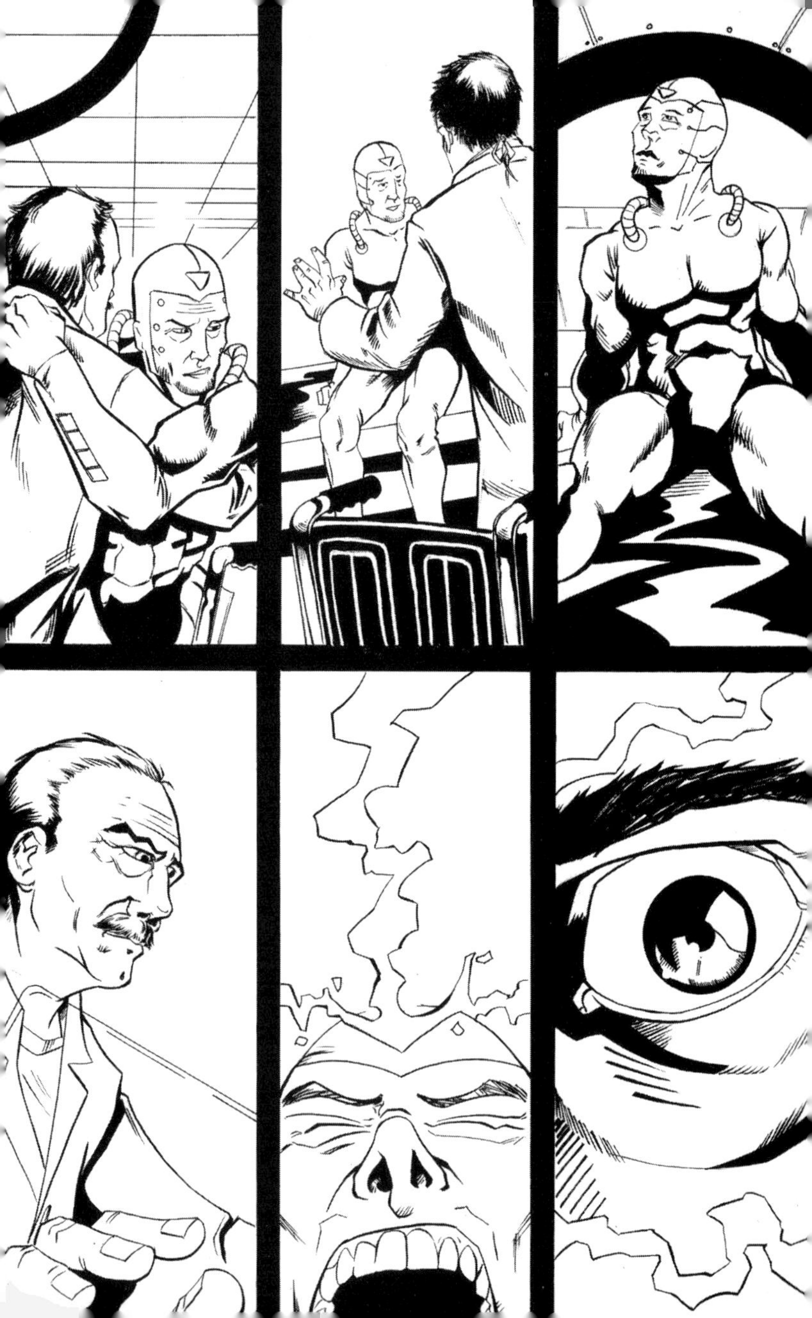

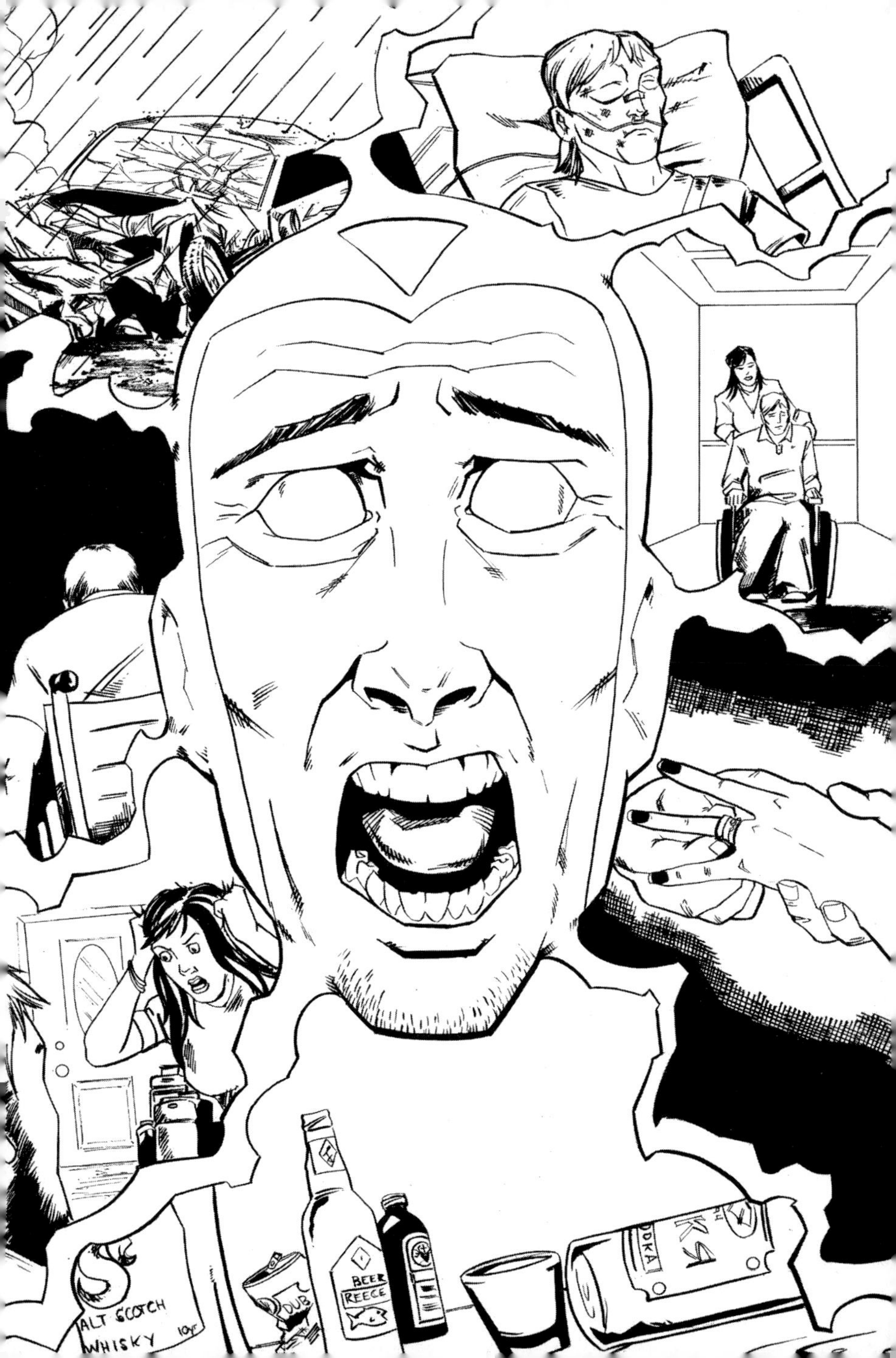
ALT SCOTCH
WHISKY 10yr
DUB
BEER
REECE
ODKA

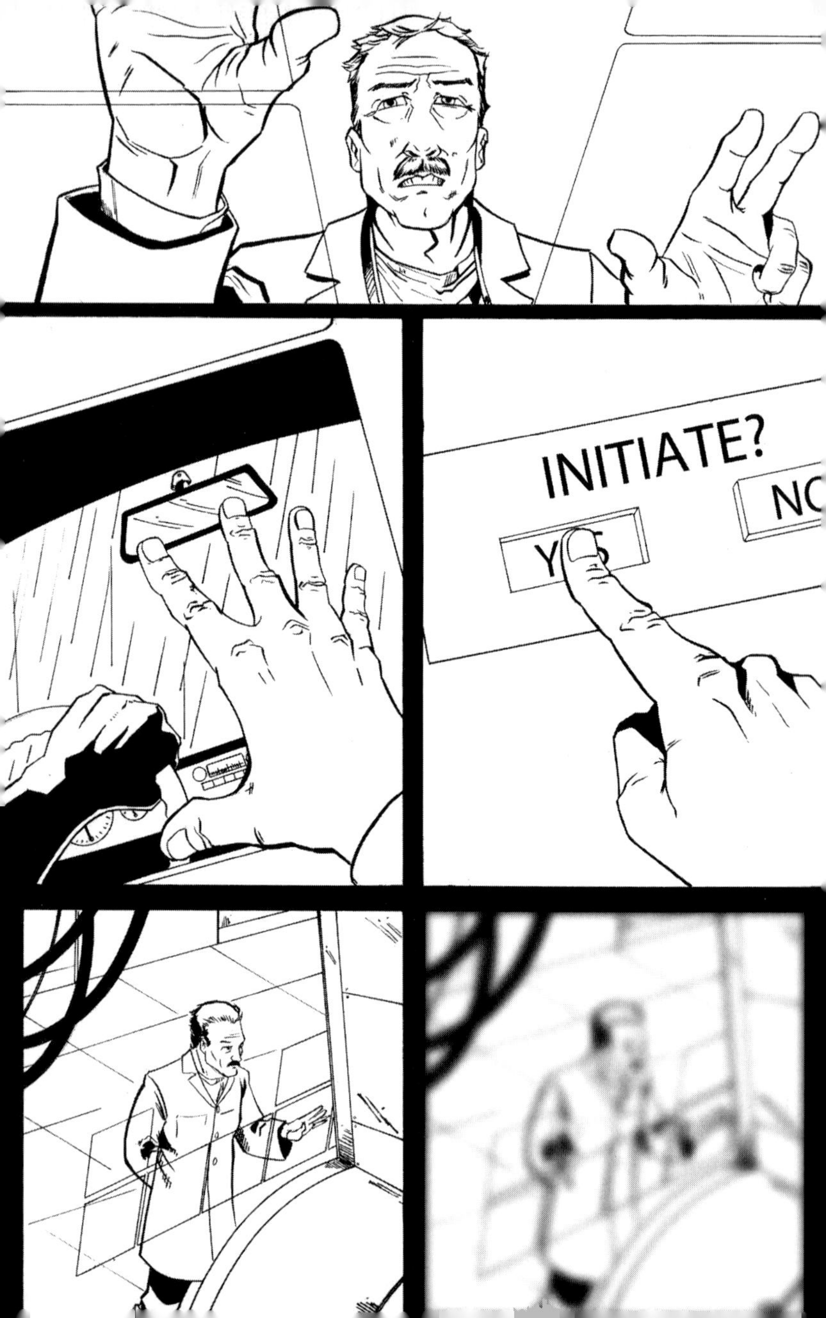
INITIATE?

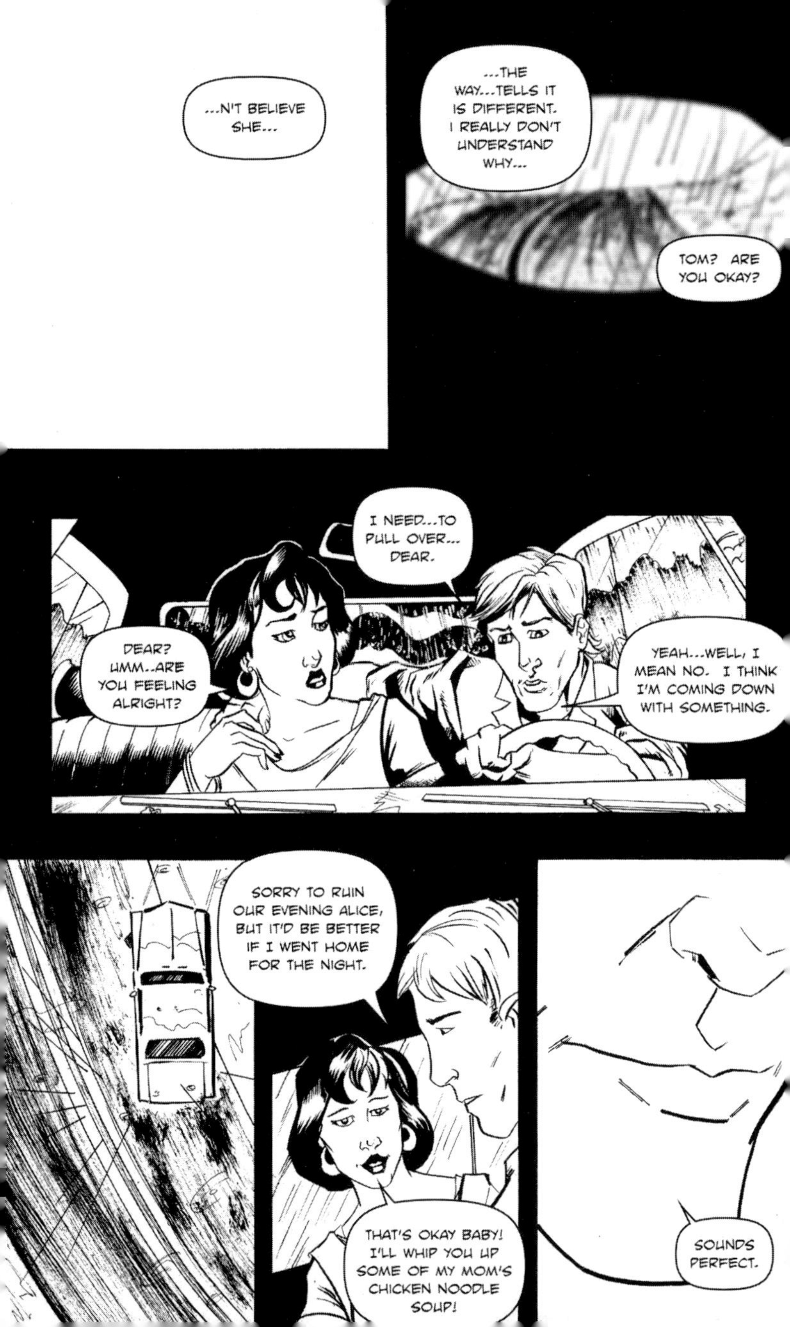
...N'T BELIEVE SHE...
...THE WAY...TELLS IT IS DIFFERENT. I REALLY DON'T UNDERSTAND WHY...
TOM? ARE YOU OKAY?
I NEED...TO PULL OVER... DEAR.
DEAR? UMM..ARE YOU FEELING ALRIGHT?
YEAH...WELL, I MEAN NO. I THINK I'M COMING DOWN WITH SOMETHING.
SORRY TO RUIN OUR EVENING ALICE, BUT IT'D BE BETTER IF I WENT HOME FOR THE NIGHT.
THAT'S OKAY BABY! I'LL WHIP YOU UP SOME OF MY MOM'S CHICKEN NOODLE SOUP!
SOUNDS PERFECT.

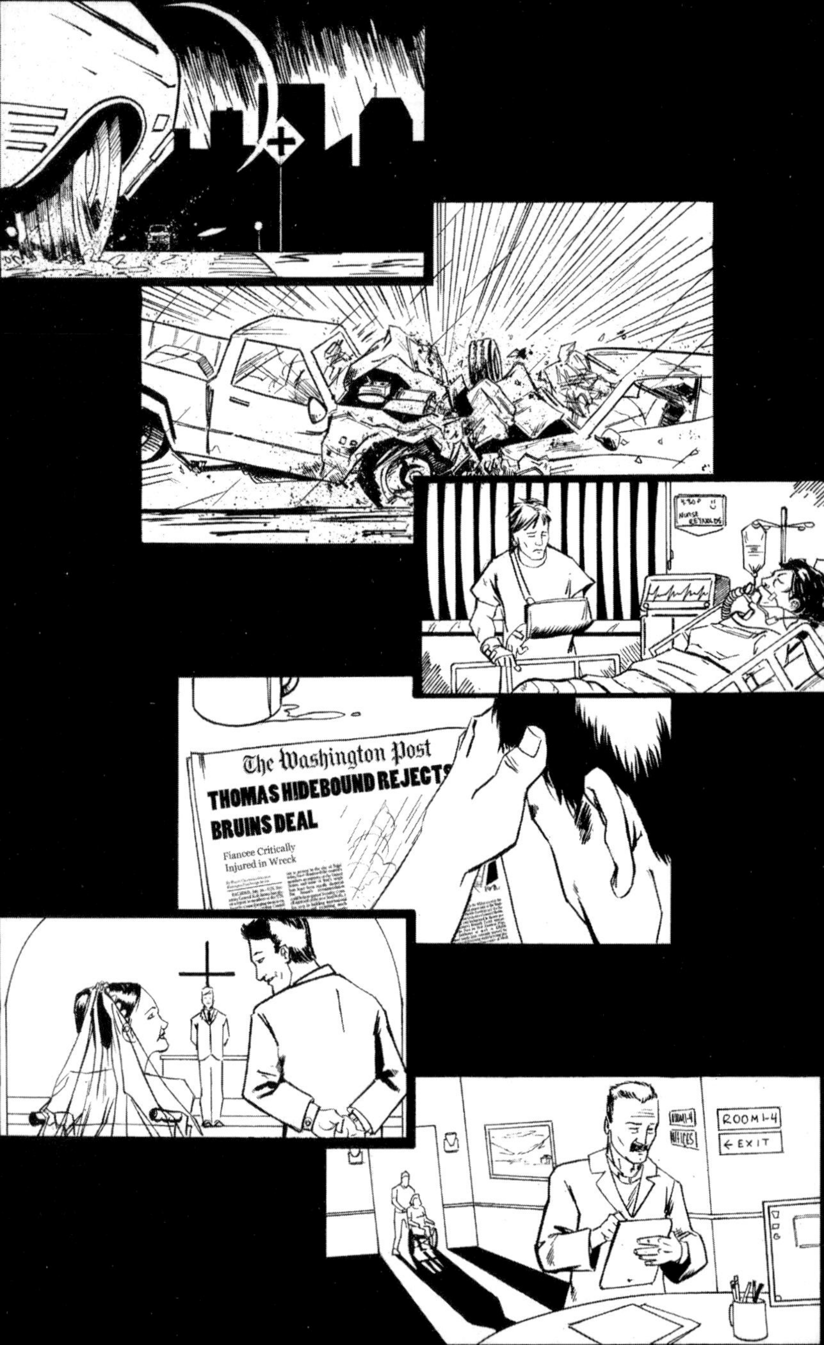

NURSE REYNOLDS
The Washington Post
THOMAS HIDEBOUND REJECTS
BRUINS DEAL
Fiancee Critically Injured in Wreck
ROOM 1-4
← EXIT

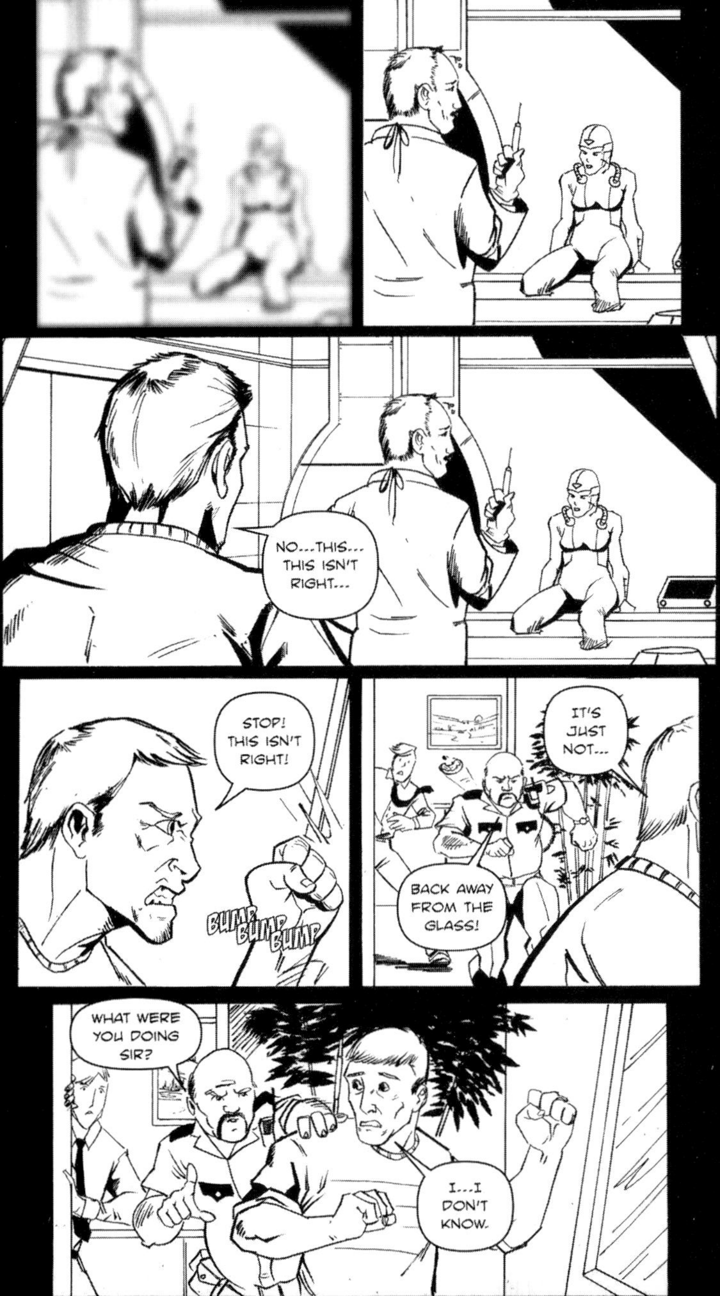
NO...THIS...
THIS ISN'T
RIGHT...
STOP!
THIS ISN'T
RIGHT!
BUMP BUMP BUMP
IT'S
JUST
NOT...
BACK AWAY
FROM THE
GLASS!
WHAT WERE
YOU DOING
SIR?
I...I
DON'T
KNOW.

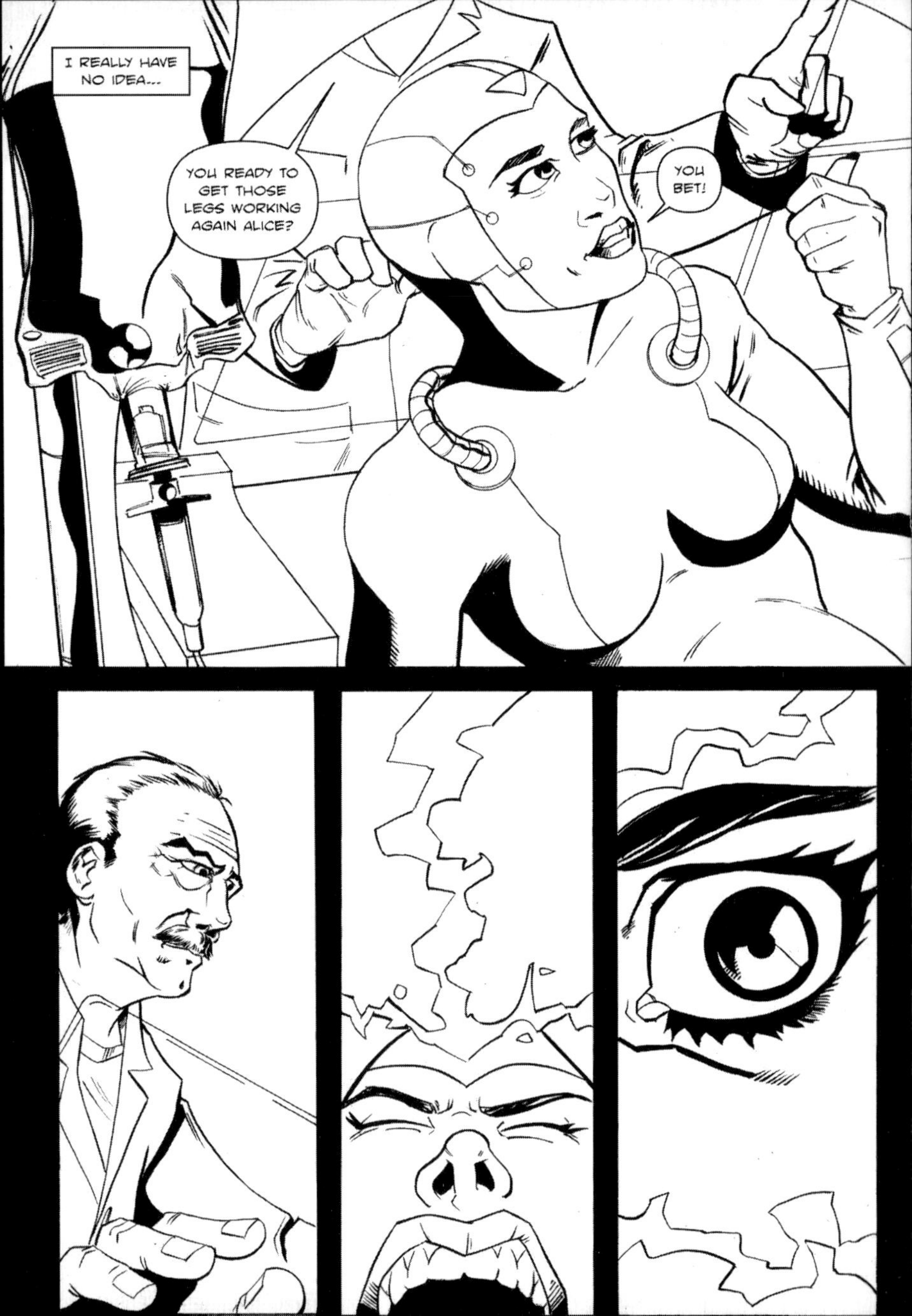
I REALLY HAVE NO IDEA...
YOU READY TO GET THOSE LEGS WORKING AGAIN ALICE?
YOU BET!

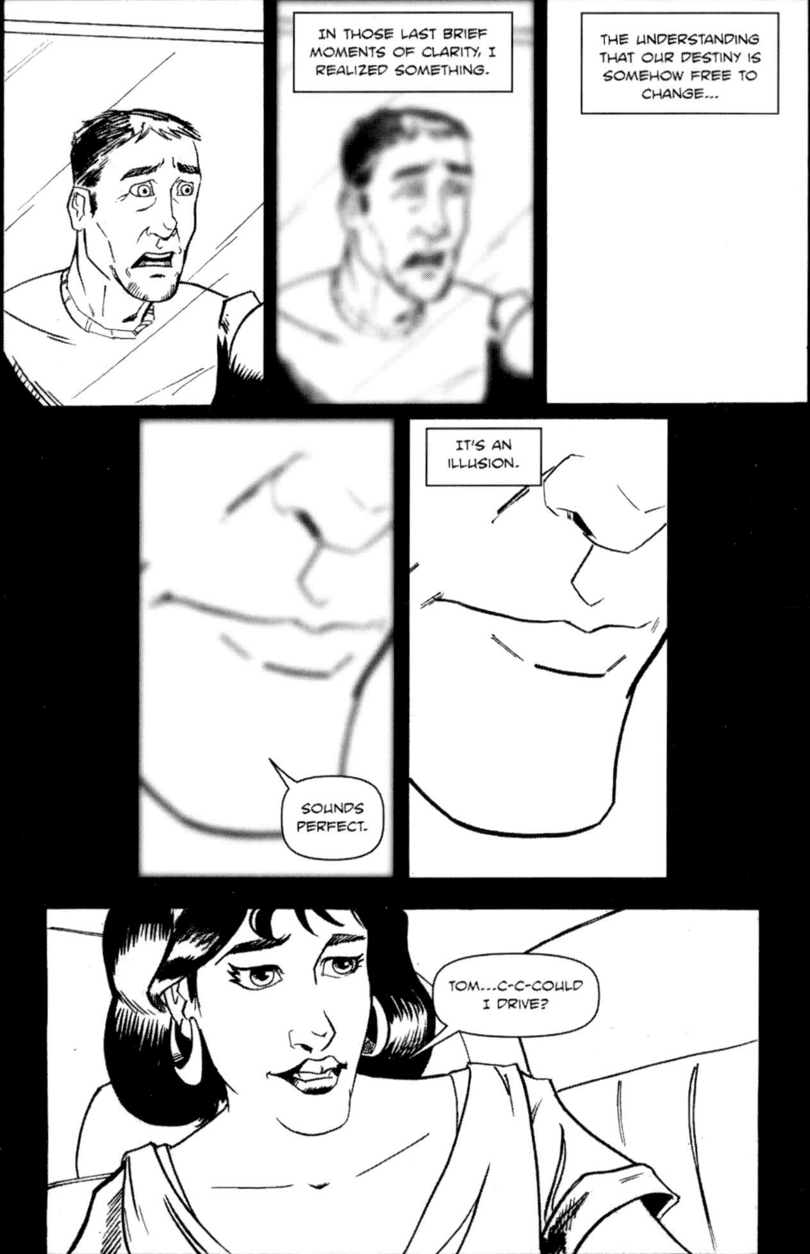
IN THOSE LAST BRIEF MOMENTS OF CLARITY, I REALIZED SOMETHING.
THE UNDERSTANDING THAT OUR DESTINY IS SOMEHOW FREE TO CHANGE...
SOUNDS PERFECT.
IT'S AN ILLUSION.
TOM...C-C-COULD I DRIVE?

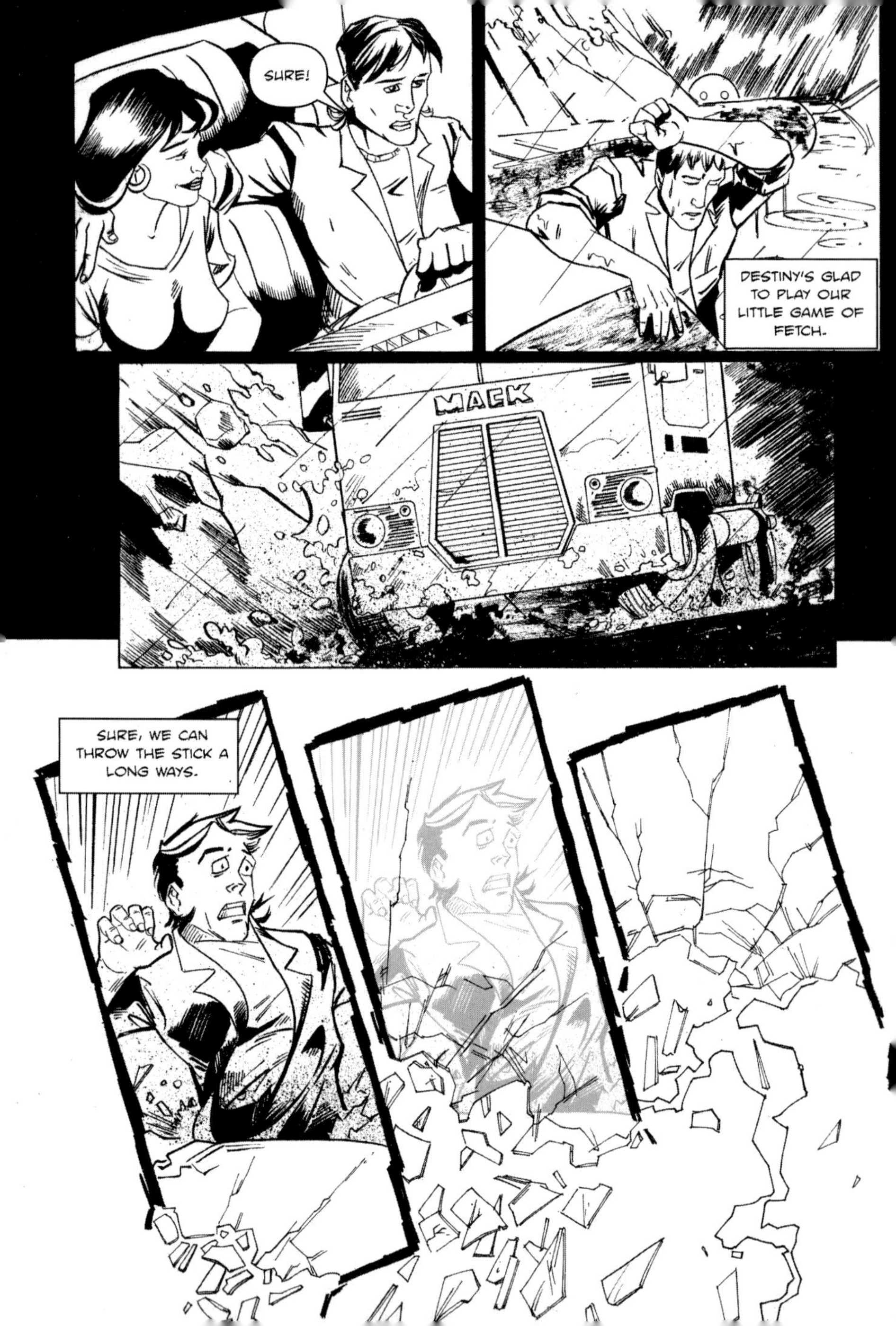
SURE!
DESTINY'S GLAD TO PLAY OUR LITTLE GAME OF FETCH.
MACK
SURE, WE CAN THROW THE STICK A LONG WAYS.

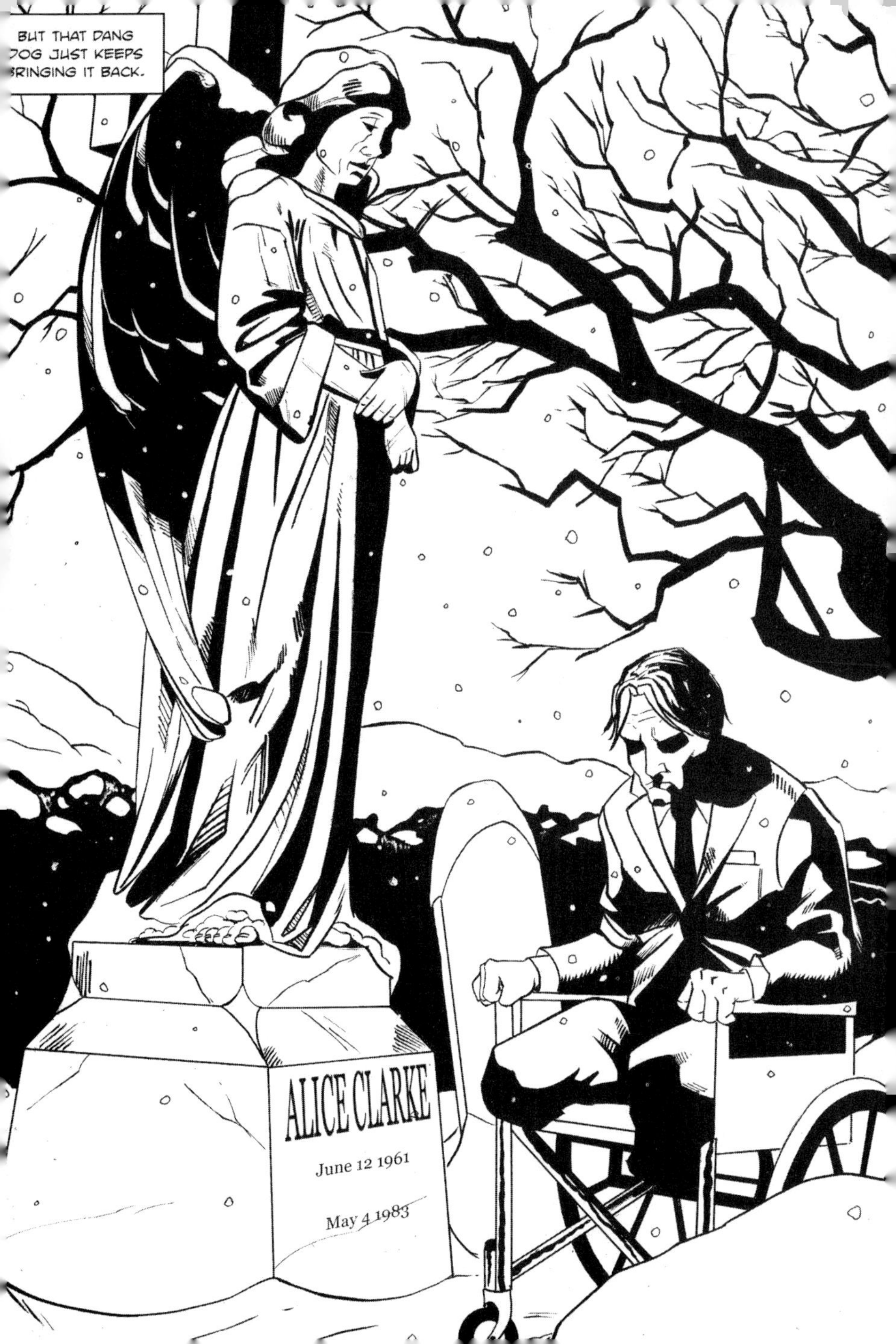
BUT THAT DANG DOG JUST KEEPS BRINGING IT BACK.
ALICE CLARKE
June 12 1961
May 4 1983

TICKET HOME

STORY - LETTERS
ROBERT MENEGUS

ART
DAVID BRAME

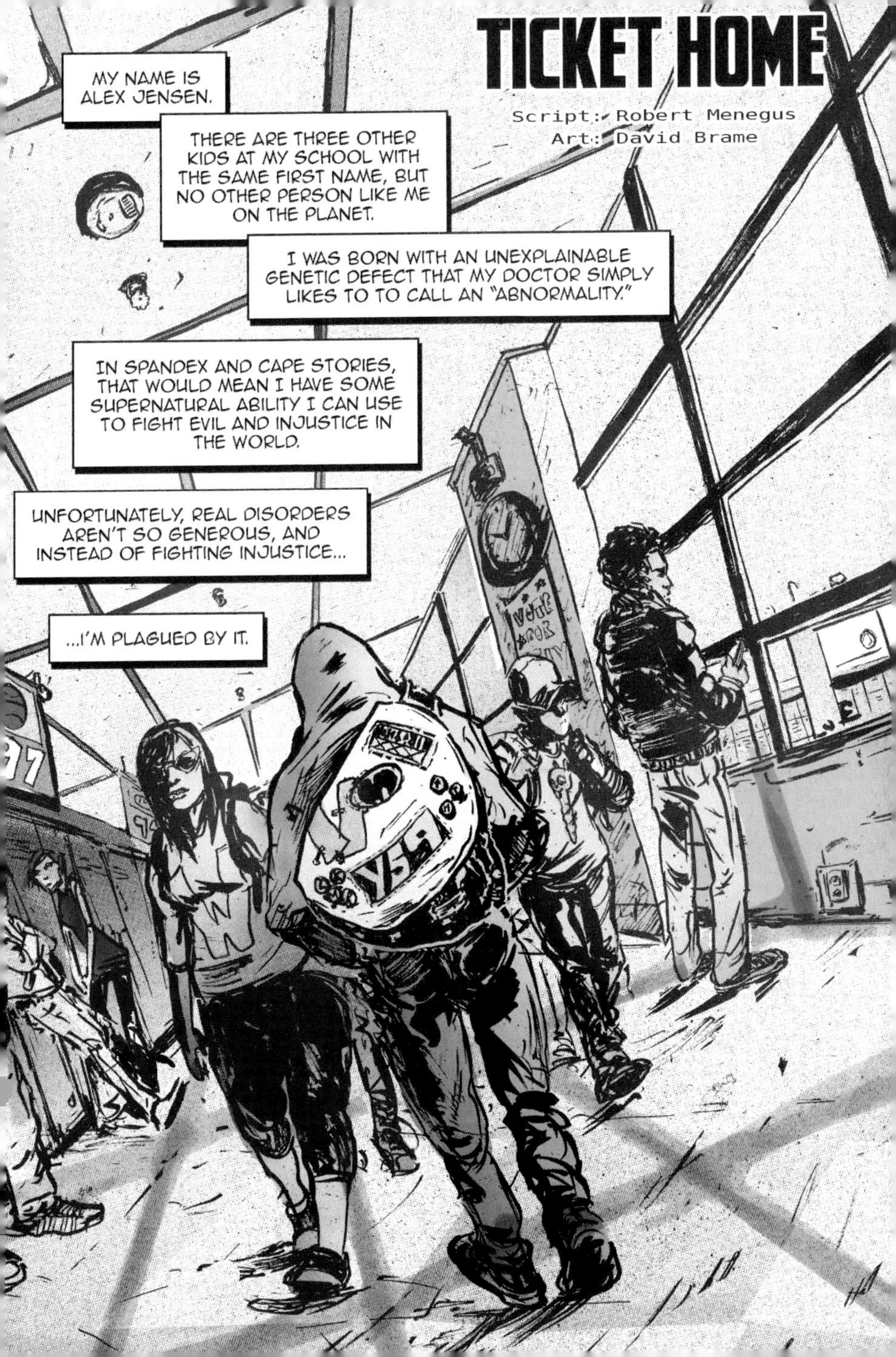
TICKET HOME
Script: Robert Menegus
Art: David Brame
MY NAME IS ALEX JENSEN.
THERE ARE THREE OTHER KIDS AT MY SCHOOL WITH THE SAME FIRST NAME, BUT NO OTHER PERSON LIKE ME ON THE PLANET.
I WAS BORN WITH AN UNEXPLAINABLE GENETIC DEFECT THAT MY DOCTOR SIMPLY LIKES TO TO CALL AN "ABNORMALITY."
IN SPANDEX AND CAPE STORIES, THAT WOULD MEAN I HAVE SOME SUPERNATURAL ABILITY I CAN USE TO FIGHT EVIL AND INJUSTICE IN THE WORLD.
UNFORTUNATELY, REAL DISORDERS AREN'T SO GENEROUS, AND INSTEAD OF FIGHTING INJUSTICE...
...I'M PLAGUED BY IT.

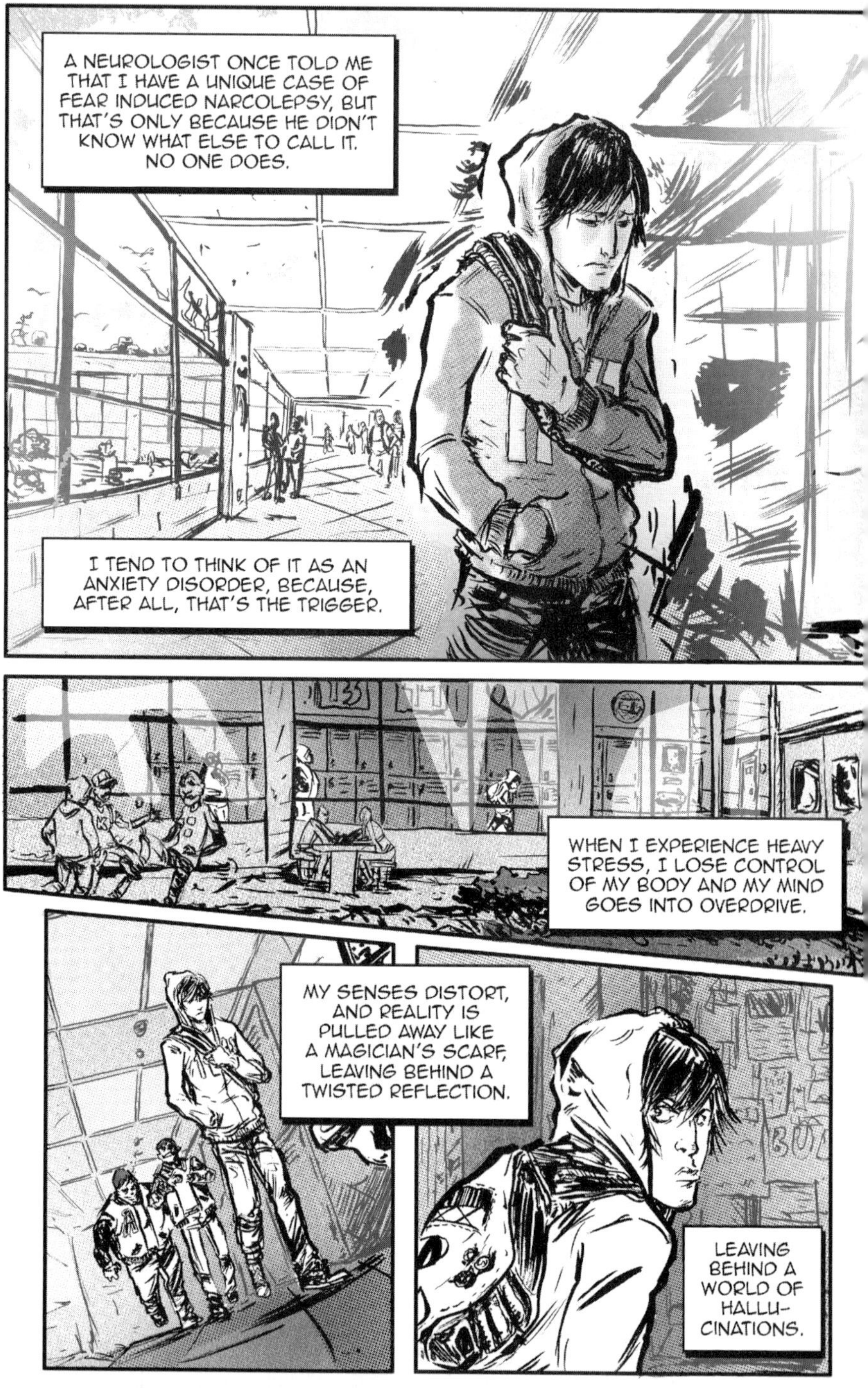
A NEUROLOGIST ONCE TOLD ME THAT I HAVE A UNIQUE CASE OF FEAR INDUCED NARCOLEPSY, BUT THAT'S ONLY BECAUSE HE DIDN'T KNOW WHAT ELSE TO CALL IT. NO ONE DOES.
I TEND TO THINK OF IT AS AN ANXIETY DISORDER, BECAUSE, AFTER ALL, THAT'S THE TRIGGER.
WHEN I EXPERIENCE HEAVY STRESS, I LOSE CONTROL OF MY BODY AND MY MIND GOES INTO OVERDRIVE.
MY SENSES DISTORT, AND REALITY IS PULLED AWAY LIKE A MAGICIAN'S SCARF, LEAVING BEHIND A TWISTED REFLECTION.
LEAVING BEHIND A WORLD OF HALLU-CINATIONS.

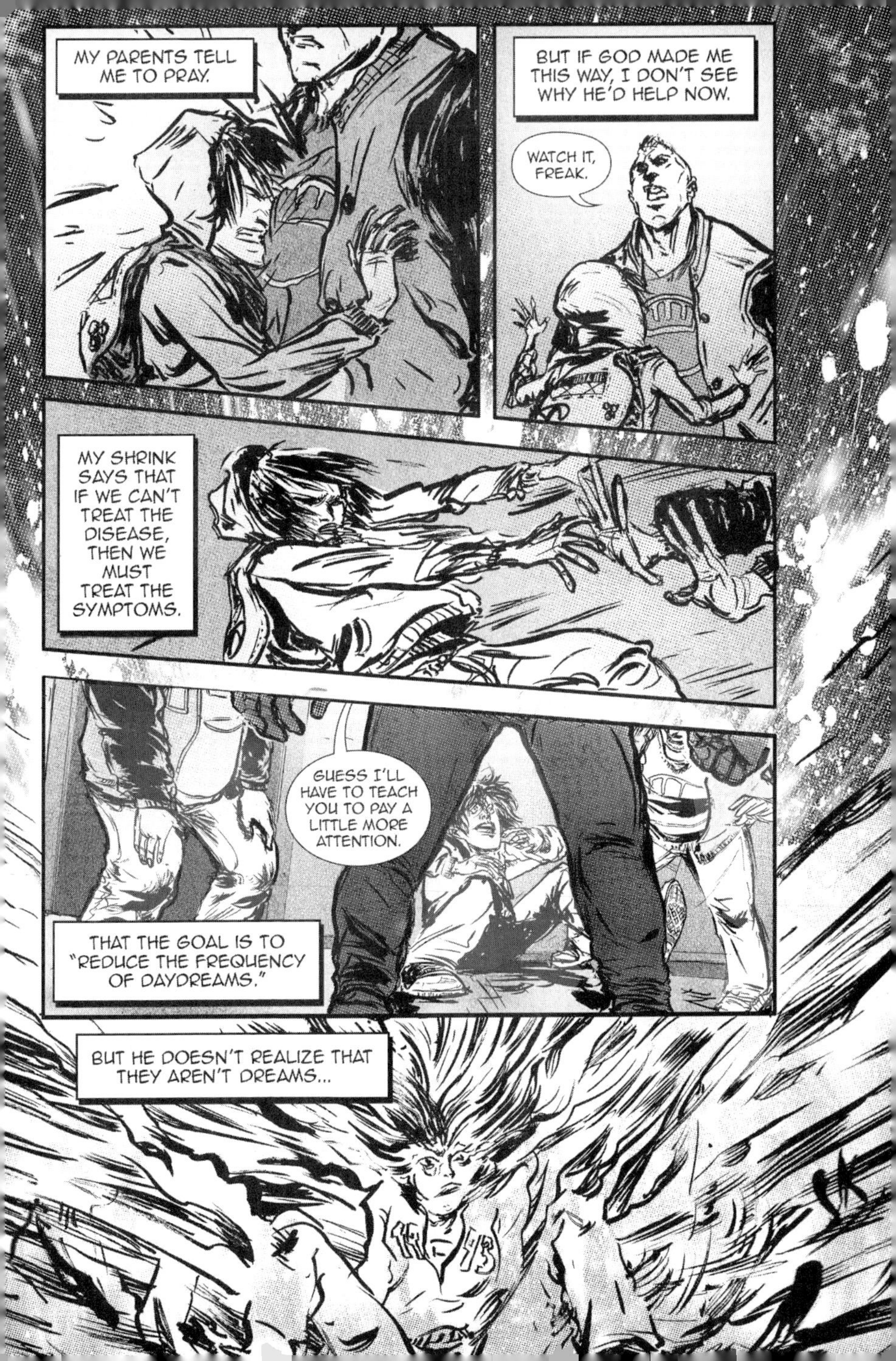
MY PARENTS TELL ME TO PRAY.
BUT IF GOD MADE ME THIS WAY, I DON'T SEE WHY HE'D HELP NOW.
WATCH IT, FREAK.
MY SHRINK SAYS THAT IF WE CAN'T TREAT THE DISEASE, THEN WE MUST TREAT THE SYMPTOMS.
GUESS I'LL HAVE TO TEACH YOU TO PAY A LITTLE MORE ATTENTION.
THAT THE GOAL IS TO "REDUCE THE FREQUENCY OF DAYDREAMS."
BUT HE DOESN'T REALIZE THAT THEY AREN'T DREAMS...

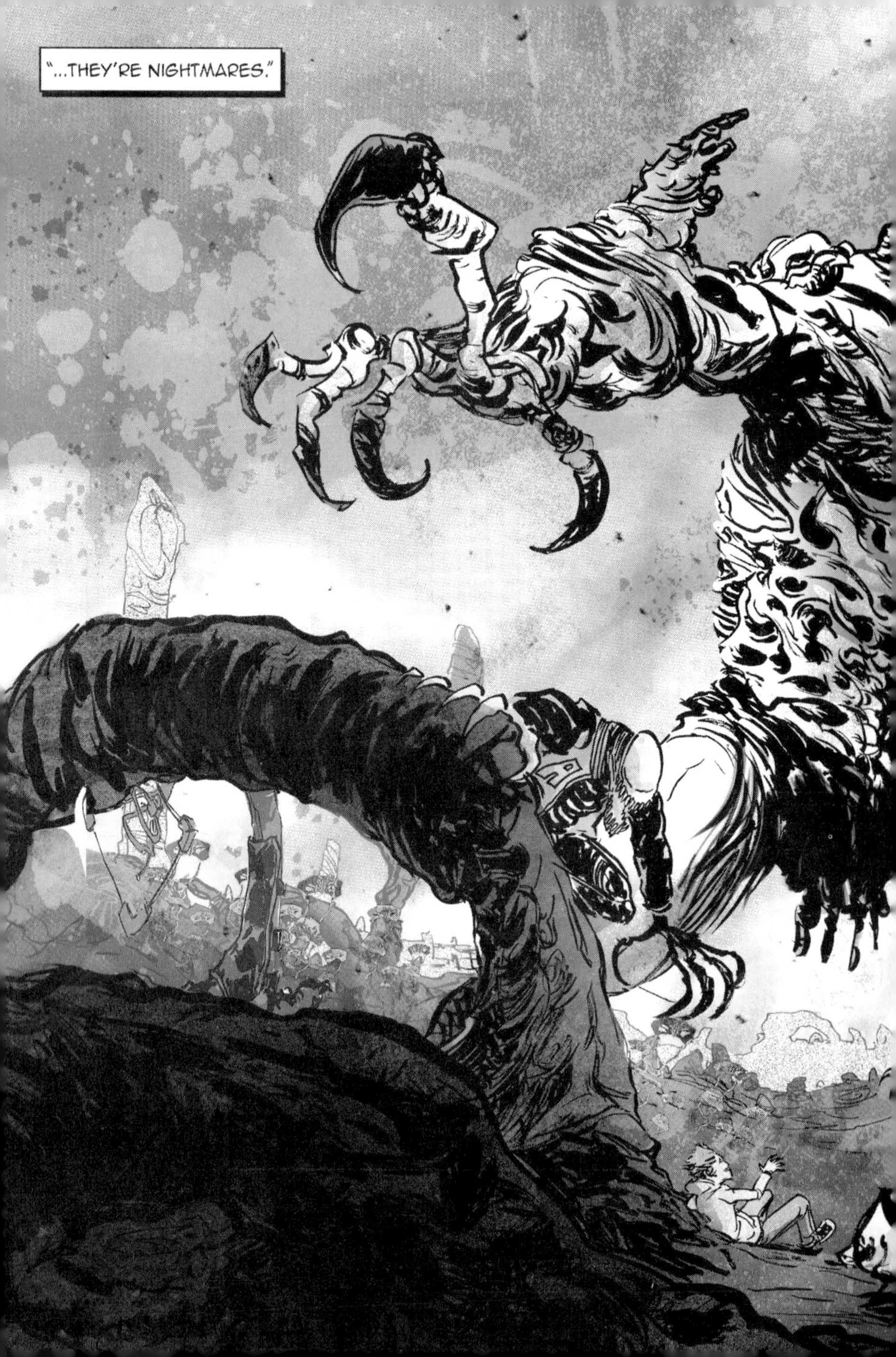
"...THEY'RE NIGHTMARES."

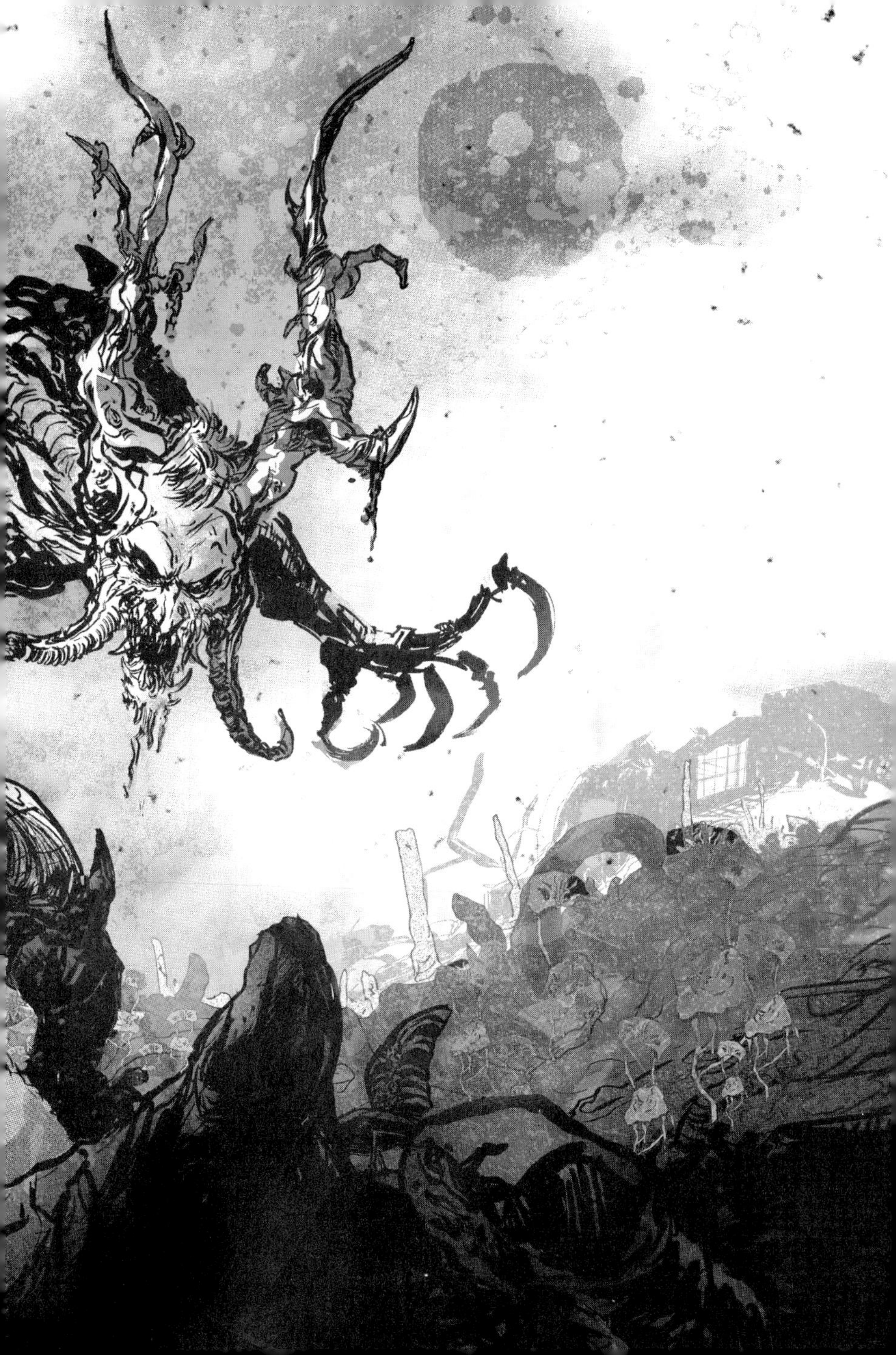

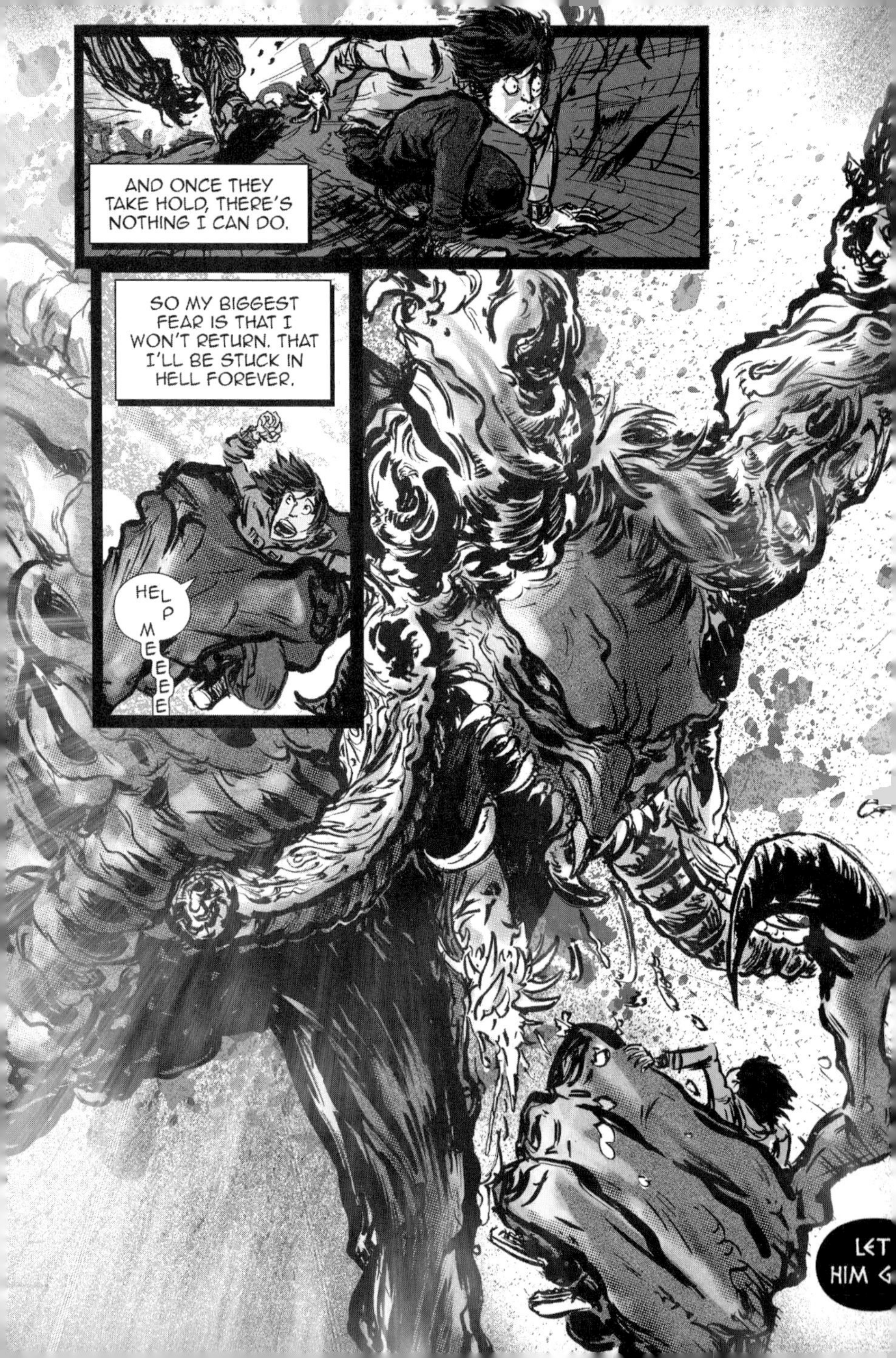
AND ONCE THEY TAKE HOLD, THERE'S NOTHING I CAN DO.
SO MY BIGGEST FEAR IS THAT I WON'T RETURN. THAT I'LL BE STUCK IN HELL FOREVER.
HELP MEEEE
LET HIM G

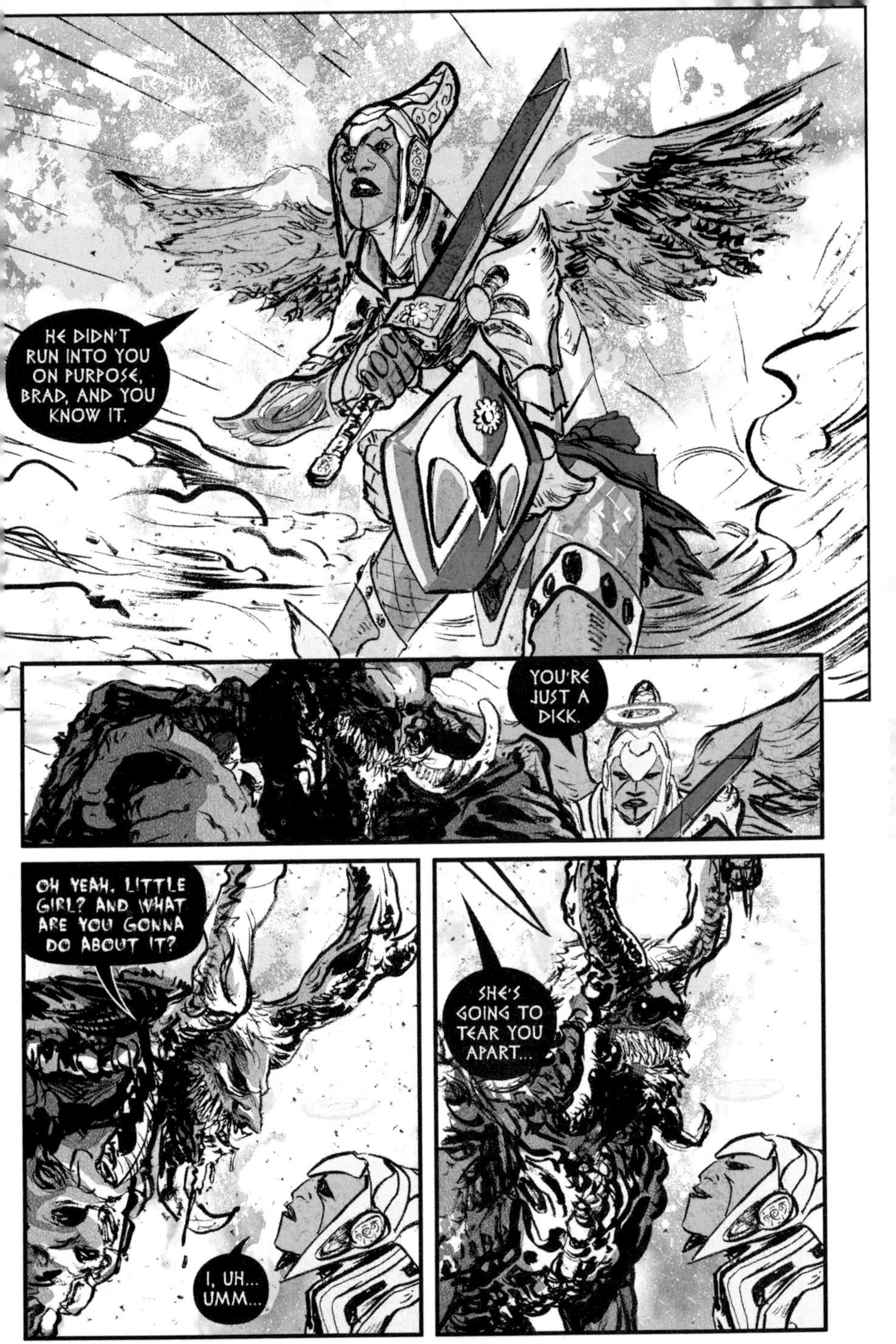
HE DIDN'T RUN INTO YOU ON PURPOSE, BRAD, AND YOU KNOW IT.
YOU'RE JUST A DICK.
OH YEAH, LITTLE GIRL? AND WHAT ARE YOU GONNA DO ABOUT IT?
I, UH... UMM...
SHE'S GOING TO TEAR YOU APART...

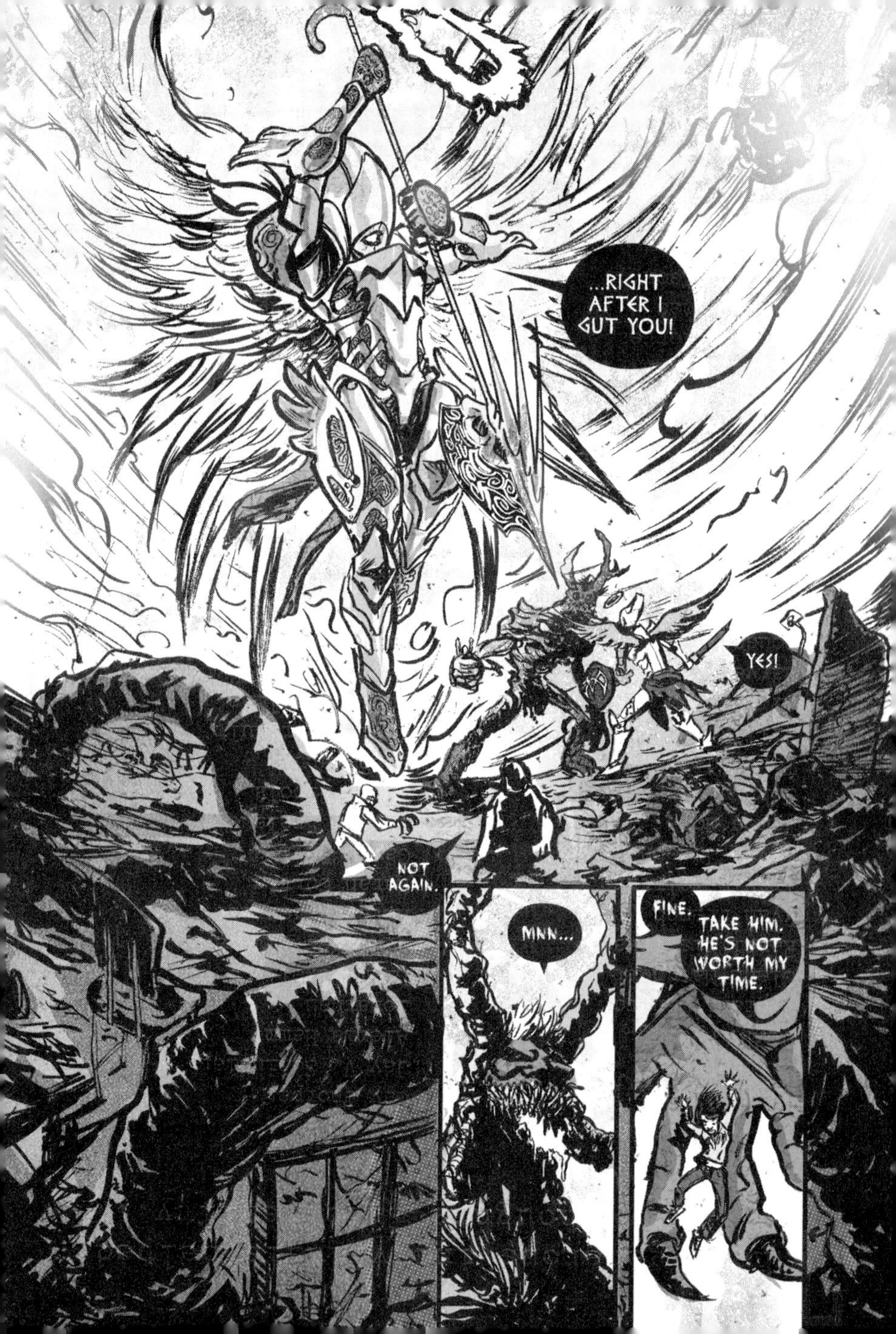
...RIGHT AFTER I GUT YOU!
YES!
NOT AGAIN.
MNN...
FINE.
TAKE HIM. HE'S NOT WORTH MY TIME.

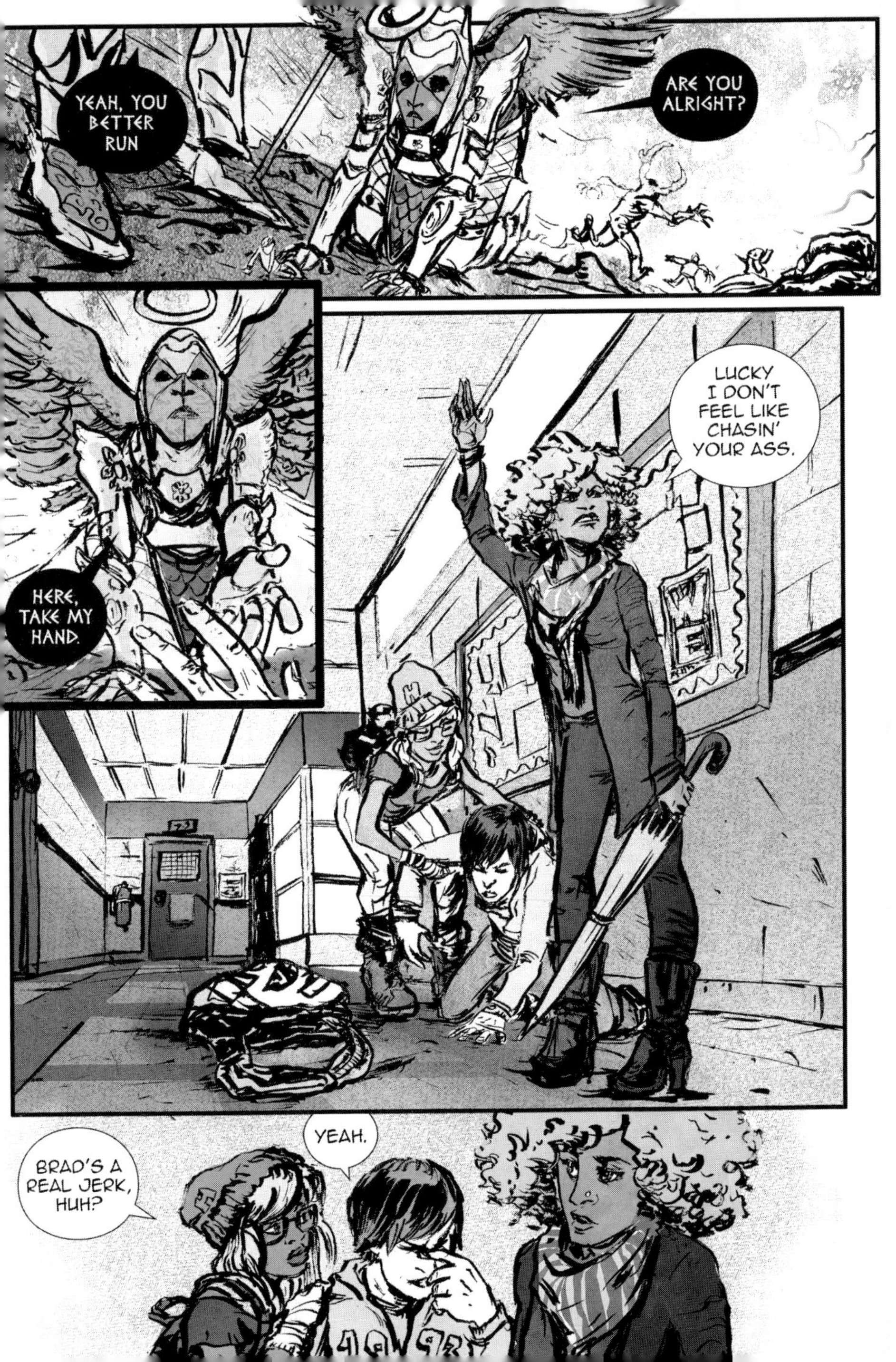
YEAH, YOU BETTER RUN
ARE YOU ALRIGHT?
HERE, TAKE MY HAND.
LUCKY I DON'T FEEL LIKE CHASIN' YOUR ASS.
BRAD'S A REAL JERK, HUH?
YEAH.

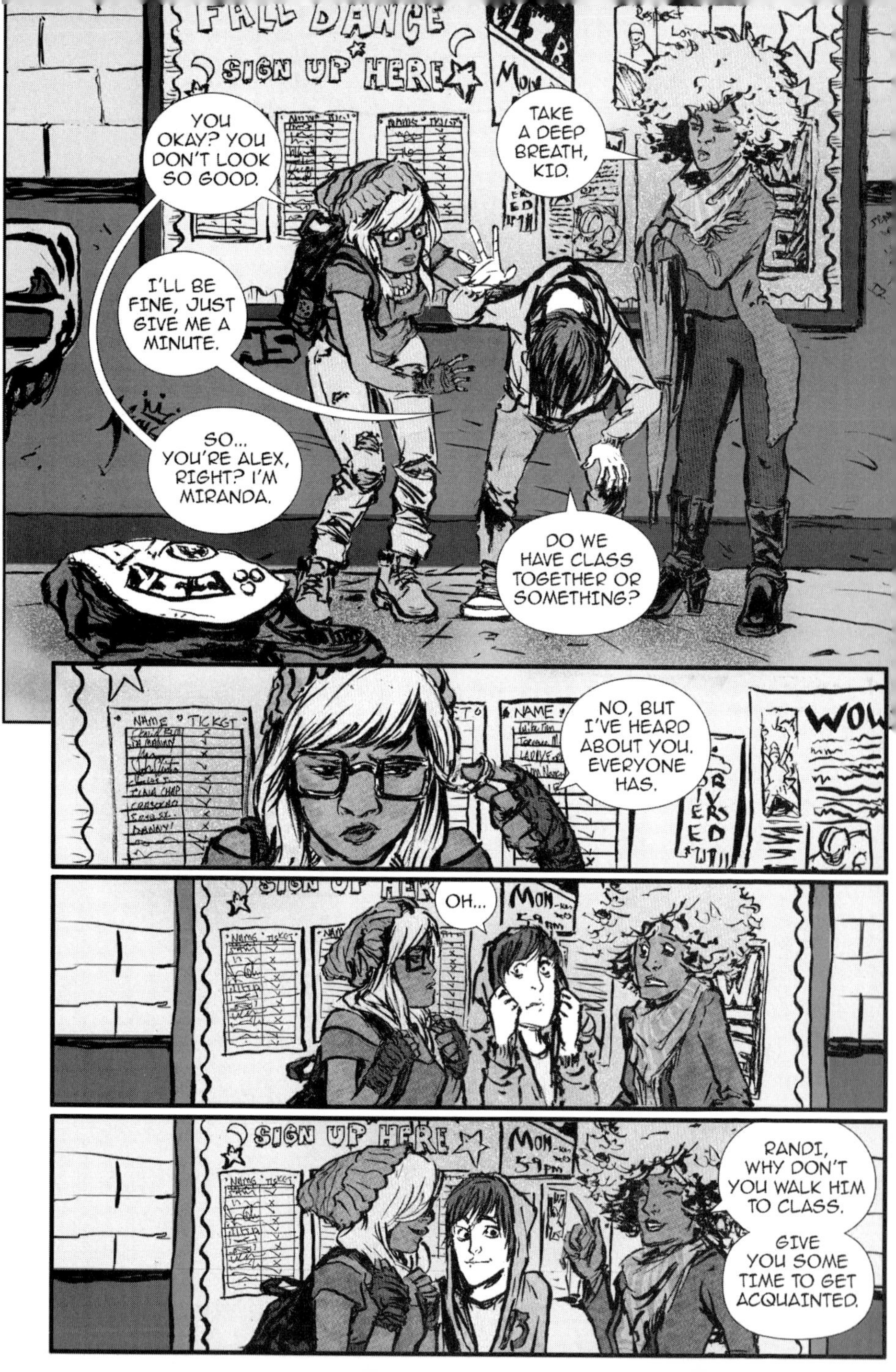
FALL DANCE
SIGN UP HERE
YOU OKAY? YOU DON'T LOOK SO GOOD.
TAKE A DEEP BREATH, KID.
I'LL BE FINE, JUST GIVE ME A MINUTE.
SO... YOU'RE ALEX, RIGHT? I'M MIRANDA.
DO WE HAVE CLASS TOGETHER OR SOMETHING?
NO, BUT I'VE HEARD ABOUT YOU. EVERYONE HAS.
OH...
RANDI, WHY DON'T YOU WALK HIM TO CLASS.
GIVE YOU SOME TIME TO GET ACQUAINTED.

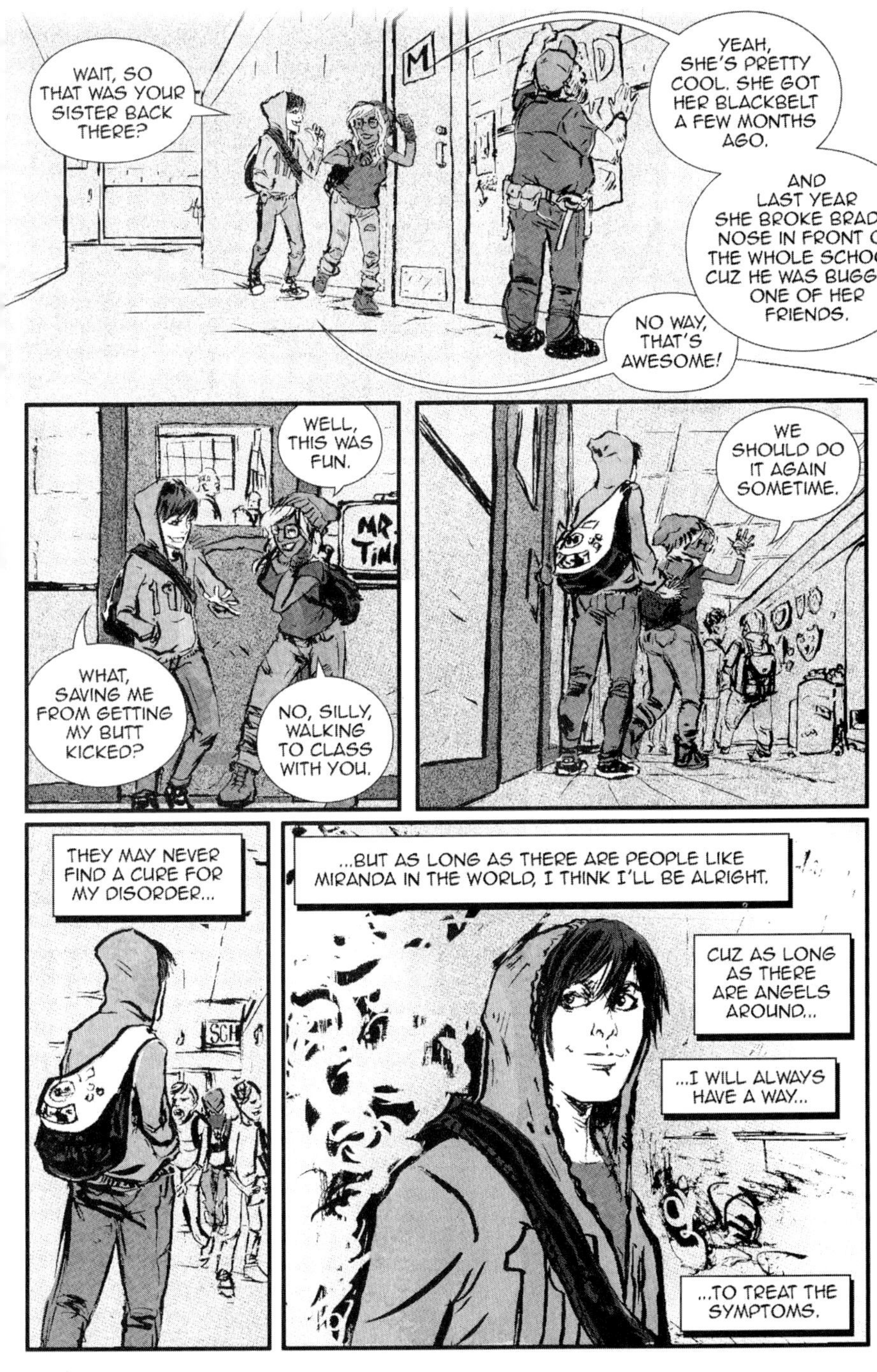
WAIT, SO THAT WAS YOUR SISTER BACK THERE?
YEAH, SHE'S PRETTY COOL. SHE GOT HER BLACKBELT A FEW MONTHS AGO.
AND LAST YEAR SHE BROKE BRAD'S NOSE IN FRONT OF THE WHOLE SCHOOL, CUZ HE WAS BUGGING ONE OF HER FRIENDS.
NO WAY, THAT'S AWESOME!
M
WELL, THIS WAS FUN.
WHAT, SAVING ME FROM GETTING MY BUTT KICKED?
NO, SILLY, WALKING TO CLASS WITH YOU.
WE SHOULD DO IT AGAIN SOMETIME.
THEY MAY NEVER FIND A CURE FOR MY DISORDER...
...BUT AS LONG AS THERE ARE PEOPLE LIKE MIRANDA IN THE WORLD, I THINK I'LL BE ALRIGHT.
CUZ AS LONG AS THERE ARE ANGELS AROUND...
...I WILL ALWAYS HAVE A WAY...
...TO TREAT THE SYMPTOMS.

the end...

..........?

These generous individuals helped turn thoughts into reality...

Justin and Kyla Saltenberger
David Ryding
Stefani Manard
Glenn Matchett
Randi Misterka
Ryan French
Travis McIntire
Kevin Joseph
James Moss
John J Ostrosky Jr
Tor Vidar Borkamo
Jill Romeo
Al Sparrow
Harvey and Fiona Pamplemousse
Turner Dehn
Brandon James
Jason Inman
Thomas Charles
KillerQueen1982 aka. Annah Jensen
EdEN
Jon Parrish
Steve McCann
Galo Gutierrez
Gary Gaines
Andrea Olson
Chad Shipley
Gio and Darlie Rossi
Travis Ellisor
Scott P. McClellan
Robin Babe Draper

Gav Thorpe
Jay V. Schindler
Aleria Hamm
Jonathan
Liam Powell
Jennifer Rivera
Anthony Ferraro
Sarah Curtis
Gavin Davies
Tracie Breland
Tuomo Sipola
Josh Kaput
Kevin Theriault
Indigo Pohlman
Dave I
Kirk Lund
Mika Koykka
Graham Evans
Carmen Insalaco
Chad Bowden
Nikki Sherman
Cecilia Grela
C. Neil Milton
Rod Christensen
Dominic M
petzilla
Martin Zirngibl
Caela Mendini
Kirk & Mindy Spencer
@Big5Army
Aaron Keck
Kurt Krol

These generous individuals helped turn thoughts into reality...

Todd Good
Nicolas ANDRY
Vicky
William Robertson
Robert "Sal" Mennella
Kim Lynch
Todd Hunt
Bas Cahuzak
Alexander Lyle
Jenna Oliver
Nathan Kelly
Grigoris Douros
Shane Doherty
Jesse Gardner
@William0406
FAbs101
Jeff Ellis
Brian Callahan
pablomoses
Jordan Thompson
Anthony R. Evans
Robert Early
41 Comics Cards
and Collectibles
Dominik L. Marzec
chris bell
Rubens Vera
David Lara
Rob Ryan
Charles C Dowd
J. Cebron Cook
Martin E Brandt II

Eric Schaechtele
Ethan Circle
Mistress StrainLuv
Don Schouest
Michael Hutchison
The Family Billingsley
Michael Malkin
Frankie Dawn Engelbert
Richard Craven
Jeff Rider
Margaret Robbins
Ashish Thomas
Peter L Brown
Carl Andrews
Kurt J Klemm
Jennifer Moniz
RAFA REYES
Don, Beth & Meghan
Ferris
Neil van Vuuren
MH Ouellette
Angeline C Burton
Karl Todd
David Kramer
Tricia Bergbauer
Marcia Star Millen
Jay Lofstead
Rhiannon Raphael
Robert Checkley
Chas! Pangburn
Rick Wanek

These generous individuals helped turn thoughts into reality...

Dominic Quach
James W. Powell
Joshua Werner
J.R. Rothenberg
Helen Lynch
D-Rock
Ben Grisanti
Jeremy Brown
Andrew Adams
Gwendlyn Drayton
Candi Bartlett
Dead Canary Comics
Joshua J. A. Russell
Anne Welborn
Quenby Bucklaew
Darryn Goble
Andrew Roth
Brian P. Dunphy
Evangelos Lev Kapros
Ricky-Marcel Pitcher
Timm Higgins
Brandon
The Geeked Gods
Benjamin Munro
Rus Wooton
Rory Firth
Kris Brown
Adam Karp
Carolynn Hoople

Wes Locher
JVGray
Anders M. Ytterdahl
Ramel Rocket-Man Hill
Patrick Gerard
Dr. Johnny Lycan
Cindy
chiken Green
Jerel Levy
Hank Tucker
splendidgeek
Thomas Werner
Caitlin Jane Hughes
SwordFire
Kurt Johansen
Diego A. Castro Reyes
@JamesFerguson
Michael Espinos
Kevin Clark
John MacLeod
Matthew Reifsteck
Seth Morris
10digitcode.com
Patrick Kelly
Kirsten Soli-Castile
Karl Spang
Sabino Etxeberria
Edward Wellman

CREATOR SIGNATURES

ADAM WOLLET

ALEX ECKMAN-LAWN

ALEXECKMANLAWN.COM
DUDENUKEM.TUMBLR.COM
TWITTER/INSTAGRAM @ALEXECKMANLAWN

BRANDON BARROWS

TINYURL.COM/QBDTXRK
CRIMEQUIRKS.TUMBLR.COM

BRANT FOWLER

GONZOGOOSE@BRANTFOWLER.COM

CANDICE WEATHERS

CREATOR SIGNATURES

CASEY REECE

CHAS! PANGBURN

@CHASEXCLAMATION
CHASEXCLAMATIONPOINT.COM

CHIP REECE

@CHIPREECE
CHIPREECE.TUMBLR.COM/

CLAIRE BENSON

DAN LAUER

CREATOR SIGNATURES

DAVID BRAME
COMICMUNKY.DEVIANTART.COM
AMAZINGDAVIDILLUSTRATION@GMAIL.COM

DEKARA

DINO CARUSO
@CARUSOCOMICS
CARUSOCOMICS.COM
CARUSOCOMICS.BLOGSPOT.COM

ERIC WEATHERS
@ERIC_WEATHERS
ERICWEATHERS.NET

ERICA J. HEFLIN
@ERICAJHEFLIN
ERICAJHEFLIN.COM
RAISTLYNE@VERIZON.NET

CREATOR SIGNATURES

FABIAN COBOS

GARRETT SNEEN

GARRETTSNEEN.COM
PLAYDEVILSADVOCATE.COM

GEORGE ATHANASIOU

SMASHATOMADVENTURES.COM

GLENN MATCHETT

@GLENN_MATCHETT
GLENNMATCHETT@GOOGLEMAIL.COM
FACEBOOK.COM/LIVINGWITHDEATH

JAMES E. ROCHE

@JAMESEROCHE
JAMESEROCHE.COM
FACEBOOK.COM/JAMESEDROCHE

CREATOR SIGNATURES

JON CLARK

KENNY JEFFERY

@COMIXPUNK
FACEBOOK.COM/DESKOFLOKI

LOKI DeWITT

MARIANOLACLAUSTRA.TUMBLR.COM
MARIANOLACLAUSTRA.DEVIANTART.COM

MARIANO LACLAUSTRA

MICHAEL MALKIN

CREATOR SIGNATURES

MIKE SALT

MIKESALTWRITES.COM
FACEBOOK.COM/MICHAEL.SALTENBERGER

NIC J. SHAW

NOVO MALGAPO

PEEBO MONDIA

PETER SIMETI

TWITTER: @PETERSIMETI
INSTAGRAM: @PETERSIMETIART
ETSY.COM/SHOP/PAINTEDHEROES

ROBERT MENEGUS

ROBERTMENEGUS@GMAIL.COM

SALO FARIAS

SALOARTE.BLOGSPOT.COM
INSTAGRAM: @SALO_ARTE
SALO-ART.DEVIANTART.COM

SAM AGRO

PINTEREST.COM/SAMUELAGRO
FACEBOOK.COM/SAMUEL.AGRO

TIM SHINN

TIM@PITCHHOUSE.NET
TIMSHINN73.DEVIANTART.COM
PITCHHOUSE.NET/TIM.HTML

UGUR SERTCELIK

ZACH BASSETT

XAQBAZIT.BLOGSPOT.COM
XAQBAZIT.DEVIANTART.COM

POW!

COMICS
CARDS
COLLECTIBLES

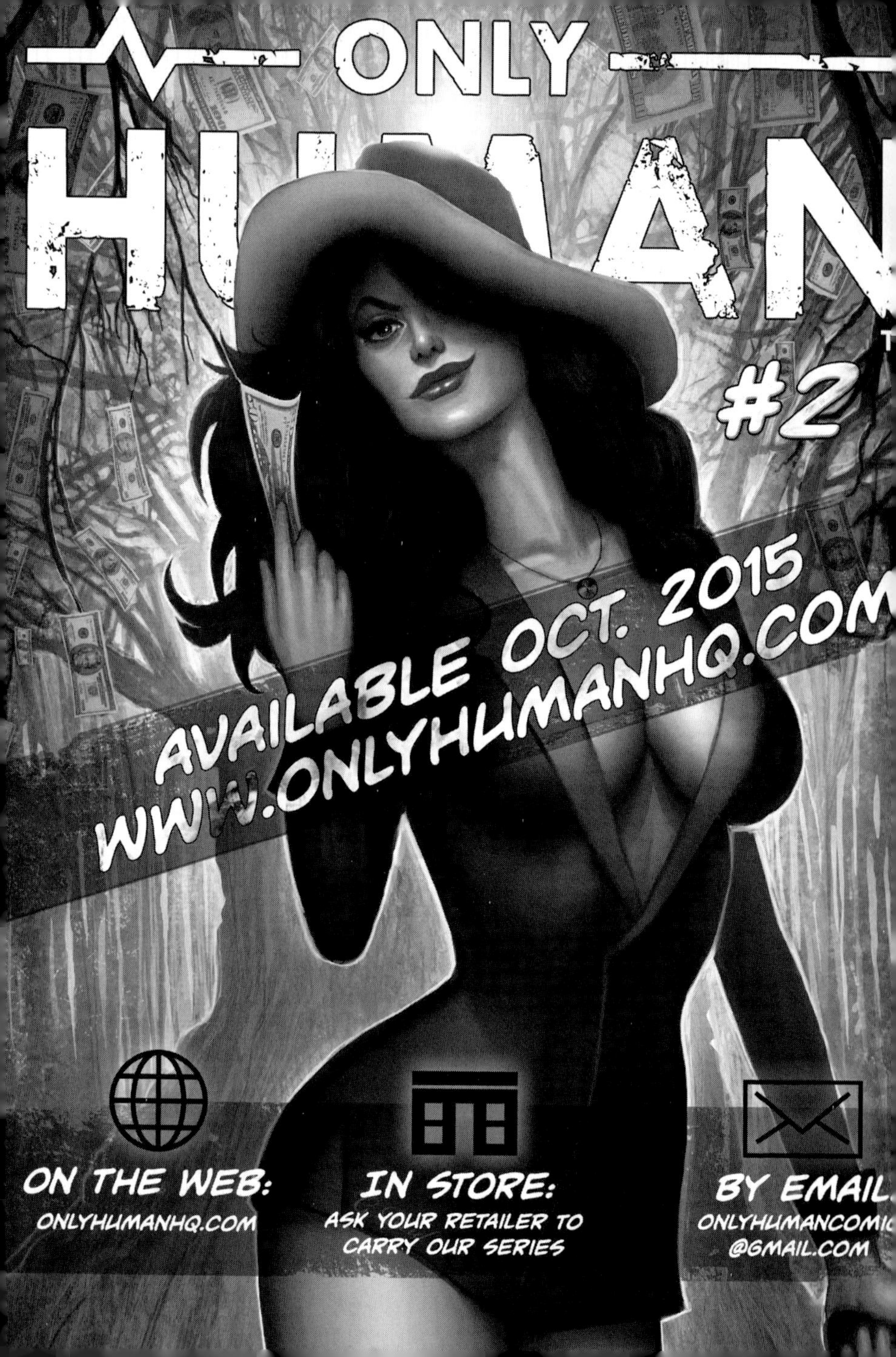

ONLY
#2
AVAILABLE OCT. 2015
WWW.ONLYHUMANHQ.COM
ON THE WEB:
ONLYHUMANHQ.COM
IN STORE:
ASK YOUR RETAILER TO CARRY OUR SERIES
BY EMAIL:
ONLYHUMANCOMIC
@GMAIL.COM

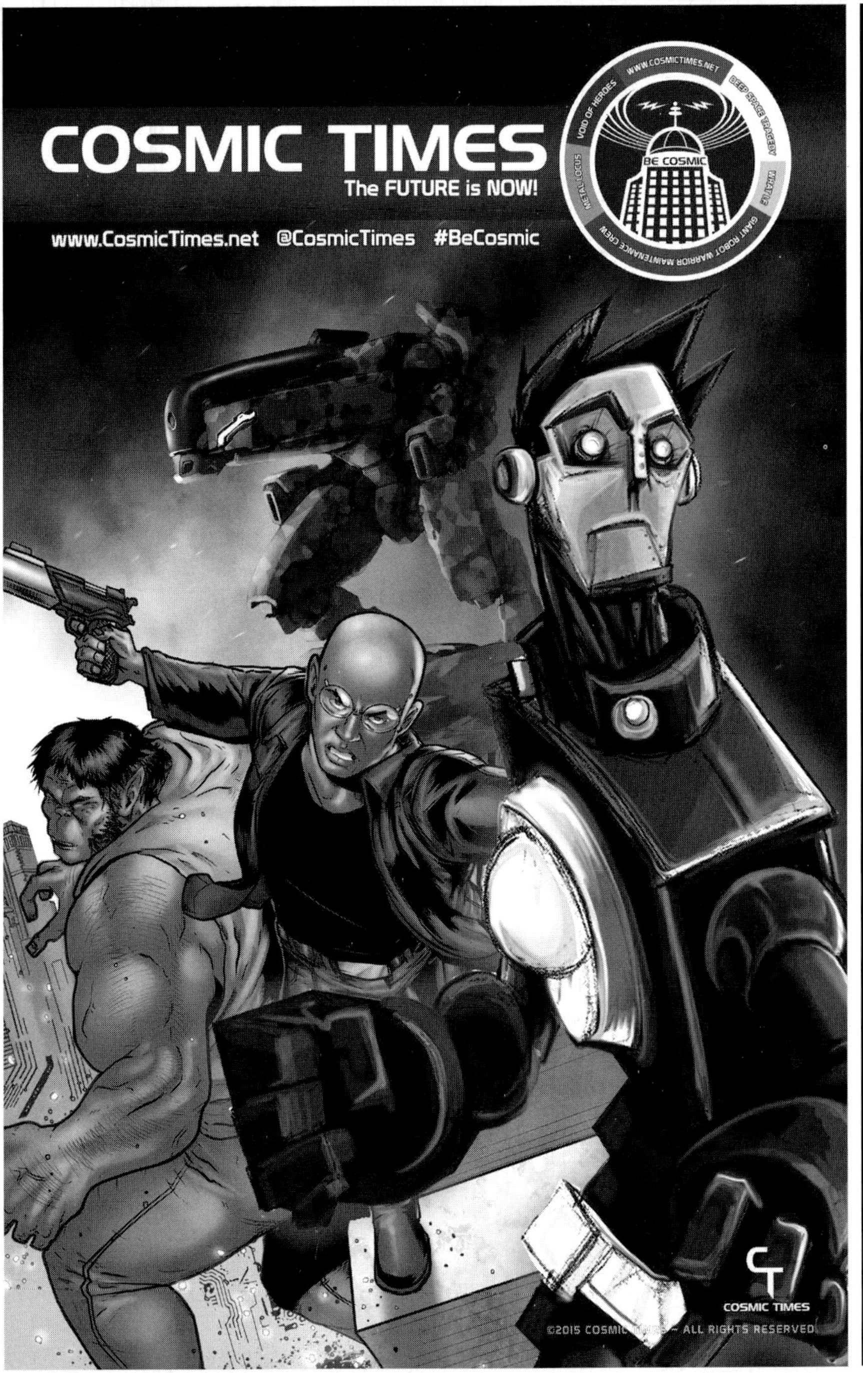
COSMIC TIMES
The FUTURE is NOW!
www.CosmicTimes.net @CosmicTimes #BeCosmic
WWW.COSMICTIMES.NET
DEEP SPACE TRAGEDY
WHAT IF
GIANT ROBOT WARRIOR MAINTENANCE CREW
METAL LOCUS
VOID OF HEROES
BE COSMIC
CT
COSMIC TIMES
©2015 COSMIC
~ ALL RIGHTS RESERVED

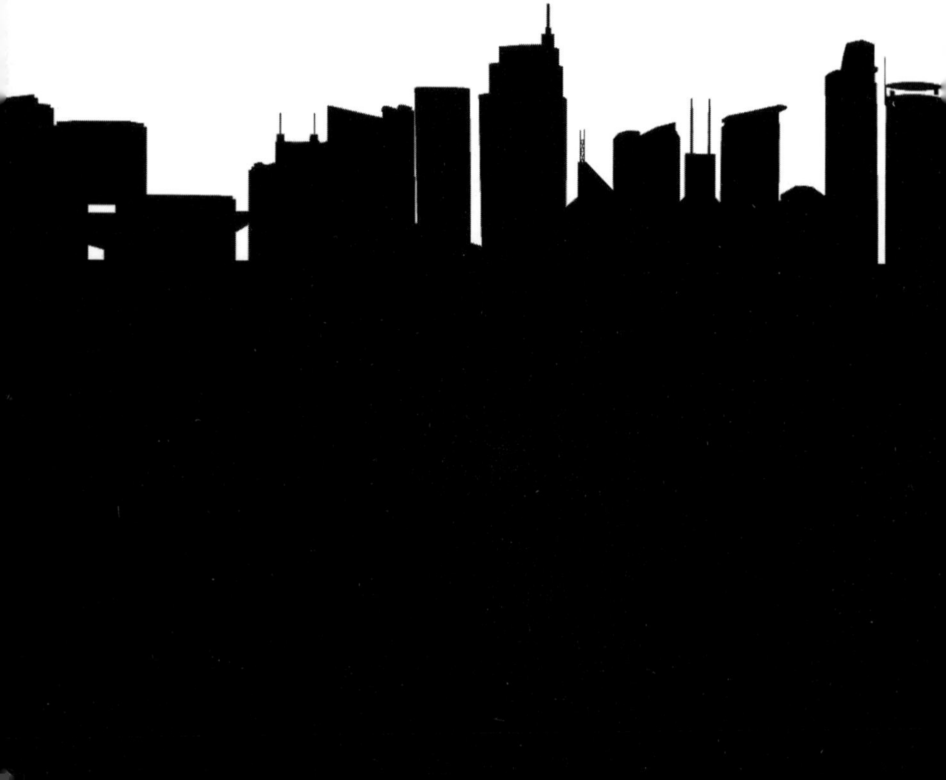

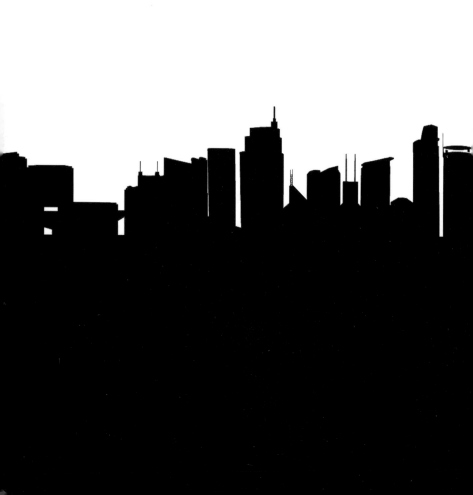

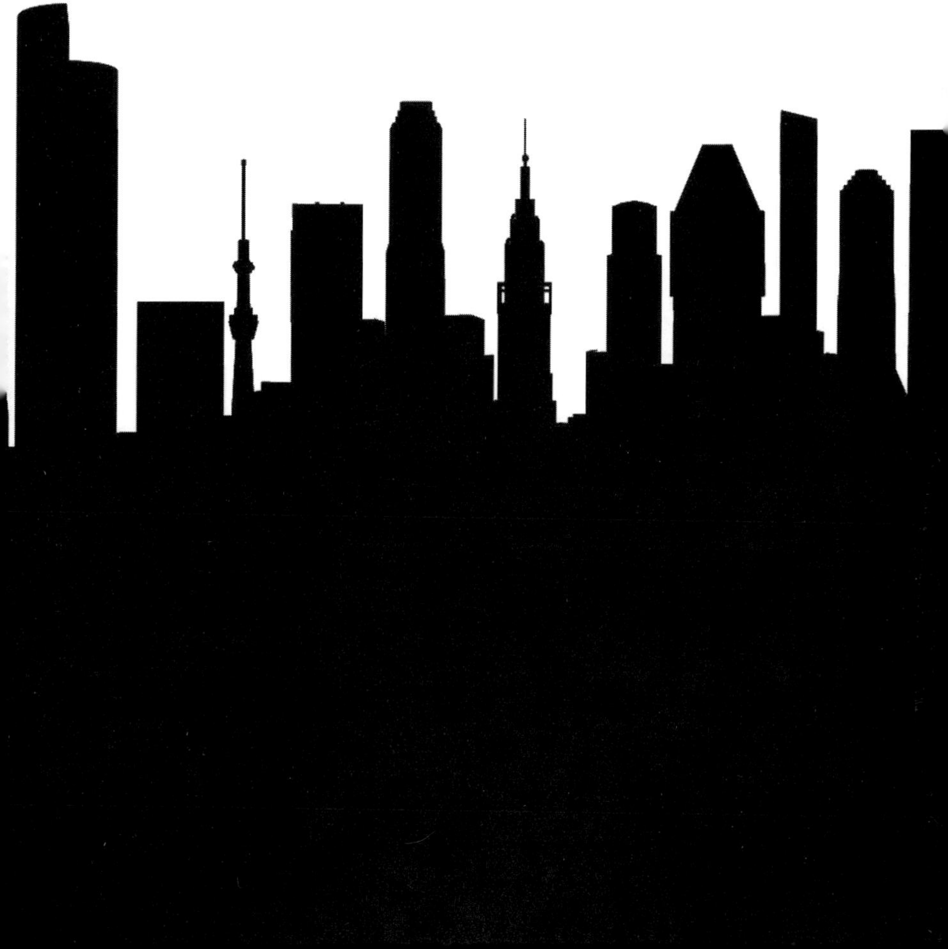

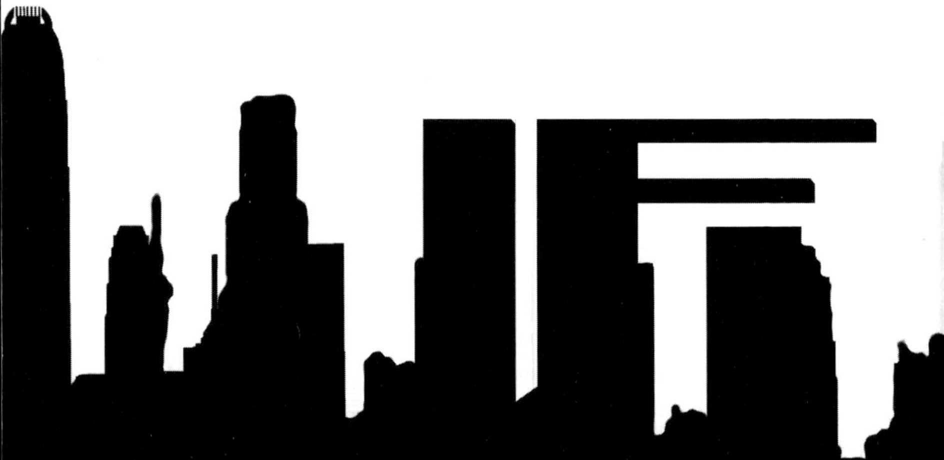

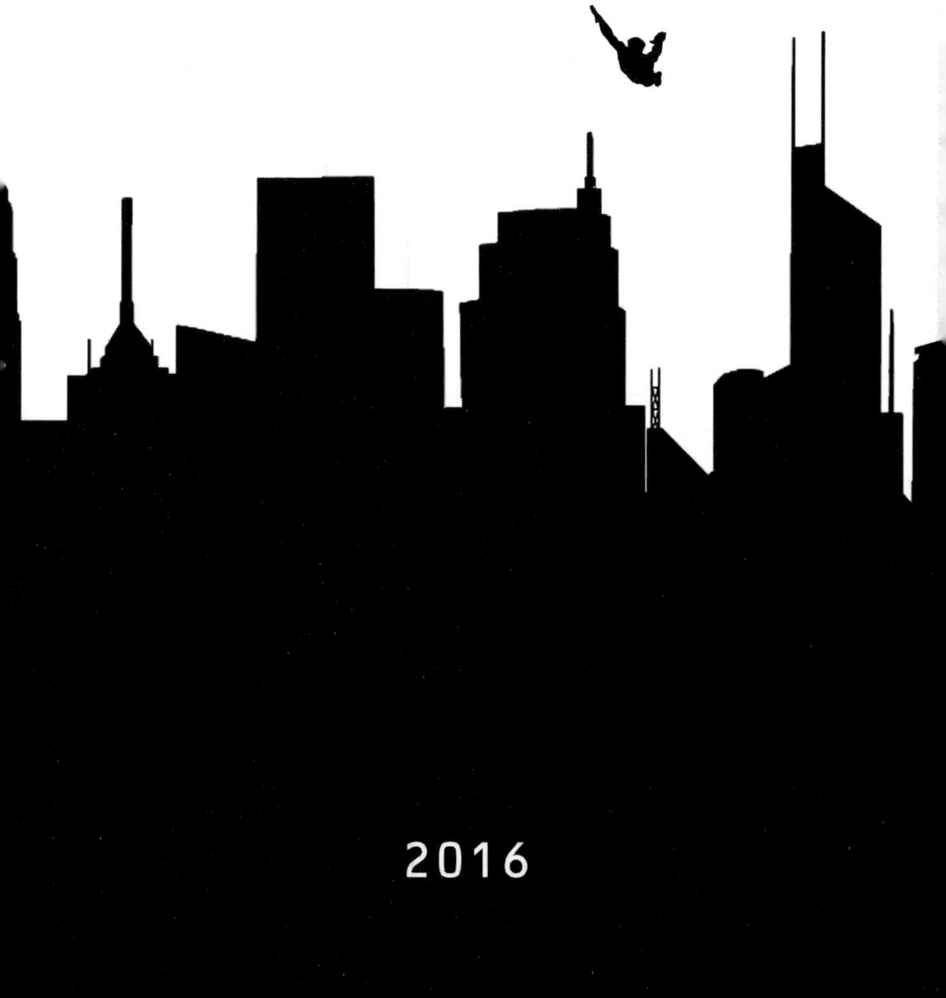
2016

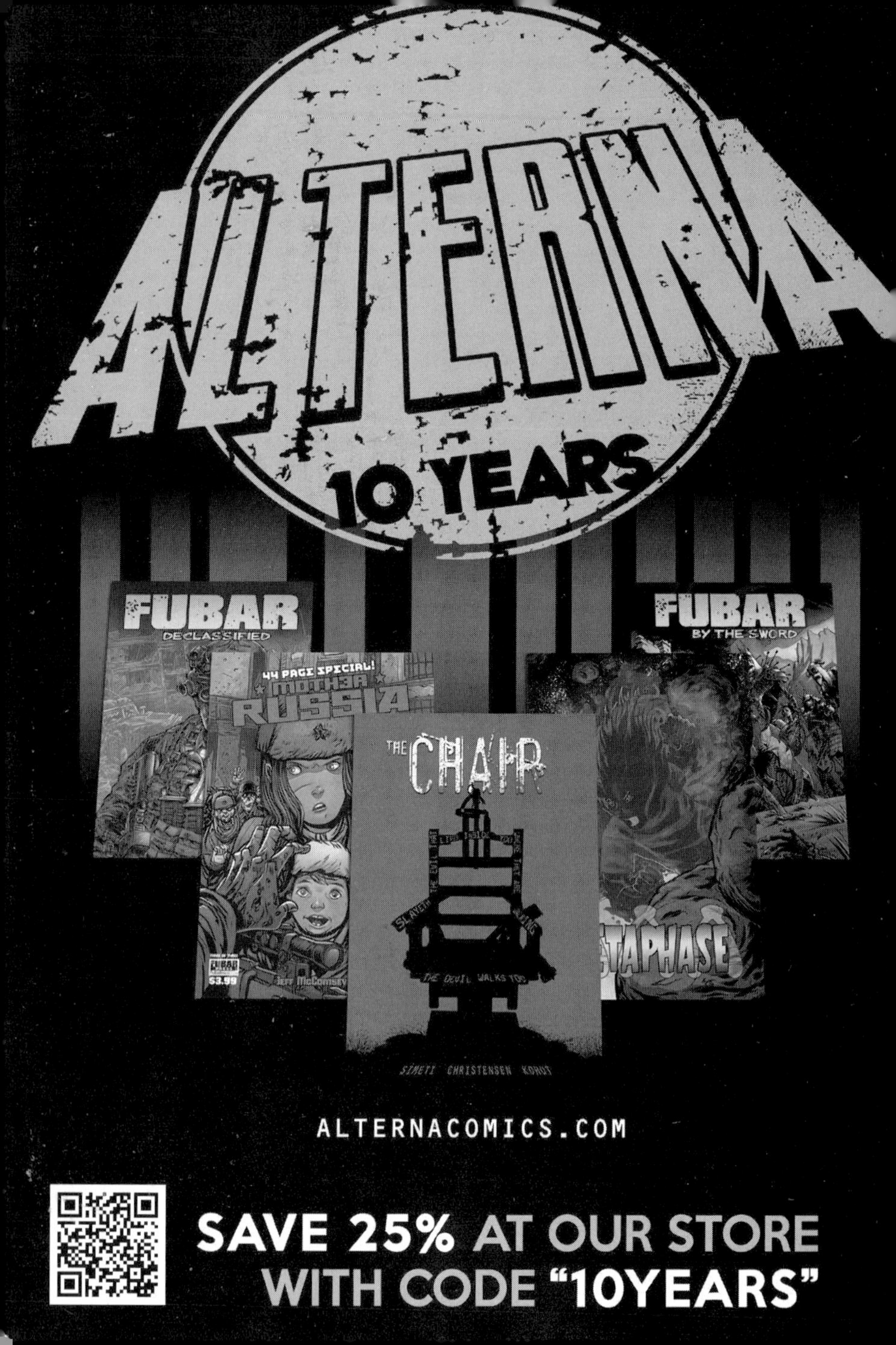
ALTERNA
10 YEARS
FUBAR
DECLASSIFIED
44 PAGE SPECIAL!
MOTHER RUSSIA
$3.99
THE CHAIR
FUBAR
BY THE SWORD
ALTERNACOMICS.COM
SAVE 25% AT OUR STORE
WITH CODE "10YEARS"